THE ILLUSION OF CIVIL SOCIETY

JON SHEFNER

THE ILLUSION OF CIVIL SOCIETY

DEMOCRATIZATION AND COMMUNITY MOBILIZATION IN LOW-INCOME MEXICO

THE PENNSYLVANIA STATE UNIVERSITY PRESS
UNIVERSITY PARK, PENNSYLVANIA

LIBRARY OF CONGRESS
CATALOGING-IN-PUBLICATION DATA

Shefner, Jon, 1958–
    The illusion of civil society : democratization and community mobilization in low-income
Mexico / Jon Shefner.
        p.   cm.
Includes bibliographical references and index.
Summary: "Addresses the success and failures of the Unión de Colonos Independientes
(UCI), a community organization in Guadalajara, Mexico. Critiques the civil society
concept and questions the strategy of political democratization as a way to assert control
over the global economy"—Provided by publisher.
ISBN 978-0-271-03385-3 (pbk : alk. paper)
1. Unión de Colonos Independientes (Guadalajara, Mexico).
2. Community organization—Mexico—Guadalajara.
3. Civil society—Mexico—Guadalajara.
4. Democratization—Mexico—Guadalajara.
I. Title.

HN120.G8S48 2008
320.972'35—dc22
2008016408

THIS BOOK IS DEDICATED TO THE UCI, FOR ALL THEY TAUGHT ME.

And to Karen, FOR EVERYTHING.

CONTENTS

ILLUSTRATIONS

FIGURES

TABLES

CHART

ACKNOWLEDGMENTS

I've been exceptionally lucky. Over the years, I've met people I've admired and who have helped me grow as a person and scholar. I am deeply grateful to many members of the UCI for their time and friendship, but especially to Tito, Ana, Agustín, Carmen, and Hermano Javier. Others in Mexico who have given generously of their time include Sofía de la Peña, Juan Manuel Ramírez Sáiz, Jorge Alonso, Mercedes González de la Rocha, Felipe Alatorre, Carlos Peralta, José Bautista, Alfredo Lopez, the de Borbolla family, and Agustín Escobar.

Through their teaching and commitment to scholarship, Diane Mitsch Bush, Stephen Mumme, Jack Goldstone, and Jan Gouldner have been models to emulate. John Walton's scholarship, integrity, and instruction in the craft of sociology has had a huge influence on me, as has that of Fred Block. Martin Tolich has helped me understand how to be an engaged scholar. Most importantly, my friend Steve Shulman has been an example of how to commit to scholarship, while refusing to leave the rest of life behind.

Others have spent their time reading my work, talking to me, sharpening my argument where I was right, and showing me where I was wrong. Much of their written work has affected me in immeasurable ways. Frances Fox Piven is a constant inspiration. Others who have deeply influenced me include Alejandro Portes, Robert Gay, Gareth Jones, George Pasdirtz, Robert Gorman, Sherry Cable, Harry Dahms, Michael Handelsman, Amparo Menéndez-Carrión, Judith Adler Hellman, Miguel Angel Centeno, Sylvia Chant, Diane Davis, Cory Blad, Julie Stewart, Denise Cobb, Scott Frey, Chip Hastings, Cecilia Menjívar, Victoria Johnson, Robert Olson, Richard Olson, Javier Auyero, Saskia Sassen, Cathy Walsh, Charlie Hale, Jon Roper, Steve McVeigh, Charlie Walker, and Paul Gellert.

In the preparation of this book, Sandy Thatcher has been a huge support; his commitment, comments, and enthusiasm were very important. Additionally, the comments of Philip Oxhorn were exceptionally helpful. Peter Ward reviewed the manuscript twice, with great care each time. His suggestions for structure, analysis, and perspective were absolutely crucial and always spot-on, and I owe him a great debt of gratitude.

If Patricia Fernández-Kelly were only my friend, I would be very fortunate. That she has chosen also to be both a colleague and mentor has added immensely to my scholarly life. Her friendship, rigorous analysis, wide networks, great generosity, and unyielding editor's pen have been crucial to my work. I am grateful to her for all these things, but most of all for her friendship.

I would also like to thank UC MEXUS, the University of California–Davis, the University of Tennessee Professional Development Grants, and the World Society Foundation for supporting my work

Sharing life with Karen, Sophia, and Isaac is the best thing to ever happen to me.

ACRONYMS

BANOBRAS	Banco Nacional de Obras y Servicios Públicas/National Public Works Bank
CEB	Comunidad de base/Christian base community
CNC	Confederación Nacional Campesina/National Peasant Confederation
CORETT	Comisión para la Regularización de la Tenencia de la Tierra/ Commission for the Regularization of Land Tenure
CROC	Confederación Revolucionaria de Obreros y Campesinos/Revolutionary Confederation of Workers and Peasants
CTM	Confederación de Trabajadores de México/Confederation of Mexican Workers
FDN	Frente Democrático Nacional/National Democratic Front
FONHAPO	Fondo Nacional de Habitaciones Populares/National Fund for Affordable Housing
IFE	Instituto Federal Electoral/Federal Electoral Institute
IMDEC	Instituto Mexicano para el Desarrollo Comunitario/Mexican Institute for Community Development
INEGI	Instituto Nacional de Estadística, Geografía, e Informática/National Institute of Statistics, Geography, and Informatics
MCJ	Movimiento Ciudadano Jalisciense/Jalisco Citizen Movement
PAN	Partido Acción Nacional/National Action Party
PFCRN	Partido del Frente Cardenista de Reconstrucción Nacional/Cardenista Front for National Reconstruction Party
PRD	Partido de la Revolución Democrática/Party of the Democratic Revolution
PRI	Partido Revolucionario Institucional/Institutional Revolutionary Party
PRONASOL	Programa Nacional de Solidaridad/National Solidarity Program

SEDESOL   Secretaría de Desarrollo Social/Social Development Secretariat

SEDOC   Servicios Educativos de Occidente/Educational Services of the West

UCI   Unión de Colonos Independientes/Union of Independent Settlers

1

IN THE STREETS WITH MEXICO'S DEMOCRACY MOVEMENT

DEMOCRACY COMES TO CERRO DEL CUATRO

On a Sunday afternoon in May 1994, a flatbed truck and a van pulled up to the dusty corner of 8 de Julio and Santa Luz streets in the southern metropolitan area of Guadalajara called Cerro del Cuatro. A group of men—residents of Cerro del Cuatro who worked with a local political organization, the Union of Independent Settlers (Unión de Colonos Independientes, UCI)—had been talking nearby.[1] Now, they stopped and walked over to help the new arrivals unload pieces of scaffolding and staging. The UCI, an alliance of neighborhood groups, had fought for more than five years for urban services, secure land tenure, and democratization. The recent arrivals were members of a nongovernmental organization, the Jalisco Citizen Movement (Movimiento Ciudadano Jalisciense, MCJ). A coalition of several groups, the MCJ defined itself as a pro-democracy organization. With the presidential elections coming in August, MCJ members were busy organizing political awareness campaigns to convince people to vote. On that Sunday, Cerro del Cuatro was the locale of the Foro Callejero, or street forum, at which local media personalities, nongovernmental organization (NGO) activists, and the local community organization, arguing for the need to democratize Mexico, encouraged area residents to take action toward that goal.

The pro-democracy activists quickly surveyed the street corner and then directed and helped the others in setting up the scaffolding. Several of the neighborhood men were bricklayers and laborers, so they worked quickly. Within a half

---

1. The UCI–Cerro del Cuatro was the main *colonos* (settlers) group using this name. At times, other UCIs emerged in other areas of Guadalajara, but these organizations never possessed the power of UCI–Cerro del Cuatro.

hour, the locals and the visitors had erected a four-foot-high stage, as well as two seven-foot-high towers facing the stage. The MCJ activists opened the van's doors and began to unload electronic equipment, including large black speakers and a soundboard. Some of the passengers started stringing wires, placing lights, and testing the equipment, while others gingerly unpacked a massive widescreen television and sophisticated video gear. With some anxiety, the newcomers and residents hoisted the cameras and lights into place on the towers.

More vehicles arrived, bringing young MCJ organizers. The newcomers joked and commented about the dust and the view of the city from the hill, and then set about unpacking props and costumes. One man donned a brilliant red devil's costume, and others wrestled with stilts. Around 5:00 P.M., the drivers of the van announced that the event was about to begin. The van slowly drove down 8 de Julio followed by scores of women, men, and children and by the fully costumed actors. Three actors, heavily made up and ten feet tall atop their stilts, picked their way precariously among the rocks, potholes, dust, and garbage of the unpaved street. While the driver of the van used a loudspeaker to exhort other residents to join the march, the devil pounded a drum and darted through the marching group, teasing kids and matrons alike. Many of the women held signs reading, "We struggle for justice!" "We want democracy!" and "We demand sewer drains!" giving the devil fodder for his teasing. "Demand!? Who do you think you are? A rich person, that we should listen to?" Another actor dressed as a skeleton urged the kids to make noise. After a short walk, the van turned around and led approximately 150 marchers back to the street corner.

Back at the stage, a woman representing Mexico was drummed to the stage by the devil, followed by his skeleton helper. They placed the woman under a gallows, where the devil broke the fake chains with which he had intended to tie her up. After his clowning, the devil retreated from the stage, which was decorated with wall hangings representing regional art. Yolanda Zamora, a radio talk show host moderating the event, welcomed the audience, thanked the people for their participation, and introduced other MCJ and UCI members. As buses on their daily routes halted near the stage, more people walked over to see what was going on. Vendors of peanuts and shaved ice hawked their wares and searched for customers. Throughout the next several hours, people would draw close, elbowing through the crowd to get a better look at the proceedings, and then stay or drift away.

Yolanda emphasized that the event was sponsored by the MCJ, a coalition of groups and individuals "working together so we can bring about a change."

She introduced a brief video detailing the history of the coalition, interspersed with footage of urban life, including protests, traffic, and sidewalk food stands. The speakers boomed out: "In 1993, the MCJ was born to rescue the rights of the citizenry, to manifest their need to be heard, in an attempt to show that democracy is not just a legal issue but a way of life. To this end, the MCJ engaged in a project of citizen education for democracy." The video continued to describe a dual strategy. On the one hand, workshops were held to help create "didactic packages," to be distributed among the citizenry. On the other hand, MCJ organizers brought consciousness-raising events to the barrios. The Foro Callejero in Cerro del Cuatro was an example of this second effort.

Yolanda resumed by stressing the independence of the group. "Many people have asked me: From what party do you come? I want to make it very clear that we are non-partisan. You all can vote for whatever party you choose, as your conscience directs. But you must demand a true representation from your elected officials. We will watch another video now, to spark a discussion of the problems in the *colonia* (neighborhood), especially the lack of sewers. But recognize, although the problems we address may be local, we struggle for change for all of Mexico."

The next video began with shots of light traffic passing calmly through the well-kept and recently renovated Avenida Lopez Mateos, a boulevard central to Guadalajara's commercial life, and a route to the city's middle-class residential areas. Pictures of other affluent areas followed, juxtaposed immediately with images of Cerro colonias. Two young bicyclists rode by a stream of sewage descending from the hills above. Children chased each other, jumping across streams of sewage that carved trenches in the pounded earth streets. Families walked by monstrous piles of garbage that choked wide areas of 8 de Julio into sections passable by only two cars. Long camera pans showed the construction common to the area, with barely completed first floors and reinforcement bar sticking up from the house roofs, waiting for the availability of time and money to finish a second story. Other houses betrayed even earlier stages of self-construction, with blue tarps covering unfinished roofs.

The video continued, showing city buses dodging huge furrows in the streets. Viewers saw a brick sewer manhole access leading to nothing, in the middle of a large open trench, testimony to construction that had begun but was never finished. These stark images were juxtaposed with shots of the community: a local woman cooking in an outdoor kitchen; people using the communal laundry, which had been built by the colonia families. The video also highlighted the

activities of the UCI by showing the group meetings that are central to its organizing strategy, group leaders walking the streets announcing meetings over
portable PA systems, and the graffiti used to propagandize.

The residents commented on the images they saw, teasing each other across
the crowd as they appeared on screen, making cooing noises as they saw young
kids bathing themselves, and saying, "How ugly!" when the pictures of the
sewage and burning garbage appeared. The video ended with upbeat images of
group meetings, ending in group hugs, and festivities, including community
meals and dances, as the voice-over intoned: "The settlement Cerro del Cuatro
in the city of Guadalajara, Jalisco, is made up of thirteen colonias. In seven of
these, sewer work began in 1990 and is still not in service. There is still no sewer
system. The organized settlers have requested a response from the appropriate
authorities because sewage discharge puts the residents' health at risk. Even
though the federal Social Development Secretariat says there is money for the
public works, the state government denies it."

The video over, the crowd's attention was captured by the devil and the
actors on stilts. One actor—mustachioed, dressed in a long black frock coat,
white shirt and tie, and a top hat—represented the corrupt Mexican system.
Two others were dressed to represent Mexico's Everyman and Everywoman, in
work clothes and straw hats reminiscent of rural backgrounds. They stood in
the middle of the crowd. The devil asked, "What do you think?"

Don Catrín, the system's representative, replied, "Well, it doesn't look all
that bad to me."

Everyman challenged the injustice of the system that created unequal access
to public works: "Why don't you supply services for the poor?"

"Well, that's why [the poverty]."

"What are you saying? What are you saying to these people here?"

Don Catrín abrogated his responsibility: "They have to work—I didn't
bring them here."

Everyman became more expressively irate: "What do you think? That they
don't work, that they are vagrants?"

"That's right."

"Is that fair, that these people who work for others get nothing? Isn't there
an obligation that there be services for all, not just for certain neighborhoods
where rich people live?"

Calling out its support for Everyman's anger, the crowd was met with comic
aggression by the devil: "Nobody asked you! Who do you think you are, all you
crazies?! Go on, get out of here!"

Don Catrín asked the crowd: "What are you complaining about? We help you—we are helping all of you! What do you have to say about Solidaridad? You know, la Escuela Digna?"[2] The audience hooted in derision.

Everyman became increasingly agitated. "What are you telling us? That we don't have the right to live with dignity?" He appealed to the crowd, "About the Solidaridad program, how can you answer him?"

The moderator entered the crowd, as catcalls about the intention and workings of Solidaridad rained down. "Wait a minute, wait a minute, this is the moment where we, the people, get to express our opinions. You, Señora, what do you think? What does your colonia need?"

A woman, with children hanging on her, answered: "Well, we don't have the necessary services. First, we need water."

"And you, Señora?"

An older woman, very solid and dignified, commented: "What we need is paving of the streets, collection of garbage, and the sewer." Further answers repeated the need for services and secure land titles. One woman commented: "Another thing, no one in the government is concerned for us. All of the work that gets done here is through our own efforts. Who put in the streets? We did! Who hooked up the electricity? We did!"

Throughout the dialogue, Don Catrín and the devil harangued the commentators, mostly to a humorous response. At one point, the devil jumped on stage, providing comic relief through his suggestion that all the people join together, get a bus, go downtown, and get an answer. He appeared crestfallen when people shouted at him that no government functionaries would be there to receive them on a Sunday. Don Catrín faded into the edges of the crowd, almost hurting himself as he tripped over the scaffolding. This, too, brought laughter.

The event continued with a folk singer singing about the Zapatista uprising. Soon, the crowd was redirected to the video screen, where a witch appeared. Heavily made up, she was dressed in a green shawl covered with numbers and odd symbols. Her face was adorned with fake moles and a false nose, and her fingernails were long and pointed. She stood in front of a steaming cauldron. The camera focused on her lips and her fingers, before panning back to a full shot. "Would you like to live in a democracy? I won't talk to you of magic, but

---

2. La Escuela Digna, or the Dignified School, was a national program that gave local schools limited renovation funds. It was one of many programs under the umbrella of the National Solidarity Program (Programa Nacional de Solidaridad, PRONASOL), commonly called Solidaridad. For an overview of the PRONASOL apparatus and programs, see Cornelius, Craig, and Fox 1994.

of things where there is a lot of alchemy, a lot of tricks." She is joined by Dedo, a phallic-looking five-foot-high finger representing the traditional system, in which the president appoints not only his successor but countless other high political functionaries. For part of the short video, the finger deflated and re-inflated, danced to martial music, and bowed, until the witch finally threw it off camera. The witch continued: "Three states of the country are currently not governed by the PRI. Despite this opening, Salinas and Dedo have continued to govern. Eighteen governors have been appointed by the president in this term alone, without elections or democratic consultation. That means every fifteen weeks or so, Salinas has changed a governor. We can't continue like this. Democracy is not a magical thing. It is the hour to pass from the *dedocracia* to the *democracia*—or no?" With that pun, the cauldron bubbled again, and the witch was gone.

After the video, several UCI and MCJ organizers mounted the stage, addressed the crowd, eliciting and responding to people's comments and questions. Ana Mondragón, one of the UCI founders, spoke first. "Solidaridad said they would pave the streets in 1990. This [promise] came at the same time as the election campaigns. The campaigns ended, and so did the works—but without being completed. This was political propaganda. They brought the [public] works, and people said, 'Okay, I'll vote [for them].' The question in 1994 is how is it that we still continue with this problem, without sewers."

When Ana's brief statement was over, the microphone was passed to Jorge Regalado, a University of Guadalajara researcher. Dressed in blue jeans and a denim work shirt and appearing uneasy speaking before the crowd, he said, "It has been years since the city promised to put in a sewer. The years have passed, and the elections, too; twice they have done this, and now they return for a third time with promises. You all have the freedom to vote for whichever party you choose. But you should never accept the trade of a vote for a public work."

Carlos Núñez, director of the Mexican Institute for Community Development (Instituto Mexicano para el Desarollo Comunitario, IMDEC), an important organizational member of the MCJ, stepped up. "How much does it cost to bring these public works here? All of this [he gestures to include the surrounding colonias] has been your effort. And still they ask you for more money. In the rich colonias, where some of us live, we haven't had to build our own homes, we don't have to burn garbage on Sundays, we don't work without stopping, without rest. Why then do all of you have to use your rest time to continue working? . . . These are all issues of justice—the problem of garbage, and of electricity. They are problems people are feeling in all of Mexico. . . . For this, for all these problems, on the 21st of August, vote for whomever you want. We are not here offering propaganda for any party. But if we don't stop being closed to change, we're all going to lose."

As the crowd's comments and questions began, the UCI representatives stayed on the stage, but it was the pro-democracy activists who answered most of the questions. Carlos Núñez responded to a woman who doubted the utility of voting. "This lady asked, 'Why vote when the same ones always win?' To think this way is to think that things can never change. But that's why we are here, struggling for change. If things could not change, we might as well be off drinking in a bar. If we want to be involved in a system where we are fooled, we will stay there. But the day that we say, 'That's enough! Only up to here!' then it will change."

Juana, a UCI member, commented that she had lived in a nearby colonia for thirteen years without running water. "Now they say they're going to install it in June. But they want to collect money first. And we have to sign an agreement. And people are a little anxious because the same thing happened with the electricity, and they overcharged, and it wasn't a satisfactory job." Many of the people in the crowd murmured their agreement, remembering previous times when they were charged more than the costs to install needed services.

As the crowd drifted away, Everywoman, still on her stilts, waded back into the crowd. "Who believes in Peace and Justice? Who will follow this route? Democracy is here living among us. Who believes that Peace and Justice still live?" The devil also got back into the act, betraying Don Catrín in the end. "You know what? It makes me happy that all of you believe in democracy. Let's demand democracy! The devil demands democracy!" The remaining spectators helped disassemble the stage, the van and truck sped away, and Cerro del Cuatro residents returned to their homes to enjoy the end of their Sunday evening.

The scene above describes a discrete moment of activity pursued by Mexico's democratization movement. The event introduces us to actors from Guadalajara who played important roles in the formal electoral reforms in Mexico. These actors include community organizations from poor neighborhoods, and non-governmental organizations whose activity has been increasingly notable in Mexico and elsewhere. The event also demonstrates the interaction of these two groups as they struggled for political change in urban Mexico. The Foro Callejero, from the speakers to the political morality play, aimed at bringing the poor neighborhood residents into struggles with goals that were beyond immediate and local demands. The juxtaposition of video images from middle-class and poor neighborhoods emphasized that the services that the poor residents fought for were taken for granted in wealthier communities. The Foro organizers contextualized the injustices endured by the poor residents within a national set of hardships, adding further explanations for the government's failure to provide for local needs. The absence of services addressing local material needs, according to the organizers of the Foro, were a result of anti-democratic politics. The movement organizers articulated a clear argument that democratizing the formal institutions of government would address the material needs of the long-suffering poor by installing the very services that Cerro del Cuatro residents had lived without for twenty years.

The scene also demonstrates how neighborhood political organizations like the UCI integrated the goal of the democratization movement into their own work. Although initiated to respond to governmental neglect of the area, the UCI pursued both the resolution of material needs and national and local democratization in alliance with a series of nongovernmental allies. Popular mobilization of many kinds helped push the Mexican government to democratize, and many of the strategies required mass participation organized by neighborhood political organizations.

Mexicans won important democratic changes through a combination of electoral struggle and social-movement action. In 2000, an opposition party candidate, Vicente Fox, won the presidency for the first time since the Institutional Revolutionary Party (Partido Revolucionario Institucional, PRI) had established political power, in 1929. The Mexican congress also transitioned to multiparty rule in 2000, a change begun many years earlier. At last, congressional seats were divided among the three major parties, requiring the formation of alliances to pass legislation and bringing to an abrupt end the rubber stamp customarily available to Mexican presidents.

The state of Jalisco and several of its important *municipios,* including Guadalajara and Tlaquepaque, were governed by opposition governors, mayors, and local congresses for the first time in 1995. By measures of formal electoral politics, then, the democratization movement had been victorious. The history and ongoing experience of Mexico's democratization presents many questions: How did neighborhood organizations move beyond seeking to satisfy local needs to join with organizations representing different social groups? How have organizations of disparate background worked together? What changes in politics and community well-being have resulted with democratization?

In addition to answering these questions, this book has multiple tasks. I seek to embed the story of Guadalajara's democratization movement in the wider political economy of globalization and to detail how global and national economic changes precipitated political changes. I address how these changes posed real consequences for the political behaviors of Mexico's poor, working-class, and middle-class citizens. A coalition of these actors, along with opposition political parties, has brought Mexico to its current stage of democratization. Global economic change precipitated national and local political change in Mexico, by driving disparate citizen groups into a coalition aimed at formal democratization.

Examining a local manifestation of this coalition movement highlights relationships among citizen groups in Mexico. The activity of civil society actors has now become a common theme in research on global and national political change. This book seeks to push the discussion of civil society beyond current limits by addressing concrete moments of change to which citizens contributed. The result of those changes differentially benefited actors in the democratization movement. In many poor Mexican neighborhoods, the fragmentation, isolation, and unequal exchange intrinsic to clientelism long defined urban politics. This tradition left many neighborhood groups focused on material goods and without networks of alliances. In contrast, much of the democratization movement's activity undercut the foundations of clientelism. I describe how this occurred through a discussion of changing politics based in one area of Guadalajara, Mexico's second largest city. Drawing on fieldwork extending over twelve years, I trace the intersection of neighborhood and coalition politics during the democratization movement.

Although civil society actors bearing the democratization banner have brought about recent political changes in Mexico, the opportunities opened to them in the wake of formal democratization have been stratified. This outcome leads to another task of this book: to examine democratization as an empirical goal within the economic and political context of the neoliberal global economy. The global economy, democratization as an empirical effort, civil society as actors and as a social science construct—all intertwined as they influenced changes in Mexico's politics. None are static, as Mexico's democratization continues to evolve and be contested. Yet current results of democratization for different actors lead me to some skepticism regarding how we think about democratization and civil society in the context of neoliberalism.

Neoliberalism, as a redefining of global capitalism, must be understood as a class project. A transnational elite has designed policy that states have implemented, policy that consistently draws wealth out of poor nations and to global elites (Harvey 2005; Robinson 1996). In Latin America and elsewhere, the effects of the project have been distinctly polarizing. Although economic opportunities have polarized, the neoliberal project has been one of political democratization. With the close of the Cold War, powerful policy makers withdrew their support of oppressive, closed regimes that they had earlier perceived as a necessary bulwark against the threat of Soviet and Chinese communist models of development. Concurrently, academic analysts and political actors alike touted the impor- tance of civil society actors engaged in struggles across the globe. Analyses of civil society actors are analogous to earlier discussions of "new social movements." Both built on the empirical reality that contemporary forms of contention were unexplained by existing theory, especially those privileging class analysis. The multiple identities of social actors demonstrated a series of social divisions (gender, ethnicity, indigenous background, sexual preference, opposition to environmental degradation) contributing to collective action in ways that were left insufficiently explained by tools such as Marxist class analysis.

The advances won by those positing the importance of collective identities to mobilization, however, appear to have become overshadowed by a new super-category, that of civil society. Although studies of civil society have pro- liferated, examination of who composes this sector, how different actors under the rubric work together, and what political change means for various subsectors has lagged behind. In many ways, civil society analysis has substituted for class analyses of resistance.

If we are to understand neoliberalism as a class project of political and economic control (Sklair 2001; Portes and Hoffman 2003), however, we may find a differentiated analysis of civil society to be lacking. I hope this book contributes to a more differentiated and nuanced discussion of civil society by recognizing the contributions made to political change and political action while simultaneously recognizing the limitations of both action and analysis using the civil society concept.

METHOD AND STANDPOINT

This book draws on information gathered over fourteen years of fieldwork in Guadalajara, eleven of them focused on the politics emanating from Cerro del Cuatro. In 1991, 1992, and 1993, my fieldwork occurred in stints of between six and eight weeks. I returned to Guadalajara in 1994 and spent the entire year doing fieldwork on the UCI and the organizations with which it worked. Follow-up visits were made in 1997, 1999, 2001, 2004, and very briefly in 2006. In all, I conducted more than 100 interviews, each between one and three hours in length, and I also conducted nearly 150 observations. Although I had not planned it, in 1994, I was fortunate to return to Cerro del Cuatro to trace the changes there over the period of democratization. I repeatedly interviewed many of the NGO activists who had participated in coalitions with the UCI over the years, as well. This long-term relationship was fostered in part by my political stance. I became a supporter of the UCI and aided its efforts in small ways. Although demonstrations of reciprocity facilitated my entry and access to the UCI and its allies, those activities came at a price, as I discuss below.

During my early work in Guadalajara, I built an extensive network of contacts. In 1992, I conducted field research on an emergent social movement that protested government negligence and inefficiency in addressing a street explosion that left hundreds dead. During this fieldwork I became friends with many of the activists who were helping the disaster victims (*damnificados*).[3] These activists graciously spent time with me during a deeply traumatic moment in their lives. I reciprocated by listening to their anguish, at both their losses and the corrupt government responses to their demands, and by serving as photographer, documenting protests and other activities. As they negotiated with police, engineers, and construction workers during the rebuilding, the social-movement organizers sometimes pressed me into a temporary role of "international journalist." I rationalized this masquerade as necessary first to maintain access, and second, as a fairly harmless way to lend some political support to subordinate groups.

In later renewing these contacts, I found that the organizers of these activists helping the damnificados enjoyed good relations with the UCI, which had been part of a citizens' coalition that supported the victims in various ways. The UCI's solidarity and organizing advice created a strong relationship between the two organizations. I had already arranged an introduction to the UCI in the hope of studying a neighborhood organization. However, Lupe, one of the damnificado organizers, offered to bring me up to Cerro del Cuatro and introduce me, before I was formally scheduled to appear on the UCI agenda. I accepted her offer, and she made an appointment with one of the UCI leaders.

On the appointed day, I traveled with Lupe up to Cerro del Cuatro. We met with Tito, who later became my good friend and most reliable informant. During this meeting, I learned a lot about the group, and he learned a lot about me. We openly discussed the issue of what I could exchange for the data I hoped to

3. Latin American disaster victims self-referentially use the term *damnificados*, meaning victims or harmed persons. For a discussion of the emergent movement and the support coalition, see Shefner and Walton 1993 and Shefner 1999b.

obtain. I mentioned that I was ready to share my results with the organization. That seemed useful, but Tito warned me that other researchers had not discharged that obligation. I explained that it would take a long time to write up my research findings, but I offered to give preliminary talks while I was doing the fieldwork. I would also deliver copies of whatever I wrote and return with a full version of the research results. This seemed satisfactory.

The following week, I returned for the formal introduction to the UCI leaders. At that meeting, I described what I hoped to do, including my interest in speaking to both the urban residents and political officials about community politics, and I then asked for questions. Ana Mondragón, one of the leaders I had met the week before, had not been impressed with me and remained quite suspicious. She questioned how I would gain access to the officials, and she voiced her concern that the government would get information about the UCI through my interviews. What she expressed were intentions frequently held by gatekeepers to "safeguard what they perceive as their legitimate interests" (Hammersley and Atkinson 1983, 65). I assured Ana that if there was any pressure to reveal information about the UCI, I would halt my interviews with government officials immediately. At that point, Sofía de la Peña—a researcher who was working as an advisor to the UCI and someone I had consulted—jumped into the conversation, supporting me by mentioning that in her own work she had interactions with government officials without compromising her loyalties.

In response to these and other questions, I talked about my political interests and organizing background in efforts protesting the U.S. intervention in Central America and other movements. The leaders expressed interest in my experience building houses in Nicaragua. I also explained why I felt it was important for U.S. academics and political organizers to understand more about Mexican organizations like the UCI. After some discussion, the UCI leaders agreed to allow me to conduct research on their organization and in their community. Five of the leaders enthusiastically endorsed my activity, while two remained silent. I had achieved entry.

The UCI leadership might have interpreted my expressions of political sympathy as mere rhetoric had it not been for the endorsement of the damnificados. My link to that group legitimized my political persona. During the initial meeting with Tito, Lupe discussed the history of our friendship at length, commenting on the long periods of time I had spent with damnificado victims and organizers, and the sympathy and aid I had offered. From some of the questions I was asked, it was clear that Tito had also shared this information with his colleagues. My contact with the damnificados had continued over several years, which helped the UCI leaders decide that I would not merely extract information from them and disappear. My efforts on behalf of other Latin American solidarity efforts reinforced the UCI leaders' perceptions of my political sympathies and activist work, which also undoubtedly helped me achieve entry into the UCI.

Nevertheless, my probationary status was clear. During my presentation, I repeated my offer to give talks and share my information, yet it was not apparent if these expressions of reciprocity would suffice. Some of the barriers to true access, I judged, were due to wide differences in status, education, and nationality. How could I overcome large social differences in order to gain access to the data that I would need to understand this community and its political struggles?

Over the next few weeks, I learned a great deal by spending a lot of time at the UCI office and reading years of archived newsletters and other documents. Tito was usually there, so I was able to talk with him frequently, and we began to forge a friendship. I provided some minimal reciprocity by translating into Spanish letters from British NGOs. But from the cool treatment I received from some leaders, I knew I was still on probation.

The day came when a UCI delegation was going to talk to the governor's assistant secretary for land-tenure matters. Because it was always important to display support, one hundred people affiliated with the UCI descended on the Plaza de Armas. This open square is bordered by the cathedral and other buildings facing the Palacio de Gobierno, which simultaneously serves as a government office building and a tourist attraction. Its architecture and murals, painted by Guadalajara's native son José Clemente Orozco, are world renowned.

As a government building, the Palacio is a constant target for protestors, and although its four entrances almost always stand open, teams of armed state police are stationed at each door. During demonstrations, even as normal daily traffic continues unabated, the state police, with reinforcements, will block protesters from entering. Today was no exception, and the guards barred UCI members' entry even though the organization had a formal appointment with the assistant secretary. After some discussion, they allowed a group of six people to go to the second-floor offices, while the guards held another group of twenty protesters on the main floor, by that famous Orozco mural, under the doleful gaze of Padre Hidalgo. The remaining UCI members were kept out of the building.

That day I was taking photographs. With camera and backpack and my Anglo features, I was indistinguishable from the other tourists. My nationality, and apparent class and status, allowed me greater freedom of movement than the UCI members had. Because of the guards' perceptions, I was able to wander in and out of the building at will, which enabled me to talk to the UCI groups in their different locations: the two groups inside the building, as well as the one outside. At one point during the course of my meanderings, Tito, with the group in the upstairs waiting area, mentioned to me in passing that he wished the group on the first floor knew about the unguarded back stairway. Unbidden, I carried this message down to the protesters stuck on the first floor, and I guided them up the back stairway to join their companions. A single police officer watched us ascend, with an expression betraying that he knew he should do something, but he didn't know what.

At a later point, Agustín, another UCI leader, left the building to make a telephone call and was then denied reentry. I helped him under the pretense of talking to an attendant at a tourist information desk in front of an unguarded entrance to the building. By the time Agustín reentered, however, and for the rest of the day, the police strictly guarded the back staircase.

The UCI members were amusedly grateful for my ability to help them unite on the second floor and carry messages from group to group when they could not. Tito, surprised when his colleagues appeared, leaned over and whispered his thanks in my ear. I had acted spontaneously, out of political sympathy for the UCI's efforts, but my actions held important implications for furthering my access to the UCI.

My next appearance at a UCI meeting demonstrated that my status had changed significantly. The organizers greeted me warmly, and I was the subject of a lot of jokes. Socorro, who had been openly suspicious of me at previous meetings, now sat next to me and joked about how she was not used to gringo Spanish, and so, unable to understand me, she had delayed following me up the back stairway. Both Carmen and Agustín, who had warmly welcomed me initially, now greeted me like an old friend. Javier, a baker as well as an organizer, immediately pushed a platter of pastries in front of me. Tito, whose friendship I had nurtured during my days delving into the UCI's files, clapped me heartily on the back. Sofía, the researcher-advisor, had yet to hear the tale, but she smiled broadly as the other leaders related the incident to her.

Ana's attitude had also changed. Up to that point, I had yet to begin interviewing UCI members, as I was still learning all I could about the organization through the archives and chats with Tito. My strategy was to first build relationships with and interview the leaders, then accompany them to neighborhood meetings that they coordinated, attend those for a while, and then, with the leaders' endorsements, solicit interviews there. In the aftermath of the demonstration, Ana asked me when I wanted to start interviewing group members. I fumbled for an answer because of my research plan and my general nervousness around her.

After patiently listening, she responded expansively, "Jon, the people await you!" In addition to joking with me, the organizers noted the political implications of tourists having easier access to their government buildings than do the citizens of Mexico themselves.[4]

The gatekeepers had opened the gate. For the remaining months of my fieldwork, UCI leaders and members aided me in many ways. I interviewed dozens of members, participated in every meeting, demonstration, workshop, and social event sponsored by the organization, and I was welcomed into the homes of many UCI members and leaders. Significantly, when I shifted to interviews with government officials and backers, the UCI leaders supplied me with an extensive, uncensored list of those I should interview.[5]

My expression of political sympathy helped convince UCI leaders and members that I was someone who could be trusted with information about their political beliefs and activity. Despite the multiple differences in social location that might have provided initial barriers to in-depth discussion, we found a solidarity around which further bonds could be built.[6] Leaders and members clearly recognized that I would leave the UCI and use their experiences to tell a story that would be more important for my professional career than for their political needs. However, my actions convinced them that my political beliefs were an important reason for my professional interests in Mexico. This perspective increased their willingness to share their history and experiences with me. Thus, my expression of political sympathy was a genuine benefit in studying an opposition organization.

However, this created ongoing expectations as well. As time passed, I was expected to take increasingly active roles in meetings, including expressing my opinion about political and economic contexts and governmental response. This led to some uncomfortable moments when I felt that I was more a part of

4. When organizers discussed the event at group meetings, my ability to enter the building more freely than Mexican citizens was used as a pedagogical device in the group's popular education efforts. The event lived on: during the planning for a similar protest seven months later, in answer to questions of what was needed for a successful demonstration, a UCI member yelled out, "Make sure Jon comes!"

5. Access is, of course, continually renegotiated. This event did not convince all UCI members that I was worth their time. I continued conversing with members about my interest in their cause and my use of the data I was collecting. I failed to convince several of my trustworthiness, and either they declined to be interviewed or our conversations were stilted. In attempting to achieve entry into a group and to remain in the good graces of gatekeepers and community members alike, one-time displays of political sympathy certainly cannot resolve all difficulties. However, this event took me a long way toward ongoing good relations.

6. As my wife and young daughter accompanied me to many events, my role as a father and husband was quite evident, so other bonds included the common joys and concerns of family.

the object of my research than my training had suggested would have been methodologically correct. One example came during a vote to decide which of the UCI leaders would become a liaison to other social movement organizations. Because I had begun to study the other organizations, I had a distinct opinion about who would be best suited for that role. I felt, however, a great deal of discomfort at being put in a position of making a decision. When asked to vote, I begged off, joking that I would be the international observer and ensure the voting process was clean.[7] Although they appreciated the joke, the UCI leaders insisted that I cast an anonymous ballot. I rationalized that the anonymity saved me from harming the relationships I was working hard to maintain, but I felt that my position as a researcher was compromised.

A similar occasion came during my study of the coalition of social-movement organizations. The Jalisco state government, under the umbrella of the federal Solidaridad program, was wooing the coalition to compete for project funds. In my view and that of many of the movement leaders, this was a transparent attempt at co-optation. When asked, I said as much. The participants responded that despite the political danger, they needed money from somewhere to proceed with their projects. They asked me if I would search for U.S.-based foundations that might fund them, so that they could escape the government's clutches. In order to display reciprocity, I fulfilled this request. My political sympathies led me, however, to take a consultative role, which pushed the organization along a course I advocated. Again this brought me into the research in ways that left me questioning my role.

My politics eased my access to the groups I studied and shaped the roles I assumed. In working with the organized poor on Cerro del Cuatro, I took positions that were similar to the advocacy roles that characterized my political life in the United States. I was always clear on the great differences between us in class, ethnicity, status, and often gender. I knew also that my political activity with the UCI was muted in comparison to that of the organization's members, and thus posed fewer costs for me than for them.[8] Yet I consistently was forced to balance expectations and analysis.

My ongoing belief in the nobility of the struggles I observed does not preclude my recognizing that my stance had costs for my project.[9] First, my political

7. This was during the 1994 presidential elections, when the government allowed international observers to document the notoriously corrupt Mexican electoral process.

8. See Sawyer 2004 for an example of particularly engaged political ethnography.

9. Much of the following discussion is the fruit of conversations with another urban ethnographer, Robert Gay. Our articulation of these issues can be found in Shefner and Gay 2002.

sympathies molded some of my expectations for what I saw and also led me to participate in ways that went beyond displays of reciprocity, such as participating in the organization's voting or in fund-raising. Both aspects had an influence on the process of study and write-up. Initially, my involvement may have compromised my ability to assess the decisions and actions taken by the organizations I studied. With even minimal involvement in decision making, my participation might have grown to the extent that it would impede critical evaluation.

Second, my strong affiliation to contentious organizations may have limited my contacts with organizations with different political perspectives. At several points during my research, I pursued interviews with both local government functionaries and pro-government neighborhood organization leaders. Indeed, one government official, finding the questions I asked to be "very hot," halted the interview to call his superior to ask whether we should proceed. Luckily, I had previously interviewed the superior, and so approval was given for the interview to continue. Although I obtained useful data from both functionaries, during one interview I asked questions of an official that made him extremely uncomfortable. With less charged information and sentiment, I might have obtained the same information in a less anxiety-producing setting.

Additionally, during the interviews with pro-PRI neighborhood organizers, I talked with many people who directly opposed the UCI. I was careful to hide some information I had, but I conducted the interviews with a very cynical eye regarding the truth of the information I gathered. A more open analysis of the interview might have been beneficial. It was not clear whether the interviewees knew of my affiliation with the UCI. If they did, however, it is likely that they carefully filtered the information they gave me. Thus, my political sympathies may have corrupted my ability to get the full picture of the urban political moment.

The question of political sympathies may also highlight researchers' arrogance in expecting that we have something to offer in a situation so foreign to our own experiences. The political environments in the United States and in Latin America during the 1980s and 1990s were vastly different. During the six-year term of Mexico's President Carlos Salinas de Gortari, for example, over two hundred and fifty militants from the opposition Partido de la Revolución Democrática (PRD, Party of the Democratic Revolution) were murdered (Bruhn 1997). This is not the environment in which U.S.-based scholars and activists conduct our own politics. There is arrogance in actively participating in a role and place that we have both the power and intention to leave, and this is compounded by the vastly different political environment in which U.S.-based scholars and activists work.

An additional problem emerges when we are put, even implicitly, in an expert role by virtue of our education and status. Our years of study can never approximate the years of experience with authoritarian or clientelist politics, and the knowledge those experiences generate among those we study. Nor can our often middle-class backgrounds be supplanted by living for a time in poor neighborhoods, especially in comparison to the experiential knowledge gained by a lifetime of such living. Yet I was at times placed in an expert role that created a problematic, if informal, hierarchy in the research site. This may have compromised my efforts to gather data on the politics of the urban poor. It also may have created a new informal hierarchy at the same time that those organizations and actors were striving to reform existing hierarchies.

The dilemma, of course, is that many of us participate in our research settings because we are asked to do so. I do not argue against offering something in return for the great help we receive during our research. The greatest difference between researchers and those we study, however, remains our ability to leave. Activists who struggle daily against oppressive political regimes have no such privilege. This makes them subject to responses to both their strategic decisions and those made with our consultation. Thus, our presence may generate a vulnerability well beyond our ability to either recognize or ameliorate, a vulnerability that we do not share.

Finally, my political sympathies may have engendered a problem for the research product. Research on Latin American social movements and community organizations exploded during the 1980s and 1990s, and as Kenneth Roberts noted, the work on new movements was often romantically optimistic: "The boom in the study of Latin American social movements . . . manifested a high degree of faith in the transformative potential of popular organizations" (Roberts 1997, 138). This "celebratory" literature, according to Roberts, tempted researchers into "viewing each new manifestation of popular organization as a harbinger of change in power relationships" (Roberts 1997, 138).[10]

I suspect that in my own work and that of others, our celebration of social movement activities may have led researchers to overestimate the impact of the social movements and community organizations we have studied. Despite decades of popular struggle across Latin America, researchers must continue to question how much the material well-being and political rights of the Latin American poor have improved due to these efforts. Yet few of us have left the field with a realistic evaluation of the outcome of popular struggle. It is only much later, with the passing of current history and further forays into the field, that we are

10. Haber (1997) makes a similar argument.

able to assess how much has actually changed for the urban poor—and how much of it is due to popular action.

This cautionary tale should not be read as advocating the return to a Weberian value-free sociology. But like Jacqueline Adams's (1998) suggestions about reciprocity, I believe that the impact of our sympathetic politics on our field studies in Latin America is insufficiently analyzed. And like many, I recognize that the very participation in the act of research suggests a taking of sides. I do not suggest that we abandon our political stances in the field or later, but that we recognize them for the opportunities and filters they provide us. I believe that my ongoing engagement with these organizations, and the long period of study over the UCI's fluctuating fortunes, allowed me to recognize organizational successes and failures, clear my mind of romantic preconceptions, and eventually tempered my bias. But this tempering took time, removal, and return. As we discuss our roles as researchers, we must be careful about how our politics influences our standpoints. Political change relies on good data as much as does social research.

BOOK OVERVIEW

The following chapters discuss the participation of the UCI in its struggles for material goods and its participation in the democratization movement. Chapter 2 provides the economic and political context. The intersection of mobilized citizen groups cannot be understood without examining the global economy's influence on Mexico. Neoliberalism's famed effort to remove the state from the economy attacked Mexico's state-centered political tradition. The literature on clientelism helps frame the political processes in which the UCI engaged, which were different from traditional political action found in clientelist neighborhoods. The electoral trends in Mexico, and specifically in Jalisco, provide further context for the discussion of the democratization movement. Finally, Chapter 2 engages in a critical analysis of discussions of civil-society activity and influence.

Chapter 3 provides an empirical introduction to the case and research site, examining neoliberal shifts that affected politics in Cerro del Cuatro over a period of urban explosion and economic change in Guadalajara. As the Guadalajara Metropolitan Zone grew, Cerro del Cuatro emerged as a locale where families could build their own homes. The early history of politics in the zone reveals that the development of the Unión de Colonos Independientes followed a familiar path. Organizers built on a foundation created by religious workers, who organized CEBs to discuss new visions of the Bible and liberation theology's preferential option for the poor, to mobilize neighborhood groups, block by block, across the zone. With the aid of a Jesuit social change organization, organizers united the separate neighborhood groups.

Chapter 4 discusses the early years of the UCI as it focused on the provision of basic services, such as water, sewers, and electricity, as the goals of its political action. To achieve these goals, the UCI consistently confronted old structures of PRI control, such as neighborhood groups. Additionally, new structures of representation, such as Solidaridad committees, provided another field of contention. Throughout this period, the UCI relied on its self-help efforts and the direction by a Jesuit social promotion group, Educational Services of the West (Servicios Educativos de Occidente, SEDOC).

Following its early years, the UCI became further involved in increasingly partisan work, as Chapter 5 demonstrates. As the PRD became institutionalized after its 1988 birth as a temporary coalition, it pursued strategies to build on its popular base. Recognizing that many popular movements supported it, the PRD opened its electoral mantle to many of these organizations. At the urging of SEDOC, which remained at the its helm, the UCI ran several candidates from Cerro del Cuatro. In so doing, the UCI continued to work toward the goal of national democratization. Its intense efforts and new partisan ties, however, displaced some of the efforts to address local needs. Popular support diminished with this organizational change. The influence of the Jesuit organization at this juncture demonstrates some of the problems with an undifferentiated concept of civil society.

Chapter 6 discusses the costs incurred with the turn to partisan participation. The Jesuit hierarchy reacted unfavorably, as did many of UCI's constituents. A crisis followed, as the UCI simultaneously sought support and direction. UCI leaders recognized the source of the diminishing popular support but did not want to give up their wider political efforts. The UCI sought balance between work addressing basic needs and democratization. But as SEDOC withdrew, the PRI increased pressure and the organizing field became increasingly complex.

Chapter 7 details research done in the late 1990s and the early 2000s as the democratic transition took root in Jalisco and Mexico. I returned briefly to Guadalajara several times, but I spent much more time revisiting Cerro del Cuatro, the UCI, and many of their NGO allies in 2001 and 2004. What changes accompanied democratization, I wondered? I address how democratization had influenced basic needs provision and political organizing on Cerro del Cuatro, and the strategies pursued by civic NGOs. The differing experiences of the UCI and their supporters during the Mexican transition return me to my concluding discussion of political change, neoliberalism and democratization, and the illusion of civil society in Chapter 8.

2

FROM GLOBAL ECONOMY TO LOCAL POLITICS

Economic globalization has imposed a series of pressures across the world. Many of these pressures have shaken the foundations of national politics, leading some nations to greater authoritarianism and others—like Mexico—to greater democratization. Once national politics are changed, their local manifestations are likely to be altered as well. In this chapter, I discuss changes in the global economy and then turn to consequent economic and political changes within Mexico, the contexts that frame the activity of the UCI. I also discuss local clientelism as the prevailing tradition of urban politics. Changes that demonstrate an increasingly vibrant civil society challenge many state- and party-centered political systems, such as clientelism. Finally, I consider the ways in which political change has been understood by those analysts who have researched civil society. Civil society analysis has become increasingly important for those examining democratization. I suggest that researchers' fixation on the unity of civil society leads us to ignore its strata.

NEOLIBERALISM AND THE ASSAULT ON THE STATE

Neoliberalism is characterized largely by "market deregulation, state decentralization, and reduced state intervention into economic affairs in general" (Campbell and Pedersen 2001, 1). The hegemony of the neoliberal economic and political project, achieved at the expense of other policy alternatives, arose largely in response to the international debt crisis of the late 1970s and early 1980s. Beginning in 1973, oil prices increased precipitously, with important results. Western recessions were deepened by increasing oil prices, "thus limiting the number of attractive lending opportunities and willing borrowers" (Weaver 2000, 172).

Banks, holding large amounts of OPEC capital, aggressively increased lending to developing and socialist nations, often disregarding the capacity of the new debtors to repay the loans. Confronted by balance-of-payments deficits resulting from steadily rising import prices, domestic infrastructural needs, scarce domestic capital, and growing poverty, these nations borrowed at unprecedented levels. The debt crisis soon ensued, with interest rates soaring, trade volume diminishing, and foreign exchange reserves depleting in debtor nations. As debt service climbed, debtor nations approached default.

Neoliberal economics gained prestige contemporaneously with the indebted nations' difficulties in paying their debts. Neoliberalism builds on liberal economics, which holds that "economic life should be as untrammeled by constitutional, legal, and administrative constraints as it is possible to achieve, consistent with the maintenance of a stable society and marketplace" (Colclough 1991, 1). Neoliberals differ from their liberal predecessors, however, by recognizing that the comparative advantages offered by national resources is insufficient protection in the global economy (Gustafson 1994). Comparative advantage is an inadequate avenue for development, in this view, if the state continues to intervene in the economy. Instead, economies grow by cutting social-service expenditures, decreasing industry protection, freeing interest rates, privatizing state-owned enterprises, and setting realistic currency exchange rates. These policies will simultaneously reduce state intervention while increasing competition and investment. The resultant economic growth will address poverty, the defining characteristic of the developing world. As the prestige of neoliberal economics grew in the graduate programs of economics departments in U.S. universities, a generation of soon-to-be policy makers were inculcated into the new orthodoxy (Babb 2001; Centeno 1997). When international development agencies and bank officials attributed the success of newly industrializing Southeast Asian countries to neoliberal policies, neoliberalism became further entrenched (Colclough 1991).[1]

Starting in the 1970s, renegotiations of both debt repayment and debt-service relief entailed neoliberal economic policy prescriptions. Developing nations were required to accept agreements with the International Monetary Fund (IMF), as that institution in effect became the collection agency for large international banks: "The IMF, aided and abetted by the World Bank, organized the

---

1. Despite neoliberal rhetoric about divorcing the free market from state intervention, the Asian NICs "were in fact state-managed economies" (McMichael 1996, 125). Amsden (1985) confirms this point, and the debt crisis that hit Southeast Asia in the 1990s also provides support for that argument. See also Weaver 2000 and Stiglitz 2006.

creditors into a coherent group and discouraged a corresponding consortium among the debtor nations" (Weaver 2000, 176). Weaver points out that Latin American governments, under pressure from the IMF and banks, added to their own responsibilities by guaranteeing the loans taken by private borrowers in their countries in addition to their own public debt. With an overwhelming debt burden and facing a coalesced group of creditors, Latin American and other developing nations were subjected to a series of agreements with the IMF.

These agreements, varyingly labeled structural adjustments, austerity or stabilization policies, or even more dramatically, shock treatments, led to drastic domestic policy changes. Governments shrank, consumer subsidies were cut, and domestic industries lost their protections. Additional measures included wage freezes and social spending cuts, in areas such as health, education, and housing.[2]

The impact of debt on developing economies was devastating. From 1980 to 1993, low-income economies' per-capita GNP grew at average annual rates of 0.1 percent, while lower middle-income economies declined by 0.5 percent.[3] Even the upper-middle income countries reached average annual per-capita GNP growth rates of only 0.9 percent (World Bank 1995a, table 1).[4] Developing-world indebtedness in 1980 totaled $658 billion, rising to $1.9 trillion by 1994 and to $2.5 trillion by 1998 (World Bank 1995b; World Bank 2001). Negative financial transfers were common across indebted nations throughout the 1980s and 1990s (McMichael 1996; Wood 1986).

With the expansion of IMF influence have come new tools of structural adjustment. The IMF now uses standby agreements, Extended Fund Facilities, and Enhanced Structural Adjustment Facility loans as tools of conditionality. This expansion, added to the growth in debt, has increased the numbers of agreements between the IMF and member nations. Prior to 1986, there was a 22 percent probability of any developing nation being part of an IMF program; from 1986 to 1997 the probability increased to 51 percent (Evrensel 2002). Indeed, many member countries "have been under the IMF's care almost continuously" (Evrensel 2002, 578). Debt and subsequent national vulnerability to policy dictates of international financial agencies arguably continues to define the economic

2. See Walton and Seddon 1994 for more on neoliberal reforms.

3. As defined by the World Bank, low-income economies include much of indebted Africa, as well as some Asian and a few Latin American nations. These statistics exclude China and India. Lower middle-income economies include much of Latin America, some recently transformed Eastern European countries, and some African and Asian nations.

4. As defined by the World Bank, upper middle-income countries include developing world giants, such as Mexico, Brazil, and the Korean Republic.

policies of nations in the developing world even more now than it did twenty years ago (Harris and Seid 2000, Nef and Robles 2000).

The role of debt in politicians' decision making is arguable. The ongoing power of neoliberal orthodoxy as the intellectual root of economic policy making is not, nor is the ongoing impact of decisions based in neoliberal policies implemented by both domestic policy makers and the international financial community. The sum total of policy, at this point, has forced national governments to increasingly cast their policy perspectives outward. Despite distinct and dramatic social development needs in their own nations, the ongoing pressure of debt and the privileged position of neoliberalism has forced many developing nations to govern in ways that disadvantage their own populations while catering to multinational capital. This external economic focus has important implications for the conduct of politics in these nations.

FROM IMPORT-SUBSTITUTION INDUSTRIALIZATION TO NEOLIBERALISM IN MEXICO

Mexico provides a useful example to examine the concurrent economic and political changes driven by neoliberalism. An economic giant in the developing world, Mexico has now become an industrialized nation, as its membership in the OECD and its World Bank designation as an upper-middle-income economy attest. In 2000, manufactured goods made up 87.3 percent of Mexico's total exports, compared to 9.8 percent for petroleum products and 2.5 percent for agriculture (OECD 2002, 7). Much of the growth of Mexico's economy occurred during the post–World War II era of import-substitution industrialization.

Import-substitution industrialization (ISI) is a development strategy that is predicated on the belief that it was the historical trade imbalance that kept developing nations at a disadvantage compared to their industrialized trading partners. Rather than continue to send agricultural goods and raw materials in exchange for manufactured imports, ISI advocates argued that developing nations like those in Latin America had to create both internal markets for manufactured goods and internal strategies to satisfy those markets. To accomplish this, national governments followed a series of protectionist trade policies coupled with active investment in infrastructure, especially supporting specific industries. Socially, ISI required investment in the working and middle classes in order to nurture both the skills to manufacture new goods and the economic wherewithal to consume them.

Mexico's economy enjoyed dynamic growth under ISI, as manufacturing drove high GDP and GDPPC (gross domestic product per capita) rates. Annual increases in GDP ranged from 5.1 percent to 7.6 percent between 1950 and 1969 (Lustig 1992). Labor legislation increased the share of income devoted to the middle earning 55 percent of the population, and much of the new economically active population became absorbed within the formal economy (Dussel Peters 2000).

Import-substitution industrialization in Mexico was never fully self-sustaining, however. The need to invest in both manufacturing and social development forced policy makers to rely on resources gained in agricultural and tourist sectors of the economy. Additionally, the nation remained reliant on imports for more capital-intensive manufacturing needs because Mexican industry focused mostly on consumer and intermediate goods (Dussel Peters 2000). A bifurcation of the industrial economy emerged, as "state-owned enterprises and national private firms provided the infrastructure, producing consumer and intermediate goods, while TNCs [transnational corporations], with higher total factor productivity and profit rates concentrated their activities in relatively more advanced manufacturing" (Dussel Peters 2000, 44).

Although ISI in Mexico was unable to overcome a high dependence on imports, social development was nurtured in important ways during this period. Mexican ISI never reached the hoped-for levels of job creation, but economic growth allowed some benefits to spread across much of the nation. The successful years of ISI policies created mostly middle-class jobs, while social policy improved nutrition, housing, and public services, and levels of education, standards of living, and life expectancy rose (Levy and Bruhn 2001).[5] As debt began to define the political economy of the developing world, critics of ISI drew on the new neoliberal orthodoxy to attack the "failure," or at best, the "exhaustion" of import substitution as a development policy. The failure of ISI is less clear than these critics would suggest.

Whether ISI so dramatically failed in and of itself is debatable, because it was a casualty of the close of the Golden Age. During the 1970s and 1980s, the two oil shocks and then the debt crisis made Latin American macroeconomic management extremely difficult by limiting access to imports of essential intermediate and capital goods. Slow output growth

5. Despite gains Mexico made during its ISI period, inequality continued growing. The annual monthly increase in income for the bottom 70 percent of Mexican families was far less than the increase in GDP rates (Aguilar Camín and Meyer 1993, 177).

and inflationary pressures due to supply limitations imposed by scarce foreign exchange were virtually inevitable. Relatively low savings rates in most countries "multiplied" . . . the impacts on output of adverse external shocks. (Taylor 1999, 4)

Indeed, it may have been the success of ISI that helped it run its course. Frederick Weaver argues that, in general, the "exhaustion and need for renewal were due to government-sponsored economic growth's success in having created an industrial base, transportation and communication networks, declining population growth rates, monetized market economies, and workforces that to a substantial degree were literate, urban, healthy, and disciplined to modern work" (2000, 180). In this analysis, a changed political and economic environment required new and innovative policy to maintain growth and attack poverty, but to consider that the ISI policy's successes were a failure tells us much more about the neoliberal policy makers' ideological agenda than it does about the strength of their analysis.

Regardless of the wider success of the model, Mexican ISI contained within it the seeds of its own destruction as policy makers proved unable to move beyond dependence on capital-intensive imports. Despite increasing industrial production, the balance-of-payment inequities that ISI was designed to address continued to characterize Mexico's economy, which became even more vulnerable with the oil-price spikes in the early 1970s. High imported-oil prices required high levels of borrowing. Ironically, the discovery of oil reserves drove further borrowing as Mexican policy makers labored under the illusion that a long-lasting oil boom would allow them to pay debt and pursue economic and social development (Otero 1996).

By 1982, Mexico was overwhelmed by its debt and declared its inability to pay its debt service. It became apparent that "Mexico had exhausted agriculture, oil revenues, and indebtedness as means to subsidize a protected industrialization process, and new avenues for economic growth had to be found" (Otero 1996, 7).With the neoliberal opening of the economy, the debt burden overwhelmed the government's ability to ameliorate the social costs of the new policy.

THE COSTS OF NEOLIBERALISM

Neoliberal policies have reduced wages and increased unemployment and the number of households in poverty. Comparing the twenty years of the neoliberal project to the previous ISI model, Alejandro Portes and Kelly Hoffman (2003) document that 5.7 percent of Mexico's population consists of its dominant class (capitalists, executives, and professionals); a second stratum, approximately 23 percent, forms the middle class (petty bourgeoisie and the nonformal manual proletariat); and the remaining 71 percent consists of the working class and working poor, whether they are employed in the formal or informal sectors.

Under neoliberalism, only the dominant class has increased its standing (Portes and Hoffman 2003, 59), while wages declined precipitously for Mexican workers. By 1997, middle-class workers earned only four times the amount considered to be a poverty-level wage, on average, and working-class incomes ranged from 2.8 to 1.9 times that wage (Portes and Hoffman 2003). Annual wage decreases ranged from 7.7 percent to 12.3 percent in an almost uninterrupted decline that lasted from 1982 through 1997. Real wages in 1998 were 57 percent of real wages in 1980; the minimum wage in 1998 was 29.5 percent of the minimum wage in 1980. The number of households below the official poverty line increased from 34 percent in 1970 to 43 percent in 1996. Growing numbers of industrial jobs brought little relief, as new factories paid wages 60 percent lower than did their predecessors (Friedmann, Lustig, and Legovini 1995; Lustig 1998; González de la Rocha 2001).[6]

It is not surprising, then, that income inequality has worsened in Mexico, as it has throughout Latin America, a region generally seen as the most unequal in the world. Julio Boltvinik notes the consistency of the trend across time, telling us that income has become increasingly concentrated across "periods of both economic stagnation (1984–89) and recovery (1989–94 and 1996–2000)" (2003, 404). That is, despite indications of aggregate economic growth, inequality has increased (Alarcón 2003). CEPAL and INEGI estimated that close to 30 percent of the population lived in extreme poverty even during the expansionist years of the late 1990s (OECD 2002, n. 48). Indeed, inequality, already high in 1992 (with a Gini coefficient of .475), had increased (to a Gini coefficient of .481) by 2000 (OECD 2002, n. 58).[7]

With the exception of a brief period in the early 1990s, unemployment has also continuously increased. The structure of employment changed as small businesses failed and fewer Mexican workers found employment in the formal

6. This section focuses on the impact of neoliberalism on Mexican workers. For an extensive discussion of the negative impact of neoliberalism and democratization on Mexico's small business sector, see Kenneth Shadlen's (2004) important work.

7. Portes and Hoffman present even more drastic evidence of polarization: a rise in the coefficient of inequality in Mexico from 6.0 in 1990 to 7.1 in 1996 (2003, 65, table 6).

manufacturing sector (Vega and de la Mora 2003; Boltvinik 2003). Households turned to the informal economy, but those enterprises offer no benefits and less pay than is found in the formal sector (Boltvinik 2003; Alarcón 2003).

Finally, although antipoverty programs were designed to ease the pain of the most vulnerable, many people have still been left behind (Portes and Hoffman 2003). When economic crisis struck again in 1995, it left even more Mexicans in dire straits. Households in extreme poverty increased by 3.4 million (Laurell 2003, 342). The shift from PRONASOL to PROGRESA, the public works and social welfare program of the late 1990s during the administration of Ernesto Zedillo, brought a drop in food subsidies (Laurell 2003). Although the late 1990s saw five years of GDP expansion, 2001 brought that trend to a halt, an outcome many see linked to the U.S. recession, since almost 90 percent of Mexico's exports are destined for the United States (OECD 2002, 30). Employment growth has slowed (OECD 2002, 11). Indeed, during the late 1990s through the beginning of the 2000s, initial decreases in unemployment and inflation and increases in investment and wages have all reversed, with the consequent expansion of informal employment as formal opportunities in the *maquila* sector and other manufacturing shrank (OECD 2002).

The late 1990s saw a temporary increase in social development spending, except in spending for rural development (OECD 2002, 51). That trend quickly halted. Because of the economic slowdown and the need to reduce debt, some of it stemming from the 1995 peso crisis and subsequent bailout, social spending fell during the presidency of Vicente Fox (OECD 2002, 12; Camp 2007).[8] Aggregate standard-of-living increases evident during the last half of the 1990s have subsequently reversed as well (OECD 2002).

Additionally, urbanization brought further political pressure to bear on Mexican governments. Mexico's urban population exploded in the post–World War II era, going from a rate of 35 percent of the total population in 1940, to 51 percent in 1960, to 66 percent in 1980. By 1995, 75 percent of Mexico's total population was living in urban centers (Gilbert 1998, 26). This massive urban growth has increased the political and economic weight of urban dwellers who, as Portes and Hoffman's analysis tells us, are largely poor. At the same time as their political

---

8. The debt, which had reached a high of 38 percent of GDP, decreased following the 1995 bailout. However, at 23 percent of GDP in 2001, the debt continued substantially pressuring the Mexican economy. From 1997 through 2001, the debt-service ratio fell from 33.2 percent to 20.8 percent, but the debt itself increased from US$148.7 billion to $190.8 billion (Economist Intelligence Unit 2002, 5).

and economic weight increased, the resources available to resolve growing urban needs declined as a result of the debt-crisis economic restrictions. For decades, the PRI's methods for political integration merged corporatism and clientelism. With the economic changes brought by neoliberalism, these political strategies became less viable.

The transition to democracy has not been accompanied by a return to material prosperity for most Mexicans. Because of the prominence of the state, its changing role has had great consequences for democratization in Mexico. Neoliberalism, both before and after the democratic transition, imposed severe costs on Mexico. Wages have been reduced, unemployment has remained high, and inequality has increased. The promised link between democratic politics and economic prosperity has been left unfulfilled.

DEMOCRATIC TRANSITIONS AND NEW GOVERNANCE

Since the mid-1980s, real-world changes have driven increased academic interest in democracy and democratization in both the South and in formerly communist nations. The emphases of this literature at first followed traditional themes, such as the impacts of material prosperity, political culture, and institutional change (Almond and Verba 1963; Lipset 1959), but the literature also addressed new elements, such as international influence and the activity of civil society. An important evolution of the discussion is the recognition of the dynamic processual nature of democratization in contrast to a dichotomous assessment of democracy versus some theorized opposite (Linz and Stepan 1996). Democratization is now understood as being a matter of degree, a transition that does not follow a particular sequence and is not an irreversible trajectory (O'Donnell, Schmitter, and Whitehead 1986). However, "once some individual and collective rights have been granted, it becomes increasingly difficult to justify withholding others" (O'Donnell, Schmitter, and Whitehead 1986, 10).

Representation and participation have consistently been central to discussions of democracy and democratization (Rodríguez 2003). Conceptualizations of representation have ranged from a Hobbesian vision of elites acting under the authority of a constituency without consulting them, to a Millsian elite representation based on the assumption of greater expertise and capacity. Others argue that true representation requires actors who mirror the characteristics, and presumably the political stances, of their constituency.

Participation is another key issue, with a variety of conceptualizations, ranging from engagement in formal electoral action to informal social-movement protests, to the activity of constituents in choosing decision makers merely through voting and campaigning (Rodríguez 2003). The influence of specific actors may differ along the chronology of democratization, as "elite factions and social movements seem to play key roles in bringing about the demise of authoritarian rule, political parties move to center stage during the transition itself, and business associations, trade unions, and state agencies become major determinants of the type of democracy that is eventually consolidated" (Karl 1990, 6).

Democratization requires a series of active social groups and strong institutions. Democratic consolidation requires "a lively and independent civil society, a political society with sufficient autonomy, and a working consensus about procedures of governance and constitutionalism and rule of law" as well as "a functioning state apparatus and a market economy" (Linz and Stepan 1996, 7). Larry Diamond, Jonathan Hartlyn, and Juan Linz echo Robert Dahl's characterization of polyarchy by identifying the crucial hallmarks of democratization: genuine, regular, and non-coerced competition among individuals and organizations for power through legitimate elections; "inclusive political participation in selection of leaders and policies" (1999, ix); and a level of civil and political freedoms that make the other elements truly meaningful. Additional features they and other researchers find important include procedural characteristics of decision making, the rule of law, state and constitutional structure and strength, strong political institutions, political leadership, socioeconomic development, especially as it influences inequality, international factors, and a vibrant civil society (Diamond, Hartlyn, and Linz 1999).

What kinds of impacts does political democratization have on economic life, and vice versa? The answers vary, although many accept Seymour Martin Lipset's belief that "the more well-to-do a nation, the greater the chances that it will sustain democracy" (Lipset 1959, quoted in Karl 1990, 12). Lipset's assumption, of course, was articulated when welfare states' capacity to resolve social needs was not under attack by neoliberal theorists and policy makers. Juan Linz and Alfred Stepan "accept the well-documented correlation that there are few democracies at very low levels of socioeconomic development and that most polities at a high level of socioeconomic development are democracies," yet they suggest that "it is often difficult or impossible to make systematic statements about the effect of economics on democratization processes" (1996, 77). Even more important than economic performance, according to Linz and Stepan, is the government's legitimacy.

Karl points out a singularly important relationship in the process of Latin American democratization, finding regime survivability to be intimately linked to who benefits from the process. In her view, the choices made regarding who wins and who loses have distinct implications for whether democratization will progress or recede (1990, 13). According to other researchers, great prosperity may not be correlated to democratization. Instead "economic performance—in terms of steady, broadly distributed growth—is probably more important for democracy than higher and higher levels of socioeconomic development . . . achieved through more pendular, disruptive, and uneven means" (Diamond, Hartlyn, and Linz 1999, 45). These researchers believe poor economic performance can erode systemic legitimacy, a crucial component of democratic transition survivability. Civil society is one of the key actors in both the building and the eroding of democratization, and one of the strategies civil society engages in is electoral opposition.

INCREASING ELECTORAL OPPOSITION

Given the decreasing wages, increasing poverty, and rising inequality, the assault on most Mexicans is undeniable. The Mexican state had great influence over the economy, in part, as the prime driver of ISI policies, but also as a legacy of its post-revolutionary design. Although PRI leaders designed the political system for maximum control, they also provided for the material welfare of the working class and peasantry. The overwhelming dominance of the PRI meant that economic failure drove the political chickens home to roost. With no other political players with whom they might share the blame for the failing economy, the PRI became the target for political change.

Until the 1980s, the PRI had a long history of *carro completo*, or a clean sweep, in elections. Until 1988, the PRI had won every presidential, gubernatorial, and senatorial election since 1929. Despite this overwhelming success, however, local inroads into PRI domination were made as early as the 1960s (Table 1).

The National Action Party (Partido Acción Nacional, PAN) ran a national candidate for only the second time in 1958, and this conservative party won 9.4 percent of the national turnout. The PAN continued to slowly gain strength into the 1980s, interrupting their competition with a protest decision not to participate in the 1976 election. In 1982, the PAN held the PRI to less than 80 percent of the electorate for only the third time in the PRI's existence. Since then, the PRI has lost substantial support for its presidential candidates.

Table 1   Presidential election results, 1952–2006

Year	Percentage of total votes			
	PAN	PRI	PRD/FDN	Others
1952	7.8	74.3	—	17.9
1958	9.4	90.6	—	0
1964	11.4	88.6	—	0
1970	14.0	85.5	—	.5
1976	—	98.7	—	1.3
1982	16.4	74.3	—	9.3
1988	17	51	31	1
1994	26	48.8	17.5	7.7
2000	42.5	36.1	18.2	3.2
2006	35.9	22.3	35.3	6.5

SOURCE: Klesner 1987; Berrueto Pruneda 1994; Navarro Fierro 1994; Eisenstadt 2004; IFE 2006.

The 1988 election decisively showed that Mexico was no longer a one-party state (Salinas de Gortari 1988, cited in Guillén López 1989, 256n). Indeed, the elections resulted in the lowest presidential turnout for the PRI in its history, only enough voters to barely elect the party's candidate. For the first time, the presence of three significant and alternative political forces were felt. Now, in addition to the PRI and the PAN—the traditional conservative opposition— there was the leftist *neocardenista* coalition, the National Democratic Front or Frente Democrático National, which would evolve into the Party of the Democratic Revolution (Partido de la Revolución Democrática, PRD).

Four registered political parties and twenty-five mass organizations and movements supported Cuauhtémoc Cárdenas' 1988 presidential candidacy (Carr 1986).[9] Dissident PRI members initiated the campaign, but other participants pushed the coalition beyond its initial focus on democratization of the PRI to a more comprehensive critique of economic policy and political structure. In addition to the official (and fiercely disputed) vote tally barely granting the PRI presidential candidate, Carlos Salinas de Gortari, a victory, the proportion of electoral districts won by the PRI in 1988 dropped to 35 percent from the 1964 rate of 85 percent (Guillén López 1989, 262). The 1991 and 1994 elections demonstrated even greater opposition to the PRI.

9. The Cardenista Front for National Reconstruction Party (Partido del Frente Cardenista de la Reconstrucción Nacional, PFCRN), the Authentic Party of the Mexican Revolution (Partido Auténtico de la Revolución Mexicana, PARM), the Popular Socialist Party (Partido Popular Socialista, PPS), and the Mexican Socialist Party (Partido Socialista Unificado de México, PSUM) all supported Cardenas's candidacy.

Table 2   Chamber of Deputies election results, 1961–2006

Year	Percentage of total votes			
	PAN	PRI	PRD/FDN	Others
1961	7.6	90.3	—	1.5
1964	11.5	86.3	—	2.1
1967	12.5	83.8	—	3.6
1970	14.2	83.6	—	2.2
1973	16.5	77.4	—	5.8
1976	8.9	85.2	—	5.9
1979	11.4	74.2	—	13.5
1982	17.5	69.3	—	12.9
1985	16.3	68.2	—	15.6
1988	18	61.4	29	1.8
1991	17.7	61.4	8.3	12.5
1994	23.8	60.2	14	2.0
1997	24.2	47.8	25	3.0
2000	44.6	42.2	13.2	0.0
2006	42	21	25	12.0

SOURCE: Klesner 1987; Barry 1992; Eisenstadt 2004; IFE 2006.

The PAN gradually increased its vote share in the Chamber of Deputies, going from 7.6 percent of votes in 1961, to 16.5 percent of votes in 1973 (Table 2). The PAN's fortunes reversed in the 1976 and 1979 elections, however. In 1976, the party suffered from the disarray sown by factionalism and the decision not to run a presidential candidate. In 1979, electoral reform cut into PAN votes. It was not until the 1980s that the party regained its previous level of electoral strength.

In 1979, the greater electoral success of smaller parties ("others" in Tables 1 and 2) was a mixed result of increased opposition and electoral reform. The 1977 electoral reforms were the first significant amendments since 1946, when the franchise was expanded by gender and age. A 1963 reform had assured proportional representation for minority parties that won at least 2.5 percent of the national vote, which was reduced to 1.5 percent in 1973.

The 1977 electoral reforms—a government response to criticism about the unfairness of the electoral system—lowered barriers to participation, allowing smaller parties to form and register more easily. In addition, the number of deputies increased, with one hundred of four hundred seats reserved for the proportional representation of minority parties. Thus, not only was the participation of smaller parties facilitated but they were also offered greater prizes for which to contend. However, the intention of the reforms was to maintain PRI hegemony by cleansing the image of the one-party state through the participation of nonthreatening political parties. Votes for the PAN and for other parties increased soon after the reforms, bringing the PRI share of the vote down to its lowest since the party's creation (Table 2).

Despite maintaining power, the PRI lost support at the rate of ten percentage points per decade from 1960 to 1982. By 1985 it was close to losing urban industrialized states like Chihuahua, Jalisco, and México, as well as losing Mexico City and Baja California. Indeed, electoral support for the PRI consistently declined in urban areas, even within individual states (Baer 1990, 43).

The 1991 and 1994 elections showed some interesting interruptions in voting trends. In 1991, the PRI made surprising gains in areas they had lost only three years earlier, while the PAN held steady, and the PRD appeared to lose much of its mobilizing power (Table 2). These election results were partially due to the PRD's lack of internal coherence in offering candidates and policy alternatives. Additionally, PRI-controlled government social-welfare planners also aimed PRONASOL monies and programs at areas where Cárdenas had had his strongest support in 1988.

In 1994, the biggest surprise was the 77.7 percent voter turnout, the largest ever recorded. This appeared to be a result of two factors. First, the 1994 Zapatista rebellion created widespread fear of a political breakdown, making the alternative to genuine electoral contestation appear to be violent confrontation. Second, a PRI defeat was widely anticipated, especially after the assassination of its presidential candidate, Luis Donaldo Colosio. The poor showing by the replacement candidate, Ernesto Zedillo Ponce de León, in a televised three-candidate debate, emphasized the vulnerability. PAN candidate Diego Fernández de Cevallos, the acknowledged winner of the debate, won support from voters willing to oppose the PRI but who did not like the returning PRD candidate, Cuauhtémoc Cárdenas. Fernández de Cevallos failed to capitalize on his debate victory, however, and he was intensely criticized for not pushing his seeming advantage during the summer campaign. Skeptics believed that he had taken a fall, choosing to limit his campaign efforts in exchange for promises of later rewards. Nevertheless, with the high turnout, the PAN did well, maintaining its strength in the industrialized north while gaining support in southern and central Mexico. The relatively poor showing of the PRD was another surprise. Despite their inability to take the presidency, however, the PRD regained support in comparison to the 1991 elections, almost reaching the level of support it had in 1988. The increase, however, was hidden by the greater voter turnout.

Since its poor showing in the 1991 elections, the PRD had splintered into three factions—whose positions ranged from negotiation with the PRI government to confrontation—that were struggling for the soul of the party. Not only were strategies contested, little coherence was reached on economic policy. Although PRD voters could be sure what they were voting against, the party had not made it clear to them what they were voting for.

Although factionalism was the source of some of the PRD's problems, it had also been more heavily targeted by the PRI than was the conservative opposition. In addition to the federal monies spent in PRD-dominated areas, the PRD was targeted for violence. The party reported that more than two hundred and fifty of its members had been assassinated by late 1994, and the violence was attributed to *priístas* (PRI party members) who were unwilling to accept the challenge the opposition posed (Bruhn 1997).

Despite the PRI's victory, the 1994 elections yielded an important change, as it was the first time the party admitted to winning less than 50 percent of the popular vote. Opposition voters from both left and right showed determination to put an end to the single-party system. In a poll asking voters why they had voted as they did, the most common answers among both PAN and PRD voters were the explicit disapproval of the PRI and the government and the hope for a change in the system (Covarrubias 1994). The PRI was forced to come to grips with an electoral situation where they did not have the absolute majority of voters, and where voter dissatisfaction appeared willing to take the most viable alternative.

The 2000 and 2006 elections demonstrate the triumph of formal democratization in Mexico. The conservative opposition won the presidency in 2000, and again in 2006, although the second election, which Felipe Calderón Hinojosa won, was marred by familiar claims of fraud. Both legislative houses were split between the three major parties, ensuring that even if the presidential election results were fraudulent, Mexico is no longer run by a one-party state.

Voting trends in the state of Jalisco showed earlier and more substantial changes than did Mexico as a whole (Table 3). Significant early opposition to PRI governance is visible although it is articulated largely through support for the PAN. In 1995, Jalisco also elected a PAN governor, Alberto Cárdenas Jiménez, as well as winning control of the state legislature and many cities, including Guadalajara. In a much more tightly contested election in 2000, Francisco Ramírez Acuña of the PAN won the governor's seat. The PAN maintained control of the office with the election of Emilio González in the 2006 elections.

The governments of Guadalajara and surrounding municipios had all changed to PAN control by 2000 if not earlier, but then they began changing back. In 2003,

Table 3   Chamber of Deputies election results for Jalisco, 1991–2006

Year	Percentage of total votes			
	PAN	PRI	PRD	Others
1991	22.6	60.3	2.6	14.5
1994	40.7	43.3	7.5	8.5
1997	43.6	34.7	11.4	10.3
2000	49.3	36	7.9	6.8
2003	38.8	39.3	6.	14.2
2006	45.7	32	12.7	9.6

SOURCE: IFE 2006; Consejo Electoral del Estado de Jalisco (CEEJ) 2003.

Tlaquepaque and Tonalá returned to the PRI. That year, the vote for deputies was extremely close in the district that includes Cerro del Cuatro. In District 16, which includes Cerro del Cuatro, the vote for deputies was extremely close, with the PRI beating the PAN by a narrow margin.

Shifts in political support in Jalisco preceded national changes, although the PAN has not gained sufficient strength to retain power in the municipios. The increase in electoral opposition is not due to any single factor. Neoliberal polices increased electoral contention, but the trends of increased opposition began before austerity programs were put in place. Neoliberal policies hastened a process of regime decomposition begun earlier, as electoral participation data have shown.

As we have seen, one of the most tangible manifestations of the democratic transition in Mexico have been new processes of governance resulting from the strengthening of electoral opposition. During the early 1980s, subnational victories nibbled at PRI hegemony in Guanajuato, Ensenada, San Luis Potosí, Chihuahua, Durango, and elsewhere. After 1988, more important inroads were made. The 1989 PAN gubernatorial victory in Baja California was followed by PAN wins in states and large cities and municipalities across the nation. However, many of the new PAN governments that were built during the 1988–1994 presidency of Carlos Salinas "emerged at the behest of the federal executive" (Rodríguez and Ward 1995, 224). This changed during the 1990s, when electoral processes were sufficiently cleaned up that preelection negotiations with the PRI were not necessary to gain office. The capacity to clean up elections was in itself a result of reforms intended to bring about a "new federalism" in Mexico (Aziz Nassif 2001). The new federalism project sought to reform both the judiciary and revenue-sharing system, achieve a real separation among the branches of government, reduce executive power while strengthening and increasing the

autonomy of state and municipal governments, and separate the PRI's equivalence with the government, effectively forcing a clear distinction between the
PRI and the Mexican government (Ward and Rodríguez 1999).

In Baja California, one researcher noted increased possibilities for political
pluralism: "political power [is]now in the hands of public institutions and
those who control them . . . specific and complex groups and nodes of power
such as municipal councils and the state legislature" (Guillén López 2001). In
Chihuahua, local PAN governments decentralized resource allocation and
broke their partisan corporatist ties to the PRI-controlled federal government
(Aziz Nassif 2001). State and municipal "PAN governments focused intensely
on fiscal initiatives designed to improve revenue generation, including tax
reform and more efficient administrative management of government finances"
(Shirk 2005, 177). Others found decentralization achieving greater pluralism of
authority in education, health care, and construction of physical infrastructure
(Díaz-Cayero 2004).

Despite the articulation of the new federalist project, and tangible electoral
gains, the achievements of decentralized governance have been incomplete.
Wayne Cornelius's statement also describes much of the democratization
period: "Subnational political regimes controlled by hard-line anti-democratic
elements linked to the PRI remain important in late twentieth-century Mexico,
even in an era of much intensified inter-party competition" (1999, 3). Alberto
Díaz-Cayero (2004) also reminds us that patron-client politics have continued
to co-exist, even thrive, with decentralized political authority. Others similarly
see trends of democratization in some of the regional political systems that is
occurring simultaneously with "backward, authoritarian, and cacique-dominated
politics" (Aziz Nassif 2001, 190).

The ongoing strength of patron-client politics is partially the result of the
continuing strength of the PRI, which remains Mexico's strongest party at the
state level (Camp 2007). It is also the result of policies of the PAN, which has
given priority to addressing transparency and efficiency over satisfaction of
popular needs. Additionally, the desire to dismantle corporatist political affiliations may have prevented building stronger popular support that would last
longer than the electoral moment (Shirk 2005).

Changing electoral fortunes have led to new configurations of power as
political authority has decentralized across Mexico. Yet the most important
conflict in Cerro del Cuatro from the 1990s into the 2000s remained that of the
fight of civil society against clientelism, as the PRI tried to return to power. On

Cerro del Cuatro, civil society activity explains many of the formal democratic changes that occurred. Before that, however, civil society sectors had to contend with long-standing clientelist politics.

PATRON-CLIENT POLITICS

Mexico's postwar political economy allowed the PRI state to reward its supporters in the middle and working classes and ensure the acquiescence of many citizens. The political system relied on corporatist state organization and clientelist relationships. The state used corporatist inclusion to bring labor, the peasantry, and the diverse urban popular sector under the PRI's big tent.

The needs created by the country's increasing urbanization provided the PRI with a medium of exchange that it used to incorporate the increasingly diverse urban citizenry and to channel that population's political participation into support for the party. With increasing housing costs and decreasing housing stock in inner cities, urban dwellers began to move to communities growing on city outskirts. In some cases, these communities were planned and coordinated by developers; often they were not (Gilbert and Varley 1991; Ward 1986). Neighborhoods could arise spontaneously when squatter groups seized land or small landowners sold their properties to people intent on building their own homes. Whether the land was purchased or only squatted on, for many families, building a house was a strategy for upward social mobility. However, this phenomenon also allowed the PRI to exploit both formal electoral roles and informal patron roles. The seizure or purchase of land satisfied only the first of the needs for these new residents. PRI political organizations formed at the neighborhood level to secure legal land tenure and to install public services, such as sewers, electricity, potable water, paving, trash removal, and so forth. These needs supplied the political system based on clientelism with the medium required to elicit the loyalty of new community members. Local brokers used their ties to the PRI to elicit the patronage resources required to resolve the needs of the growing urban periphery.

The confluence of exploding urban growth, an expanding economy, and state efforts toward inclusion created a particular variant of patron-client politics.[10] Mexican clientelism channeled dissent and demand-making into state sanctioned venues, limiting alternative organizing and recreating state power by incorporating

10. This section is drawn from classic studies of Mexican clientelism, such as Vélez-Ibáñez 1983; Cornelius 1975; Fagen and Tuohy 1972; Eckstein 1988; Gilbert 1989; Gilbert and Varley 1991; Ward 1986; Castells 1983; Roniger 1990; Roniger and Günes-Ayata 1994.

dissident groups and leaders. Initial incorporation was often facilitated when the PRI organized the sale of lands or squatting. Even in the absence of that, however, the PRI brought communities together by using local leaders, or brokers, who exploited their ties to state and party functionaries to obtain local benefits.

In return for using their influence with state or party functionaries, local leaders elicited community support for the entire political system. Party activists made it clear that allocation of resources to resolve local needs was contingent on neighborhood political support, especially at election time. Neighborhood organizations voted for the PRI and participated in conspicuous displays of support for the system. For example, brokers often mobilized communities to greet important government functionaries or attend pro-government rallies.

Clientelist community groups usually avoided protest, thinking that it could be both futile and harmful to relations with state and party patrons. Instead, groups offered to pay for urban services, exerted indirect pressure by publicizing demands in the media, and reminded visiting officials of long-felt needs. The exercise of clientelist control contradicted the emergence of an ethos of citizenship, as Peter Ward writes "resources cannot be demanded or negotiated as of right: they must be exchanged for political support, for good behavior, and compliance with those in authority" (1986, 97).

Channeling dissent into state-sanctioned spaces limited unification of neighborhood groups, despite the similarity of their needs. The very scarcity of resources, along with manipulation by state and party patrons, forced groups to compete against each other for the largesse of the state. Clientelism tends to preclude the creation of unity across organizations, weakening potential bonds of solidarity.

Uniting with groups of dissimilar needs and community makeup was even less common than were alliances among similar communities. Members of peripheral neighborhood groups mobilized to respond to local problems, not to engage in wider political participation. Local political foci limited organizations from working together, especially if an alliance offered no resources to resolve local problems. Because the system was based on personal and party contacts, independent organizing was perceived as a threat to eventual satisfaction of the community's needs.

Finally, PRI patrons and brokers represented state and party interests above those of community members. Manuel Castells wrote that the organizing of Mexican squatters "represented a major channel of subordinated political participation by ensuring their votes and support goes to the PRI" (Castells 1983, 196). Susan Eckstein emphasized that the result of corporatist and clientelist organizing of urban communities "legitimate the regime, extend the government's realm of administration, and reinforce existing social and economic inequities through overt and covert collective incorporation" (1988, 101).

In his influential study on Argentine clientelism, Javier Auyero (2000) has made it clear that clientelism does not sustain itself by material exchange alone. A network of affective relations embeds clientelism in power relations of aid and loyalty that masks the bare exchange of goods for electoral support. Studies of Mexican clientelism offer some similar evidence regarding affective networks (Fagen and Tuohy 1972; Lomnitz 1977). Carlos Vélez-Ibáñez (1983) offers us the best portrayal of Mexican clientelism that stems from examination of the social networks and subsequent affective links of both broker and clients. Nevertheless, Mexican clientelism owes more to the satisfaction of basic needs than affective links, certainly more than is true for analogous systems elsewhere. Although PRI state clientelism used the rhetoric of revolutionary legacy for systemic legitimation, the efficiency of clientelism as a mode of political control is embedded in political economy (Shefner 1999a; Roniger and Günes-Ayata 1994; Cornelius, Gentleman, and Smith 1989). It takes a certain level of resources to maintain clientelism, regardless of the presence of affective elements softening the hard edges of political exchange. As Luis Roniger and Ayse Günes-Ayata write, "Patrons and clients are not interested in the generality of equality and legal rules; they are interested in resources" (1994, 10).

In summary, then, the Mexican variant of clientelism is focused on the politics of local needs. Brokers or local leaders exploit ties to powerful outside actors in the party or state. The process of political demand making is largely deferential and based on exchange rather than rights. In large part because of the local focus and the way such politics has been channeled to legitimate the prevailing political system, neighborhood-based clientelism has had important implications for fragmenting potential opposition groups. Clientelist politics have helped keep both dissimilar and like actors apart.

It is important not to essentialize the activity of any actor, regardless of common social categories of class or locale. Research on clientelism in Mexico and elsewhere does not argue that residents of urban peripheries are incapable of united and ideologically driven political action. Instead, these organizations and their members pragmatically and strategically assess the political space in which they work. In doing so, they recognize the relative benefits of supporting a patron, the state, or a political party (Portes 1972; Leeds and Leeds 1976; Perlman 1976; Nelson 1979). A sophisticated expression of agency leads clients to make astute decisions regarding what strategies will best serve their interests. Indeed,

Cornelius (1975) emphasized that clientelism functioned only when patrons fulfilled some community needs. Clients recognized they could resolve their problems, partially and over time, by upholding systemic power.

Understanding Mexican citizens' response to clientelism as an expression of agency highlights how clientelism has structured Mexican politics. Clientelism helped the PRI state survive by acting simultaneously as a system of exclusion and inclusion. Politically, clientelism is exclusionary and anti-democratic. Those who pose political or ideological alternatives are either co-opted or excluded. As a system of political integration, clientelism supplies a narrow path that limits members from expressing dissent or disagreement outside of strictly delimited channels. Clientelism gives much higher priority to state and systemic maintenance than to the satisfaction of constituency needs (Eckstein 1988; Cornelius 1975).

Simultaneously, clientelist political participation offers a venue for airing material grievances (Gay 1998). Clientelism is a successful strategy of social control because exchange of political support has been rewarded with resources to satisfy community needs. Structurally, the most pernicious characteristic of clientelist exchange is that it works. The creation of party machines, and in the case of Mexico, state political machines, with the capacity to dispense patronage to loyal followers creates a structural logic that is difficult to challenge, especially for urban dwellers with clear material needs and few alternative strategies or resources to satisfy those needs. By participating in clientelist exchange, clients simultaneously resolve material needs, display a pragmatic agency and clear political analysis, and comply with a political system that marginalizes them.

Clientelism is an especially pervasive and flexible form of political control. As Jonathan Fox writes, "political entrepreneurs can replace rigid, antiquated controls with new, more sophisticated clientelistic arrangements without necessarily moving toward democratic pluralism" (1994b, 155). Robert Gay (1998) writes of an increasingly bald set of clientelist exchanges in favelas in Brazil that divorced any affective component from negotiations with potential patrons.

Despite many researchers' analytic focus on the material benefits to clients, it is unclear how decreasing domestic budgets influence the relative value of remaining patronage resources. If all patronage is withdrawn, the logical foundation to maintain clientelist behavior fails. Why be a client, after all, if the patron fails to deliver? If patronage decreases without disappearing, however, the relative value of such resources may indeed increase. In societies suffering increasing poverty, as did so many during the neoliberal era, the availability of even limited patronage resources may be critical to the survival of households needing assistance with housing, food, or employment. The elimination of patronage will destroy clientelist relations, but the diminution of resources in a political economy of shortage may have varied results for clientelist systems.[11]

An intersection of contexts help us understand political change in Mexico in the 1980s and 1990s. Pressures from the global economy reversed many of the hard-won gains brought by an expanding Mexican economy. Debt and subsequent government policy based on neoliberal imperatives left Mexicans with lower wages, limited access to social welfare benefits, lower physical quality of life, fewer jobs, and increasing levels of inequality. Increased electoral opposition forced Mexican politics away from a single-party state, providing new organizing possibilities for diverse citizens. The decrease in state patronage and increase in electoral contestation weakened the clientelist form of social control that had limited political alternatives while maintaining state support. The final contextual element is supplied by the "emergence" of civil society.

VISIONS OF CIVIL SOCIETY

Beginning in the 1980s and continuing today, social scientists and others have increasingly focused on the participation of civil society in social-change efforts across the globe. Depending on the analyst, civil society has emerged, reemerged, is resurgent, has reconstituted, is weak or strong. The search for civil society has occurred within the urban landscape, nongovernmental organizations, and even U.S. bowling alleys.[12]

The reasons for this analytic trend are multiple. Important empirical changes have driven these examinations. Social groups have organized outside of governments and political parties to pursue social, political, and economic needs across the globe. Nongovernmental organizations, often thought of as the new face of civil society, have been frequent participants in these struggles. Although it is difficult to estimate the number of NGOs in existence, their high growth rate has been demonstrated. First, the number of NGOs granted consultative status by the United Nations Economic and Social Council provides a proxy measure. In 1949, there were forty-one; by 2002, that figure had increased to 2,379. Second, the amount of resources controlled by international nongovernmental organizations has also increased dramatically. In 1992, INGOs "channeled over $7.6 billion of aid to developing countries. It is now estimated that over 15% of total overseas

11. I am grateful to Amparo Menéndez-Carrión for drawing my attention to this point.
12. One measure of this concept's wide spread is a February 15, 2007, Google search on the term "civil society," which elicited over eleven million hits.

development aid is channeled through NGOs" (NGO Research Guide).

These data underestimate the number of organized groups actively working for change and contained under the umbrella label of "civil society." Many researchers studying social movements, labor unions, faith-based groups, NGOs, community-based organizations, and other groups have documented social changes brought about through popular action. This empirical trend appeared simultaneously with the growing perception that governments are less likely to resolve such diverse societal problems as poverty and representation. This perception of the state, in turn, has several roots. First, the activity of what were called "new social movements" displayed the variety of challenges to the state and the increasing numbers of activists whose answer to inequality was not the capturing of power but culture change. The failure of governments to address the needs of certain constituencies led many of these movements and their chroniclers to reject the potential of states to address a series of social ills.

Additionally, the fall of communism in the Soviet bloc caused a crisis among analysts who had championed active state intervention in economic and social policy. As communism fell, the popularity of state-centered resolutions to social needs declined. The civil-society concept became increasingly popularized in response to the crisis of authoritarian states and "became embroiled in a demonology of the state, often serving as an idealized counter-image, an embodiment of social virtue confronting political vice: the realm of freedom versus that of coercion, of participation versus hierarchy, pluralism versus conformity, spontaneity versus manipulation, purity versus corruption" (White 1996, 179). The fall of right-wing governments in response to challenges launched by civil society also led to the lionization of those groups.

The failure of revolutionary options similarly brought state-centered solutions into question. The palpable optimism brought by the celebration of a revolutionary government in Nicaragua, and the hopes raised by revolutionary alternatives in El Salvador, Guatemala, and for some in Peru and Colombia, were dashed by the 1990s. The failure to take and hold on to state power seemed to further convince many analysts that states are not the actors to take progressive political action. Almost by default that function fell to civil society.

Perhaps most important to the real world activity of civil society and its academic documentation was the impact of neoliberalism on state policy. Neoliberal reforms target state efforts to provide for the social welfare of the citizenry. The withdrawal of the state from its traditional roles of welfare provision led to civil-society activity in two related functions. First, organized groups protested the changed state policy. Second, many organizations stepped up to fill the social vacuum left by states, taking on tasks of health care, education, and development, as well as other basic survival needs (Clark and Kleinberg 2000; Hellman 1997).

Although one can find civil society as a unit of analysis or a descriptive term in ever-wider usage, the trends described above suggest that three elements of the discussion are crucial to this book. One is the relationship between civil society and the state; the second is civil society's efforts to democratize political power; and the final element is how civil society responds to neoliberal policy.

"A central feature of the revival of democracy in Latin America in the past two decades has been the awakening, or reawakening, of civil society" (Feinberg, Waisman, and Zamosc 2006, 1). This largely accepted position leads the editors of a recent book to ask "how civil society has contributed to the strengthening of democratic institutions" (Feinberg, Waisman, and Zamosc 2006, 2). *The Illusion of Civil Society* helps answer that question. Civil society, I will show, mobilized in a way that strengthened the vote in Mexico, making it a viable tool for political change after seventy years of single-party rule. Mexican civil society also strengthened democratic institutions that observed and legitimated the voting process. Finally, Mexican civil society significantly strengthened the system of competitive political parties, often recognized as crucial institutions of democracy. The following chapters offer detailed description of how a community organization, nurtured by a Jesuit social-change group, worked on all these fronts.

This book also turns the question cited above on its head by asking: how has democratization strengthened civil society? To pursue the answer, I ask a further question: how can we describe the characteristics of civil society?[13] Before I offer my preliminary answer to this question, I examine some recent discussions of civil society's relationship to democracy, the state, and neoliberal policy.

Notwithstanding their critique of the diverse and inconsistent uses of the concept, Richard Feinberg, Carlos Waisman, and León Zamosc conclude that "regardless of how the term is defined and of what mechanism is postulated as a link between civil society and democracy, the core idea [is] that the existence of a dense web of private associations based on all major classes, interest groups, and value communities constitutes a foundation for a strong and durable democracy" (2006, 2). In their view, agreeing on a definition is less important than recognizing civil society's contribution to democratization.[14]

13. I am grateful to Pennsylvania State University Press reviewer Peter Ward for sharpening this research question.

14. For discussion of the multiple and diverse definitions of "civil society," see Cohen and Arato 1992; White 1996; Eberly 2000; and Waisman 2006.

There is wide agreement on the importance of civil society to the functioning of democratic institutions, as well as to the political philosophy underlying democratic systems. Civil society is seen as crucial to articulating the discourse of democratic values and forming the propensity to seek democratic resolutions to shared problems (Cohen and Arato 1992; Elshtain 2000; Bellah 2000). Others emphasize the role of civil society in training citizens in the "arts of deliberation, compromise, consensus-building, and reason-giving" (Glendon 2000, 305). Evelina Dagnino argues that political actors perceive civil society and its organizations as "crucial terrains and agents of democratization" (1998, 55). Sonia Alvarez, Dagnino, and Arturo Escobar (1998) find the concept useful because it has helped categorize social movements as actors important to democratization processes.

Civil society plays varying roles in the democratization process. "A strong civil society directly supports democracy by widening participation in several ways" including "educating and mobilizing citizens generally to exercise their right to participate . . . encouraging previously marginalized groups into the political arena to participate, and building a complex net of groups . . . and by deepening policy accountability to its citizens" (Blair 1997, 28). Civil society can also "alter the balance of power between state and society in favor of the latter," "disciplining" the state in a quest for verifiable standards of accountability, influencing how a formal political system interacts with citizens, and "redefining the rules of the political game along democratic lines" (White 1996, 185–87). L. E. Hedman (1997), as well as others, sees a strong associational life as indicative of democracy.[15] James F. Hollifield and Calvin Jillison agree that civil society is important during transitions to democracy because "not only must a society be strong enough to weather the transition without a complete breakdown of political order, it must also be capable of providing alternative sources of rule and leadership" (2000, 10).

Civil society is often counterposed to the state, for the reasons that I have offered above. Much of the discussion assumes a zero-sum space of political action, in which the sole actors are the state, political society, and civil society. If one actor expands its power, space contracts for the others. The zero-sum game is alluded to in analyses that describe "increased participation" by civil society (Gomá et al. 2003). Dieter Rucht refers to the zero-sum space, describing how "the modern nation-state, with its monopoly of formal power and its tendency

15. See also Avritzer 2006; Levy and Bruhn 1999; Oxhorn 2006; Pye 2000; and Waisman 2006.

to assume more and more responsibilities, was widely perceived as a potential threat to civil society. Strengthening civil society became synonymous with reducing the role of the state" (Rucht 2003, 215). Elizabeth Jelin's comment can be read similarly: in her view, new movements in Latin America (consistently listed as civil-society actors) emerged largely due to "the closing of institutionalized channels of participation" (1998, 79). As political space closes, civil space opens.

In the current era, the state's relationship with civil society leads it to respond to neoliberalism. Many analysts see civil society providing important sources of resistance to neoliberal policy. These actors offer protest and representation and even advocate for alternative policy in the face of internationally inspired and nationally imposed austerity policies. "Civil society has a double origin: in neoliberalism's need for stability and political legitimation, and in grassroots organization for the sake of survival in the face of structural adjustment" (Yúdice 1998, 363). Jude Howell and Jenny Pearce note the wide varieties of popular challenge to neoliberalism, finding "the most common thread is the use of the concept of civil society to legitimize their right to resist the prevailing development paradigm" (2001, 36).[16]

There is a vast literature analyzing civil society, and here I have necessarily examined only a minimal amount of that material. However, the commonalities mentioned above reveal that analysts understand civil society to consistently be in counterposition to the state—especially crucial in transitions to democracy—and to be an important actor in responding to neoliberal pressures. In discussing the activity of civil society in these realms, analysts often describe civil society in terms of its strength and weakness or emergence and reemergence.

Rather than describing characteristics intrinsic to civil society, however, I believe those traits are actually describing the relationship between the state, civil society, and the global economy. For example, Leonardo Avritzer (2006) addresses how civil society emerges in different ways depending on state configurations of authoritarianism, traditions of democracy, economic liberalization, or modernization. The characteristics of emergence and reemergence also suggest that states are influenced by a global political and economic context that may provide independent reasons for civil society to emerge or fade. For example, repressive Latin American governments that sided with the West during the Cold War received ideological and material support as they crushed civil

16. Many researchers take similar positions. For a sample, see Kleinberg and Clark 2000; Oxhorn 1995; Veltmeyer and O'Malley 2001; Broad 2002; and Sklair 2002. For a dissenting view, see Roxborough 1997. He notes that civil society declines as neoliberal reforms deepen.

society. In contrast, as many have noted, civil society has emerged in response to economic hardships stemming from global neoliberal pressure on states.

Weakness and strength are also measured through a comparison to the state, and by determining the degree to which organized groups can influence policy makers. What some analysts identify as strength or weakness may instead be a reflection of how groups within civil society can mobilize in the face of societal threat and which social groups are willing to organize and contend with the state. For example, Carlos Waisman assesses strength on three dimensions. Density is the degree to which identifiable interest groups and communities are mobilized; autonomy "implies self-rule, rather than absolute independence from the state" (2006, 23); and self-regulation means that the organizations of civil society play within the accepted rules of society, such as obeying the law. Using these criteria, argues Waisman, we can differentiate between weak and strong civil societies. I do not argue with Waisman's choices of criteria by which to assess the strength or weakness of civil society, but fundamentally, his notion of strength and weakness mirrors that of others who describe power in relation to the state. Thus, the concepts used to characterize civil society instead characterize its relationship with the state.

Finally, analysis assessing the strength or weakness of civil society repeats some of the errors of an analogous literature discussing the state (Dauvergne 1998; Migdal 1988). To better understand civil society, it is not strength or weakness that is important but rather an examination of what civil society does and whom it benefits.

Whether Mexico has a weaker or stronger civil society is not important, in my view. Instead, the character of civil societies depends on social divisions, and on the resources that different groups possess that allow them to pursue change in the face of threat. Thus, we have to examine more than strength or weakness, but history, tradition of mobilization, level of social immiseration, and other traits of specific social groups. Rather than discuss weakness or strength, emergence or reemergence in this book, I question how and which agendas are put forth, and how they differentially influence different actors within civil society. My examination leads me to question the unity of civil society.

Perhaps the most commonly accepted characteristic is the unity of civil society. The very willingness to describe and theorize disparate organized groups as a single entity demonstrates how many analysts consider civil society to be a unified totality. The language used to discuss civil society confirms the willingness to consider it unified: as a whole it emerges, is weak or strong, or is autonomous from the state.

Certainly some analysts have articulated their doubts regarding the unity of civil society. Even amid their largely optimistic analysis, Alvarez, Escobar, and Dagnino identify civil society as a "terrain of struggle mined by sometimes undemocratic power relations and the enduring problems of racism, hetero/sexism, environmental destruction, and other forms of exclusion" (1998, 17). Gordon White goes further, arguing that "different sectors of civil society have different power resources at their disposal . . . civil societies contain inequalities and domination, and the resolution of any competitive game between components of civil society depends heavily on its internal balance of power" (1996, 188). Yet few note that understanding civil society requires understanding the activity of differentiated groups that have entirely different political interests, some of them conflicting.

Indeed, the most important characteristic of civil society is that it is stratified in the classic sociological sense of that term. Civil society is differentiated by social, economic, and political power manifested in the social hierarchies pertinent to the particular society under examination: class, gender, ethnicity, geography, and status, as well as intersections of these. This stratification has important implications. How and whether civil society unites to respond to particular social threats will depend on what sectors are affected. A large generalizable threat, such as the impact of neoliberal economic policies or anti-democratic political policies, may give impetus to a general response from many sectors within civil society. But it is illusory to assume unity beyond a common response that the state is not acting as it should. From that point of unification, the stratified nature of civil society will define the response. And it is likely that more powerful sectors of civil society will have greater influence over the strategies pursued to redress social threats than will less powerful members.

At times, we can demonstrate wide societal action, as in Mexico's democratization effort or the mobilization of opposition during revolutionary situations, such as the one in Nicaragua during 1978–1979. At various times, the Filipino people have also demonstrated a wide societal expression of an attempt at social change (Silliman and Noble 1998; Schock 2005). The examples of social upheaval are multiple and varied, but within them, different groups are working in different ways, with differing levels of resources and power to decide and implement strategy.

If the defining characteristic of civil society is division, then organized groups representing societal sectors will be fragmented along interest lines reflecting those societal divisions. The existence and power of organized groups within civil society reflect the divisions, histories of mobilization, and state-society relationships within societies. This may not always be the case, for example, when an authoritarian structure overrules division, as in a fascist state. But, in most cases, the webs of association that many talk about reflect specific and not generalized interests.

When are these disparate sectors brought together? Unification occurs when some monolithic and palpable threat overwhelms most sectors of society. Natural disasters may provide such a threat, but such threats do not need to be defined by spontaneity and dramatic tragedy. Instead, they could be a product of long-standing or accrued societal harm. Anti-democratic governance and many forms of neoliberal economic policy may inflict sufficient damage on enough segments of society over a period of time that civil society will unify over the shared hardship and then mobilize together against the identified threat.

The strata into which a society is divided represent the most definitive hierarchies of that particular society at specific historical moments. Because civil society is divided, the threat around which civil society unites will have differential impacts on its separate strata. That is, different social sectors will be more or less vulnerable depending on their place in the society's hierarchy. The unity of civil society is illusory because it is temporary and dependent on whatever social, economic, or political pressure to which organized groups are responding; the more consistent character of civil society is its stratification.

It is illusory to expect that civil society as a whole generates strategy, or to assume some equity of effort, power, or participation in decision making. That is to say, even in its efforts to respond to threat, civil society is as stratified as the society it attempts to shape. The activity civil society embarks upon provides opportunities to examine the decisions made, alliances pursued, and relationships forged with the state. The illusion of civil-society unity may be dispelled by careful examination of who acts, how, with whom, what strategies are employed, and the outcomes of those strategies. Examining real decisions and strategy allows us to discern the strata rather than assume only unity.

The overwhelming harm inflicted by neoliberalism has created some semblance of unified resistance among large sectors in much of the developing world. They have worked together to combat neoliberalism in many nations, culminating in the "pink tide" of recent leftist elections in Latin America. Yet unity in resistance does not equate to equality in strategizing about what tactics should manifest resistance. The strategies that civil society chooses provide evidence of its division. Different strategies will yield different benefits for different sectors by virtue of their location on society's hierarchy.

Democratization, in this case, must be understood as a strategy that Mexican civil society chose to pursue to ameliorate the damage of years of neoliberal policy and anti-democratic governance. Evaluating the strategy of democracy is only one way to reveal civil-society's strata. Another way is to assess which actors have benefited from the outcomes of democratization and which have not.

Examining state relations, basic-needs satisfaction, and democratization as strategies are key to assessing how different kinds of strategic decisions were made at varying times, and with differential effects on civil-society strata. This book examines exactly that—how different members of one coalition targeting Mexico's democratization interacted throughout the struggle. Despite the articulation of common goals, how do groups differentiated by class and status work together? In the aftermath of democratization, how did the different coalition members fare? What does post-democratization political action look like? These are the questions for the rest of this book. Throughout the course of the following chapters, the experiences of different civil-society actors suggest that the differences among them are as important as their similarities.

3

CERRO DEL CUATRO AND THE ORIGINS OF THE UCI

How did trends of political economy and political change affect the lives of Mexican citizens on the urban periphery of Guadalajara? Economic changes in Guadalajara drove working-class families to search that periphery for affordable housing. Many came to live in Cerro del Cuatro, a zone without urban amenities that would be the birthplace of the Union of Independent Settlers (Unión de Colonos Independientes, UCI). Local PRI activists, working to maintain clientelist authority, nurtured the growth of the new settlement. However, the clientelist system's failure to provide infrastructure occurred simultaneously with the organizing efforts of the popular church that was deploying the new ideological weapons of liberation theology. The arrival of a Jesuit organization mandated to promote social change further nurtured the residents' efforts to mobilize outside of the traditional clientelist system.

ECONOMIC GROWTH AND URBAN CHANGE

Economic change in Guadalajara reflected national changes. From the nineteenth century until the 1960s, Guadalajara remained a regional commercial and industrial center, relying on small and medium-sized companies that produced items for domestic consumption, such as shoes, clothing, and food (Gilbert and Varley 1991; Vásquez 1989). These goods found a secure market niche because of their cheap prices, a consequence of relatively low wages (Walton 1978; González de la Rocha 1994). Small family-run enterprises were the norm for Guadalajara's industry until national and transnational firms established factories in the city.

Foreign investment in Jalisco expanded significantly from 1960 through 1975. Between 1940 and 1959, only eight foreign enterprises operated in Jalisco.

In contrast, between 1960 and 1970, twenty-four foreign enterprises moved to the state, including Ralston Purina, Ingersoll Rand, Pepsicola, Kodak, General Mills, and Phillip Morris. By 1975, an additional twelve large corporations had arrived, including Nabisco, Ciba Geigy, Pennwalt, and IBM (de León Arias 1988, 291–92). These firms found Guadalajara attractive because of its large regional market, favorable urban environment, peaceful labor history, low wages, and the incentives offered by local authorities (Walton 1977).

Into the 1990s, large industry increased in Guadalajara, but the city was still characterized by its predominantly small- to medium-sized industries coexisting with large, capital-intensive, high-technology production (Vásquez 1989, 102; Gilbert and Varley 1991; 63). In 1974, the appearance of maquiladora plants in Guadalajara's industrial sector was an important change. These foreign-owned assembly plants, attracted by special low-tax regimes, were a key component of Mexico's economic development policy for several decades, and they helped to significantly expand the country's industrial production. Initially intended to operate along the U.S.-Mexico border, to provide access to materials in the United States and facilitate export shipping, the program proved so successful that the maquiladoras expanded throughout the country, including to Guadalajara in West Central Mexico. With the establishment in the late 1970s of Burroughs de México and Semiconductores Motorola, electronics production increased. It continued to grow with the arrival in the mid-1980s of two Hewlett Packard plants, which used Guadalajara's central location "as a jumping off point to attack the Latin American computer market" (Sklair 1993, 152). By 1998, the electronic industry of Jalisco (much of it concentrated in Guadalajara and surrounding areas) accounted for 83 percent of the state's exports (Román, Flores, and Govela 2004, 34). Nevertheless, although maquiladoras did much to diversify the region's industrial sector, they were never the major element of its productive structure (Sklair 1993, 144, 146).

In the mid-1990s, manufacturing in Guadalajara increased dramatically. Foreign-owned plants, not necessarily maquiladoras, predominated, and huge factories in new industrial parks encircled the city, while older Mexican-owned plants were still located in the traditional industrial area, between the downtown and the city's southern border. By about 2002, of Guadalajara's 75,606 formally recognized economic producers, 9,190 were manufacturing plants, employing 125,665 of Guadalajara's 470,075 workers and producing over half of the municipio's gross product (INEGI 2003, table 8.7). Guadalajara's thirty-seven maquiladora plants employed 4,059 workers (INEGI 2003, table 9.3). Among the top employers were manufacturers of food and drink, clothing, chemicals, plastics, furniture, and metal products, with smaller but still substantial numbers of workers employed in computer and electronic fabrication (INEGI 2003, table 9.2). During the first half of the current decade, maquiladora growth slowed dramatically in Guadalajara and throughout Mexico (Román, Flores, and Govela 2004, 37). However, foreign direct investment in the state of Jalisco has continued to grow, reaching 6.8 percent of all investment in 2001, compared to 0.6 percent in 1994 (Román, Flores, and Govela 2004, 32). Manufacturing, then, has become a result of capital investment, a characteristic of globalization, rather than a state-directed program, such as the maquiladora policy.

Guadalajara's expanding industrialization coupled with declining fortunes for small landholders throughout Mexico drove the city's impressive urban growth. Between 1940 and 1960, the city increased its land area by 78 percent (González de la Rocha 1994; Walton 1978). The city outskirts continued to expand through the 1970s and into the 1980s. In the 1980s, major commercial centers were built, many copying the design of U.S. shopping malls and, for the most part, serving the mobile, higher-income households. To the south and northeast of Guadalajara, low-income settlements grew. The total population of the Guadalajara Metropolitan Zone, which comprises the municipios of Guadalajara, Tlaquepaque, Zapopán, and Tonalá, grew from 2,244,725 in 1980 to 3,458,667 in 2000 (Ayuntamiento de Guadalajara 2003, 33). The borders of the city expanded to meet these formerly separate urban areas. Although the municipios maintain independent civic structures, they share the urban problems that bleed over their borders: traffic, pollution, crime, and insufficient housing and employment.

The population growth was driven by immigration. By the early 1980s, two out of every three Guadalajara residents had been born outside of the city (González de la Rocha 1994, 46). After the 1985 Mexico City earthquake, migration from the capital increased that ratio. As the metropolitan population grew, the search for land on the city's periphery intensified.

Prior to the 1970s, land developers in Guadalajara often subdivided available land in cooperation with government officials. Despite official sanctioning of such subdivisions, land sales were often illegal. Some of the property that was sold was nontransferable *ejido* land.[1] When developing land for the urban poor and working class:

1. "An ejido is a tract of land controlled by a group of peasants as the result of a Mexican land reform process in which the title to certain agricultural property is granted by the government to the peasants' village or other residential unit ... the land may be farmed collectively or distributed as individual or family plots" (Ronfeldt 1973, 2n). Most ejidos were distributed during Cardenas's presidency

most subdividers failed to provide the promised services, and the limited
infrastructure that was installed failed to meet the municipal specifi-
cations. The authorities registered the subdivision but failed to check
whether the subdivider had complied with the legal service requirements.
The sale of plots was approved (or simply went ahead) before services
were installed. In many cases, the municipal authorities were eventually
obliged to install the necessary infrastructure with the residents again
paying for services which were already included in the price of their plot.
(Gilbert and Varley 1991, 80)

Such land deals left neighborhoods waiting for years and paying double to
obtain the urban services promised to them with their lot purchases.

In the 1970s, ejido land sales became more common because the expanding
margins of the city reached these protected areas. PRI-affiliated union federations
often controlled the land sales, continuing earlier developers' roles by working in
illegal complicity with agriculture ministry officials, as well as with state and
municipal officials. Convinced by PRI-affiliated organizations to sell their land,
the *ejidatarios* were promised, but frequently never got, a portion of the sales
proceeds. The PRI organizations relied on their ties to municipal officials to quietly
cheat ejidatarios and dissident settlers alike (Gilbert and Varley 1991).

Guadalajara's urban expansion into ejido land was significant. By 1989, eight
hundred thousand people occupied ejido lands that had been illegally transformed
into residential areas by individual landowners or PRI-affiliated organizations
(Vásquez 1989, 103). "Irregular areas" accounted for 20 percent of the city's land
area, not to mention irregular settlements in the surrounding municipios. In 1970,
that figure had been only 1 percent (Vázquez 1990, 103, 122). The development of
ejido lands had important implications for the settling of Cerro del Cuatro.

THE BIRTH OF CERRO DEL CUATRO

Cerro del Cuatro, a community overlapping the southern borders of Guadalajara
and Tlaquepaque, emerged when local authorities were increasingly challenged
to satisfy urban needs.[2] Until the late 1960s, Guadalajara's southern border was

---

(1934–1940). Ejido lands were nontransferable until 1991, when the Salinas administration passed legislation giving ejiditarios the right to sell or rent their parcels (Austin Memorandum 1994).

2. I asked various friends where the name Cerro del Cuatro (Hill Four) originated, especially
when nearby hills bore more elegant names, like Cerro del Tesoro (Treasure Hill). One longtime

Colonia Lomas de Polanco, located beyond the "industrial zone." In 1974, then-director of the city public works agency, Enrique Dau Flores, "recognized for the first time the existence of an irregular settlement in the city" (del Castillo 1994). By 1994, the irregular settlement, home to three hundred thousand people, extended for several kilometers, almost to the top on both sides of a high hill (del Castillo, 1994).

Avenida 8 de Julio, Cerro del Cuatro's main street, begins in Guadalajara's downtown as a four-to-six lane avenue. It runs the distance to the hill, where it narrows abruptly, continuing as a pockmarked and dusty road. In 1994, 8 de Julio petered out at the end of the populated area on Cerro del Cuatro, becoming a trail passable by only one car at a time, as it descended the southwestern side of the hill. By 2000, the avenue had been paved and fed into the Anillo Periferico, the eight-lane urban highway that encircles the metropolitan area, and which was, at one time, considered to be its outer limit.

In 1994, approximately ten colonias perched precariously on the northern and western sides of Cerro del Cuatro.[3] The homes on the hill itself either face nearby Cerro del Tesoro (Treasure Hill), an aptly named middle-class to wealthy subdivision to the west, or they face the city center to the north. Residents began settling the area in the 1970s, and the community continues growing, up to the present time. La Mezquitera, one of the oldest colonias, stands nearest the bottom of the hill close to Avenida 8 de Julio. Nueva Santa María, a sprawling colonia that extends across both sides of 8 de Julio, was established concurrently with La Mezquitera. Buenos Aires, the third oldest colonia on the hill, borders La Mezquitera, and climbs the hill almost to the fenced radio transmission facility at its top. Loma Linda, Los Colorines, and Lomas del Tepeyac are all small colonias bordering Buenos Aires. Lomas del Tepeyac housed one of the few churches in the area; the other was located on Avenida 8 de Julio in Nueva Santa María.[4] To the southwest, Colonia Francisco I. Madero runs from Avenida 8 de Julio up the hill to where the colonias of Guayabitos and Lomas de San Miguel are located. Guayabitos borders Francisco I. Madero and is the occupied area of the hill farthest from downtown Guadalajara.

Guadalajara resident told me that the area was named Cerro del Cuatro because, being on the city outskirts at four kilometers from Guadalajara's main train depot, it had been the final station stop for the metropolitan area.

3. More colonias are located on Cerro del Cuatro's eastern flank, but on three sides, growth threatens to top the hill. My research was, for the most part, limited to the hill's northern and western flanks.

4. Various Catholic religious orders established homes and small places of worship all over the hill. The two churches had satellite facilities, staffed by nuns and students, at different locations on the hill.

The residents of the colonias on Cerro del Cuatro bought their lots from several sources. Smallholders possessing title to the land sold some lots, and ejidatarios and members of the indigenous community Santa María Tequepexpan sold others. Prior to 1991, when a major constitutional reform changed the law, ejidatarios and the indigenous *comuneros* were forbidden to sell their lands, although local PRI bosses illegally sold ejido tracts.[5] At times, these lots were sold and resold, forcing families to contend over the ownership of a single land parcel. Indeed, the PRI-affiliated land sellers often sold lots with no permission from the real owners of the land. Many of the subsequent problems in Cerro del Cuatro arose from these questions of property ownership.

In 1990, the economically active population of Cerro del Cuatro was mostly unskilled or semi-skilled labor. Workers were split almost evenly between the secondary sector, which includes industry and construction, and the tertiary commercial and services sector. Of those workers, 74 percent identified themselves as employees, 10 percent as peons or day laborers, and 15 percent as self-employed. Their occupations included factory work, construction work, domestic service, and taxi and government driving. Many were self-employed in the informal sector as small merchants or *tianguistas*, working in the mobile markets that sell all kinds of merchandise throughout the city. For the most part, the earnings of workers in Cerro del Cuatro were small: 17 percent earned less than one minimum salary per month; 54 percent earned between one and two minimum salaries per month; and the remaining 29 percent earned between two and five minimum salaries per month.[6]

Starting from Avenida 8 de Julio, the streets initially climb the hill at a gentle incline, but this abruptly halts in the face of blocks-long steep slopes. In 1994, some of the streets close to 8 de Julio were paved with irregularly set stones

5. An important exception were areas settled with the aid of militants from the Democratic Front for Popular Struggle (Frente Democrático de Lucha Popular, FDLP), a coalition of several organizations including university groups. The FDLP sold lots they did not own and collected money for services, in the same way as the PRI did. When a new governor acquiesced to some of their university-linked demands, the students stopped participating, effectively killing the coalition. The students' victories in their own university setting apparently lessened their interest in popular colonias (author interviews; see also López Rangel 1987).

6. These statistics are based on 1990 census data compiled by INEGI, Mexico's national census and statistics bureau. They are drawn from the basic geographic areas that INEGI calls Áreas Geográficas de Estadística Básica (AGEBs), geographical units that do not conform to civic or colonia borders. I identified nine different AGEBs that were entirely contained within the Cerro del Cuatro area, although large parts of the hill area were not counted in the 1990 census. The AGEBs I drew data from included portions of older colonias, like Buenos Aires, and newer colonias, like Francisco I. Madero. Despite the missing geographic coverage, I assume that the statistics I compiled are reasonably representative of other portions of Cerro del Cuatro. Nevertheless, INEGI may misrepresent the extent of urban

interrupted by pits, dips, potholes, and bare spots. Those streets that were paved for several blocks served as bus routes, but most roads only had paving for a block or two and ended in unpaved sections on which stacks of pre-formed concrete curbing remained unused for months awaiting the start of improvement projects. Most streets were hard-packed earth, crisscrossed with rivulets cut by streams of wastewater and sewage. Where small streams converged, or where water cascaded down the hill during the rainy season, large trenches had formed in the streets. Small canyons were common on the hill, and residents often used them as trash dumps since garbage collection is sporadic or unavailable.

The area consists of a mix of homes and small stores. Much of Avenida 8 de Julio is dedicated to stores, and some of them, near the neighborhood called La Mezquitera, are quite large. Clothing stores, government commissaries, chain pharmacies, liquor stores, coin laundries, and other relatively large concerns fill both sides of the avenue. Up the hill from the main street, tiny stores selling canned goods, soft drinks, and snack foods were most often found on corners. Small hardware stores satisfied many of the area's owner-built construction needs, although larger building supply centers were located closer to the industrial zone on Avenida 8 de Julio. Entrepreneurs commonly sold loads of bricks from the backs of trucks.

Other neighborhood enterprises included butcher shops, tortilla factories, and pharmacies. Several video stores used garish posters to advertise both Mexican and U.S. movies. In the newer colonias, stores were fewer, indicating the weaker consolidation, as well as the difficulty that trucks have in delivering goods over the rutted streets.

The urban modernity exemplified by the video stores and the forest of TV antennas on the roofs contrasted sharply with other aspects of life on Cerro del Cuatro. Goats, cows, and chickens walked the streets, feeding in overgrown lots or were tethered on people's properties. Horsemen riding down the hill would whip at the dogs that tormented their horses, while buses idled behind them. Dogs were everywhere, playing with children, running in packs, fighting, or chewing themselves raw. Open-air butcher shops, with no running water or refrigeration in sight, displayed big slabs of pigs and cows. In the one-room storefronts housing tortilla factories, primitive-looking machines ate raw dough and belched out tortillas.

---

services available to Cerro del Cuatro residents. INEGI bases its data not just on independent census counts but on information provided by municipios and public works agencies, which have political reasons to misrepresent the urban services available in popular colonias. In addition, the 1990 census omitted the newest of the Cerro's settlements. For both reasons, application of INEGI data to the rest of the hill is likely to overestimate the quantity of urban services.

HOUSING ON CERRO DEL CUATRO

The colonias on Cerro del Cuatro differed only in their chronology of settlement, reflecting the length of time that residents had lived in the community. Long-time residents finished houses, built sidewalks, and established more stores, while in younger colonias, construction was still in its early stages. This difference is not absolute, however. In 1994, not one interviewee considered their homes to be completed, regardless of how long they had lived there. On return trips, I continued to notice that additions had been made to various houses, yet few of the owners claimed they were done. Moreover, the outer limits of older colonias like Nueva Santa María and Buenos Aires are continually expanding, and new housing continues to climb the hill and fill every open spot.

Owner-built housing in Cerro del Cuatro followed a familiar pattern. Families built their houses only as quickly as time and funds permitted. Most of the people on the hill initially lived in houses of cardboard, with roofs of either laminated plastic held down by rocks or blue tarpaulins tied into place. The fear that their land might be resold if they did not maintain a consistent presence on the lot forced many families to live there long before they were able to build a house.

The first step in building a more substantial home was buying and stockpiling materials. Block, brick, and rebar filled lots, while small sheds sheltered sacks of concrete and stucco mix. Elsewhere, temporary walls of unmortared brick bordered the lot, waiting to be made into permanent walls. The family's first priority was to build a brick or concrete-block room so they could leave the cardboard or wood-pallet temporary home. Permanent walls of concrete or block, bordering the lots, often preceded the house building. Those walls provided security in case of others' claims on the land.

About 77 percent of the homes on Cerro del Cuatro had two to five rooms, although half had only one bedroom. Once one room was completed, almost all of family life was conducted in that single space, as they waited for money to buy materials and the free time to build more rooms or perhaps a second story. About 60 percent of the homes in Cerro del Cuatro in 1990 had kitchens, but in those that did not, the women in the family would cook outside, under an over-hang, using either a wood-burning or propane-fueled stove. Before finishing the kitchens, all families cooked outdoors. Similarly, most families began with out-houses, before building more permanent facilities. Only 60 percent had finished floors of cement, tile, or wood; the rest were made of hard-packed earth.

Power lines hung overhead throughout most of the colonias. In 1994, some blocks were notable for their electric meters, which showed they had legal access to electricity. More commonly, residents, who had grown tired of waiting for the Federal Electricity Institute to connect their houses, had illegally tapped into the overhead lines. INEGI data documented that 57 percent of area homes had electricity, but no estimate was provided on the number of illegal hookups. According to the 2000 census, 96 percent of houses had electricity legally (INEGI 1990, 2000).

In 1994, water was even less available than electricity. Only approximately 21 percent of the homes had water piped in, while another 11 percent possessed some water access on the property. Public hydrants, simple house pipes anchored to wood or concrete blocks that dispense water through four faucets, stood on many street corners. At all times of the day and night, these faucets were connected to hoses extending the length of the block. Residents would take their turn with a hose, then knock at a neighbor's door and pass the hose through the window. Because water was not always available from the hydrants, which were often shut off without explanation, whoever was at home when the hose arrived—usually the women—stopped whatever activity they were involved in to fill all possible water-storage receptacles. In 1994, about 68 percent of the households on Cerro del Cuatro lacked access to hydrants or piped-in water, and they had to rely on the *pipas,* tanker trucks that roamed the street selling water. Women and children would supervise the truck driver as he filled the family's receptacles.

Even in the small canyons, where house construction is extremely difficult, all possible building space had been exploited. Stone and dirt paths led down cliffs to the canyon houses, which were built right up to the cliff walls. During the rainy season, the cliffs turn into muddy waterfalls, threatening to wash away the houses. The residents also suffered because people from other parts of Cerro del Cuatro used the canyons as garbage dumps.

The walls of the canyon homes are a combination of masonry and makeshift materials, such as wood and wood pallets or discarded box springs. The roofs are also pallets, or sheets of plastic and blue tarpaulins, or recycled sheets of corrugated metal held in place by rocks. None of these houses are painted, except the doors, which are often left open, with blankets hanging down as mosquito netting. The facades of many houses are exposed block, leaving them a dull grey. A few walls may be finished and stuccoed before family resources and time runs out. Once stuccoed, the walls are painted to provide extra protection. Other small decorative aspects include exterior plants, or small ledges that jut from the bricks to which painted coffee cans containing small plants are attached.

By 2004, more families had moved to Cerro del Cuatro. Some began building their own homes with greater resources, while others repeated the cycle of shanty to a more complete building. Long-term residents also added further to their homes. The result was a greater variety of homes on the hill. With the passage of time came greater variety of economic fortunes to Cerro del Cuatro households, and the variety became manifest in home construction. Some homes on the hill appeared completed, with features like fancy windows, steel grille work, ornate masonry, finished concrete sidewalks, and polished wood doors. Ornamental houseplants decorated small patios tiled in the typical mosaic fashion, and verandas are a common second-story feature. Bright paint also distinguished these houses. Upper floors still showed indication of auto-construction, with steel reinforcement bar sticking pointing to the sky, unfinished concrete or block work, girders sitting on the top of unfinished brick walls, or dried mortar oozing through the brickwork.

Most families bought land on Cerro del Cuatro to avoid the increasing prices and decreasing availability of rental housing in the city. Almost 90 percent of the homes on the hill are owned by the people who reside in them. In addition to escaping high rental prices, the lots and houses represent a legacy that adults can leave to their children. Self-built housing is not merely a survival strategy of the poor, but also a mobility strategy, a way to provide some patrimony for the family's future (Gilbert and Varley 1991; González de la Rocha 1994).

The residents' building efforts demonstrate great self-sufficiency in pursuing both survival and social mobility. Their self-building process contrasts sharply with the reliance on the government or the PRI, defined by clientelism. As Mercedes González de la Rocha suggests, "while self-construction demands the action of the household members, and their immediate and closer relatives—and, sometimes, neighbors—self-urbanization demands the collective action of all those sharing the problem: the regularization and legalization of the land, the introduction of drinking water, electricity, sewerage, bus lines" (1994, 243).

The patchwork of urban services on Cerro del Cuatro tells the story of popular origins, clientelist political control, and dissident contention. Although much of Cerro del Cuatro lacked urban services, the spotty existence of services provided residents with evidence that over time their needs would be satisfied through traditional political exchange. The clientelist networks remained strong in part because they characterized the community from its very beginning.

CLIENTELISM ON CERRO DEL CUATRO

Most of Cerro del Cuatro is within the borders of the municipio of Tlaquepaque, immediately south of Guadalajara. One of the PRI's corporate organizations, the

FIG. 1   Water tanks and rebar on rooftops, awaiting service installation and second floors. Cerro del Cuatro, 1994

Revolutionary Confederation of Workers and Peasants (Confederación Revolucionaria de Obreros y Campesinos, CROC) governed Tlaquepaque for forty years. The 1991 elections passed the municipio into another PRI faction's hands. Although the municipio president was not a crocista, the CROC continued to dominate Tlaquepaque, wining several internecine battles during the 1991–1994 period.

The CROC is a national labor union affiliated with the PRI-controlled labor confederation, the Confederation of Mexican Workers (Confederacíon de Trabajadores de México, CTM). Although it is a union, the CROC was able to stake territorial claims to control in much of urban Jalisco because of its link to elected officials. In the neighborhoods on Cerro del Cuatro, neighborhood PRI leaders usually affiliated themselves with the CROC because of its efficiency as an urban political machine that dispensed patronage in the form of jobs and urban services to loyal neighborhoods and punished non-supporters by withholding those goods. In addition, the neighborhood CROC structure provided mobilization in favor of its candidates and against other contenders for local power.

The CROC maintained its power over Cerro del Cuatro by using a multitude of strategies and resources. Many residents bought their land from CROC militants, who assured lot buyers that urban services would be forthcoming and collected money under the pretense that through their efforts, the residents of

FIG. 2   Raw sewage runs down a street in Cerro del Cuatro, 1994

Cerro del Cuatro would obtain the much-needed water, sewers, electricity, and other services. For years, Tlaquepaque mayors confirmed the CROC militants' promises during meetings with settlers (del Castillo 1994).

   If the land selling and promises of services were insufficient to impose social control, the PRI/CROC could also dominate the neighborhood associations

FIG. 3   Sewage canal delimiting the bottom of Cerro del Cuatro, 1994

(*asociaciones de vecinos,* or *juntas de vecinos*) that were the formal local power structures. The state of Jalisco mandated neighborhood associations to petition for, obtain, and monitor urban services. These associations were empowered to collaborate in the "promotion, execution, and maintenance of infrastructural public works; in the contribution of public services necessary for the coexistence of the inhabitants; and in general, in the development of better conditions of life in human settlements" (Ley Orgánica Municipal, art. 109). The state further imposed restrictions on membership and leadership to nurture democratic participation in the neighborhood groups. Membership in the neighborhood associations, for example, was limited to residents and landowners of the represented area, and the association officials were prohibited from holding municipal office. Local association heads were mandated to represent their constituency without regard for political, economic, or religious affiliations, and meetings were prohibited from dealing with partisan political issues (Ley Orgánica Municipal, art. 109–16).

The neighborhood associations on the hill violated these legal stipulations. Local PRI power brokers were also often the neighborhood association heads, so that the restriction barring neighborhood committees from tackling partisan issues was often disregarded. Even when the letter of the law was observed, and

FIG. 4   Building stages: A small house with a brick pile, which testifies to its ongoing construction; next to it, a house that is more completed. Cerro del Cuatro, 1994

local needs were not mediated through partisan language, the prerogatives available to PRI block committee presidents maintained support for the PRI.

Although I describe them as two separate loci of power (land selling and service delivery through party affiliation and formal authority structures), in practice, they were intertwined. Local PRI leaders' connections to party and government functionaries facilitated both immediate patronage and the making of promises to alleviate local needs. The lack of local infrastructure provided one medium of clientelist control; the need to legalize land tenure provided another. The PRI-affiliated land sellers first misrepresented the legality of the sale, and then assured the buyers that secure land titles would be shortly forthcoming. Javier Reyes Beltran commented: "[I bought the land] under the condition that they were going to give us *escrituras* [title deeds], and there was not going to be any problems with the property. It was a pure lie, because we were sent documents saying that our land was ejidal land, not [small-holder's land] like they said" (UCI archives).

In Colonia La Mezquitera, local PRI leader Elisa Cantero sold settlers many of the lots. Even some residents who were relocated to the new colonia by the

FIG. 5   Multiple stages of construction on Cerro del Cuatro, 1994

state sewer agency when a public works project displaced them from their former homes were forced to buy their lots from her. In addition to providing some clientelist carrots, Cantero tried to pressure dissidents to get off the land. Some stood up to her and demanded that she provide proof that she could legally displace them. Those who challenged Cantero kept their land, although she continued to threaten to cut off the few services that became available to the colonia (Gamboa Rodríguez and Mancilla Soto 1991).

In Colonia Buenos Aires, Jesús Guillén, along with his follower Flora Magnón, were the main land sellers, and in Guayabitos, Abraham Meza, another PRI leader, was responsible for many of the land sales. In Colonias Francisco I. Madero and Nueva Santa María the selling became more complicated. In Francisco I. Madero, activists from the Unified Socialist Party of Mexico sold lots, working with militants from the previously mentioned FDLP (López Rangel 1987; Gamboa Rodríguez and Mancilla Soto 1991). In addition, Jesús Díaz Capistran, a PRI-affiliate, also sold a great deal of land. Both PRI-affiliated and independent land sellers, it turned out, sold the land without the owners' permission.

Nueva Santa María was built on legally nontransferable land that belonged to the indigenous community of Santa María Tequepexpan. The impoverished landowners sold settlers some individual lots. For the most part, however, the comuneros were coaxed into selling their land to CROC militants, especially María Luisa Ibarra, who worked closely with Alfredo Barba, leader of the CROC

FIG. 6   A Cerro del Cuatro street, 1994

in Tlaquepaque and who was, at various times, municipal president and federal deputy (del Castillo 1994; author interviews). The CROC workers then represented themselves as the original indigenous comuneros, a strategy they used to both sell the land and strengthen their positions when disputes over land regularization erupted. The CROC members gave property purchasers worthless documents, which the sellers claimed provided clear title to the lot (Gamboa Rodríguez and Mancilla Soto 1991; author interviews).

To make the land tenure issues even more complicated, BANOBRAS, the Mexican development bank, laid claim to some of the land in the colonia. In 1984, the governor backed its claim by sending in heavy machinery and riot police. After several houses were destroyed, thousands of residents gathered together to stop the destruction. After a two-day standoff, Governor Enrique Álvarez del Castillo called off both the police and the machinery and suggested talks be held between the owners and the residents. When the federal land regularization agency was finally brought into the discussion many years later, they denied BANOBRAS its claim in the colonia (Gamboa Rodríguez and Mancilla Soto 1991).

The lack of secure land titles made settlers on Cerro del Cuatro fear that they would be dislodged from their homes. Ana Mondragón, one of the founders of UCI–Cerro del Cuatro, remembered a threat to Buenos Aires: "Some houses were destroyed in the colonia. On May 23rd, in 1986, four in the afternoon. They violated my human rights, with the presence of the police, the riot police. There were about five pick-ups. They destroyed about five houses. They also tried to destroy the school and the little market. And immediately two thousand people came around, easy, in that moment."[7]

Apart from the disturbing land-ownership issues, the lack of urban services provided the medium for clientelist exchange. The first settlers had no urban amenities. Doña Julia Contreras, one of the earliest settlers of Colonia Buenos Aires, described it this way: "There was no water—we always had to go down to the canal. There really were no services; no water, electricity, nothing. At that time, we had to get everything from below. The closest stores were in Polanco; the buses ran only to the canal and then turned around. I carried 10 kilos of tortillas on my head from below. And eggs to sell, thousands of chilies. Everything, casks of water from below, had to be carried up. We bathed in the creeks also."

Once the colonias were more heavily populated and the initial stages of housing construction under way, PRI leaders came to the residents raising money for promised urban services. In Buenos Aires, local PRI leader Jesús Guillén, with the aid of Flora Magnón, sent his followers to collect money for services that never arrived. Ana Mondragón remembered: "Before, when they were telling us that the services would come, we paid some fees to the PRI committee, so that there would be roads so they could bring pipas." Doña Julia had a similar memory: "Señor Guillén ordered his people to come around every week to collect [money], and they began to have meetings and promise the water and the electricity, and the this and the other. And this happened year after year and nothing was done."

Even in the absence of the delivery of the promised services, the neighborhood association leaders made it clear that the PRI was the only source to petition. When services arrived, they were often linked to electoral campaigns. In 1987, during Guillermo Cosio Vidaurri's campaign for governor, water hydrants were installed in Buenos Aires. Other exchanges of party support for material benefits were common. For example, PRI-affiliated neighborhood officials dispensed coupons so residents could buy tortillas at a discount.

7. Unless otherwise cited, all quotations are from interviews with the author.

In La Mezquitera, Elisa Cantero demonstrated her power when the city put her in control of dispatching the water trucks throughout the colonia. Water delivery was made contingent on support for the PRI-controlled neighborhood association. When the state Family Services Agency made charity foodstuffs available to the colonia, Cantero also gained control of this resource. The control of these resources sent very clear messages about the political behavior that was expected. Thus, when Cantero called meetings devoted to petitioning the government for urban services and asked for "voluntary donations," her request carried some bite. Residents were expected to vote for the PRI, attend neighborhood events, including campaign stops, and occasionally board buses and attend rallies for PRI candidates (author interviews).

María Luisa Ibarra, famed in Nueva Santa María for her land-sales manipulations, controlled the government dairy outlet in the colonia. Not only did her control send clear messages about what kind of political behavior was required to obtain milk, the outlet was used as an office by the neighborhood committees controlled by the CROC (Díaz Betancourt 1993). Guillén and Magnón in Buenos Aires tried to control the Solidaridad committees, and Abraham Meza brought busloads of residents from Guayabitos and Francisco I. Madero to petition the government for land regularization. Cantero, who had won the honor of a street named after her in La Mezquitera, continued to try to take control of the Solidaridad committees. All of these PRI-linked neighborhood powers intensified their efforts as elections approached. Those who had promised benefits to their colonias in the recent past threatened the residents with further delays, and those who had control of resources threatened their revocation. The PRI clientelist strategies on Cerro del Cuatro continued until the PAN victory.

ALTERNATIVE IDEOLOGY AND THE CREATION OF THE UCI

Mexican clientelism relies less on an affective ideology to sustain the economic relationship than do some other variants of clientelism (see Chapter 2). Yet affective or ideological components must exist to legitimate a patronage system, even when it is primarily focused around provision of material goods. For the PRI, it was Mexico's revolutionary legacy that provided the ideology of inclusion even when the political process of the party's mass organizations belied it. During the period of Mexico's healthy political economy, the revolution and the party's populist image offered affective hooks for those benefiting from clientelism.

For some time, Mexican clientelism enjoyed a legitimacy based on citizens' "highly positive orientations towards institutions such as the presidency and the official political party . . . especially insofar as these institutions are associated with the stated goals and symbols of the Mexican Revolution" (Cornelius 1975, 54). The one-party state relied on its control of education, the media, and its own rhetoric to preserve its position as the heir of the Mexican Revolution and standard-bearer of revolutionary goals.

According to Wayne Cornelius, a majority belief that federal and local governments could be trusted, that the institutions noted above "contributed to the welfare of the country," and that the government was the most likely source of concrete benefits for poor communities legitimated the government's authority. Cornelius' classic study of new migrants to Mexico City in the early 1970s found that residents of poor neighborhoods had overall favorable attitudes toward the federal government, its fulfilling of the promises of the Mexican Revolution, and its capability to supply concrete benefits to urban dwellers (Cornelius 1975). Responses to open-ended survey questions indicate the level of support accorded the PRI system:

> The government does good things like building roads and improving colonias *proletarias*. . . . They're concerned about things like that.

> The PRI . . . does a lot to help the people. It gives classes in sewing and has laundries for poor people. It gives breakfasts for schoolchildren.

> I support the PRI because it has always concerned itself with the people of the country. To the peasants it gives credit so that they can work the land, and to the workers, better employment. (Cornelius 1975, 58)

Other excerpts from the same study lauded the government and party's provision of medical care, oil stoves, letters of recommendation, public housing improvements, and so forth. Conspicuously absent were demands for democratic decision making.

The institutionalization of exchange relations created both affective and pragmatic ties as well as structuring political action. The urban poor were consistently organized into neighborhood associations, and their reliance on brokers and government "encouraged a sense of dependence on the government" (Cornelius 1975, 176). The political system structured the repertoires of demand making by the urban poor so that they would follow a pattern of reciprocal exchange based on a defined hierarchical channeling and a reliance on powerful individuals. The structural result was that politics was kept local, fragmented, and focused on material needs. To challenge such a system required new ideological and organizational resources. On Cerro del Cuatro, the mobilizations in the mid-1980s in response to the threatened demolition and displacement had opened possibilities for alternative organizing. So, too, did the entry of several Jesuit students.

In a political system defined by deferential exchange relations and limited popular conceptions of state obligations and citizen's rights, little ideological foundation is available with which to frame calls for justice. The sharpening of genuine material needs helped to uncover the empty revolutionary rhetoric of the ruling party that had, until then, served to frame the demands of the urban poor. But the poor residents on Cerro del Cuatro seeking to work outside the PRI apparatus needed an alternative ideology to help them recognize their rights and launch new demands. Liberation theology provided that new language.

Berryman offers a succinct definition of liberation theology: "(1) an interpretation of Christian faith out of the suffering and hope of the poor; (2) a critique of society and of the ideologies sustaining it; and (3) a critique of the activity of the church and of Christians from the angle of the poor" (Berryman 1987, cited in Levine 1992, 39). Liberation theology identifies the struggles of the poor as a locale for active intervention by the Catholic Church. Fr. Gustavo Gutiérrez, one of the doctrine's best-known proponents, views theology and action as inseparable elements of the struggle for social justice. For Gutiérrez (1973), liberation is made up of three integrated elements: liberation from oppressive social, economic, and political conditions; true human autonomy; and emancipation from sin and acceptance of new life in Christ.

Yet it is insufficient for the church merely to preach such values and ideology; it must practice them by actively accompanying the poor in their political, social, and economic struggles. Christian base communities (comunidades de base, CEBs) became the organized expressions of the new theology. CEBs in Mexico have not had the same high profile as they have had in other Latin American countries, such as Brazil, largely because of opposition from the Mexican Church hierarchy (Tangeman 1995). Despite the conservative Catholic Church in Mexico, Bible reflection groups have had significant effects on organizing in both rural and urban communities. By 1988, more than five thousand CEBs were organized in Mexico, heavily concentrated in six states, including Jalisco (Castañeda 1993, 212).

Latin American CEBs are not homogeneous in their makeup or political and cultural impact (Levine 1992). Their memberships range from radicals, who focus more on "social action and consciousness raising," to conservatives, who depend more on the Church hierarchy and focus their activity on Bible study and discussion. For the most part, Mexican CEBs have worked toward explicitly political goals. A 1977 meeting of the CEBs of the eastern region stated their goals: "To unite in political actions, to mutually aid the construction of the kingdom of God on earth, by bringing greater consciousness-raising to the people [about] the defense of their rights, to realize the obligations and the search for solutions to common problems in an organized manner" (quoted in Ramírez Sáiz and Hermosillo 1994, 25).

In addition to their orientation to political change, the system-challenging character of these groups comes from their impact on popular education. In CEB Bible discussions, poor people find not only that they have opinions but that their opinions are valuable. "If all can read and comment on the Bible, the value of popular insights is enhanced and traditional distinctions of rank in religious life are undercut" (Levine 1992, 40). Once a political project is explicitly joined to the religious project, the poor can apply their critique more generally to the stratification of power by political and class distinctions. Liberation theology influenced alternative organizing on Cerro del Cuatro when religious workers committed to social change founded small groups for Bible discussion and political action.

THE POPULAR CHURCH ON CERRO DEL CUATRO

Until the late 1980s, no church existed on Cerro del Cuatro. In the mid-1980s, Jesuit students and faculty from Guadalajara's Jesuit training school, the Free Institute of Philosophy and Sciences (Instituto Libre Filosofía y Ciencia), and missionaries from the religious group Holy Spirit (Espíritu Santo), organized small groups that began to meet in separate colonias. These groups followed the paths of politically oriented CEBs elsewhere, first studying the Bible, then looking to put its teachings into practice through social struggle.

The absence of a formal parish on Cerro del Cuatro facilitated the growth of independent Bible reflection groups, as there was no formal Church hierarchy with which to contend. According to Padre Luis García Orso, the coordinator of CEBs on Cerro del Cuatro during the 1980s, parish leaders often guarded their congregations jealously: "I found in some sites, the old religious leaders were very jealous of their roles, and they didn't want other religious people, or priests, to intervene. They wanted to continue organizing on their own . . . they wanted to keep their independence from other advisors." A national meeting of CEBS in nearby Ciudad Guzmán invigorated the Jesuit students and faculty, and they pushed the local diocese to increase organizing efforts, without much success. On Cerro del Cuatro, however, popular church workers were welcomed because of the absence of the official Church.

The CEBS helped heighten the consciousness of those who were later to work with the UCI. Agustín Martínez, a UCI leader, told me: "I worked in some of the CEBS, reflecting on the situation. About the text that we read. We read, and we began to act. And I began to be motivated, to feel the necessity to do something. Basically, it was through the CEBS that I began to do the work of the organization."

Tito (Miguel Ángel Juárez Medina), a paid organizer of the UCI, reflected on the importance of the CEBS in his experience both with the UCI and growing up in nearby Lomas de Polanco.

> It was the first school to make me more knowledgeable of reality, of the colonia, the barrio, of the country, little by little. It was the way I started reading the Bible, and the way I learned of the necessity, the demand to change the situation, and the way to become more committed to participate in organizations. Not just about religious questions, or that of the Bible, but to be able to look for spaces to increase faith, about the Christian exigency to commit oneself a little more, or a lot more, to change reality.

The CEBS in Guadalajara were most active in the early 1980s. Although they continued meeting throughout the 1990s, their influence waned after the arrival of conservative Cardinal Juan Jesús Posadas Ocampo in 1986. Padre García Orso remembered:

> Cardinal Posadas arrived in July of 1986. From this moment on, the CEBS started to go down. They weren't well liked by the archbishop, and a new period of pastoral work began, and a new direction for the diocese. So they went down, from 1986 on. I saw during the time of this Posadas that there was no support. The CEBS became distant from each other in their sites all over the city. They began to delink, disunite. They were focusing only on their own pastoral work in their own parish, but they began to lose the linkage, the organization, and the information among themselves. There was a lot of tension with the previous advisor named by the diocese, and he left for another diocese.

The popular church responded to the conservative Church hierarchy by finding new ways to organize. Influenced by a theology that stressed action on behalf of their rights, the future UCI members began to work collectively to address local problems. Ricardo Herrera, a Jesuit student, came to Cerro del Cuatro in 1987 as part of his pastoral work, along with other Jesuit students. After making contact with several of the CEBs, Ricardo helped settlers in Colonias Buenos Aires, Francisco I. Madero, and Nueva Santa María form separate residents' groups. These groups circumvented the PRI neighborhood associations and directly petitioned government officials for sorely lacking urban services. Working individually, the unnamed groups enjoyed some success in obtaining more frequent water delivery and the establishment of a community laundry in Buenos Aires. Building on these successes, the CEB coordinator urged a local Jesuit social-promotion agency to unite the separate groups. Padre García Orso explained:

> From what I remember, there were various people who had demonstrated interest in urban services for the Cerro before the government, and these people didn't belong to any organization, either civil or religious. . . . These people, who had always demonstrated interest, dedication, work, generosity, were part of who became UCI, as [it became] more organized. But they existed before, as a united group of colonos. Then we saw a moment when it was necessary that this union would organize itself better. Organize itself better, and unite the distinct unions, because there were distinct unions, right? It seemed important to us to ask Padre David Velasco, who was working for SEDOC, why don't they advise this larger union, and in this way, the UCI was formed. A proposal from us to Padre David Velasco and SEDOC. And SEDOC thought about it, and decided, and advised us, and this is the way the UCI began.

SEDOC ENTERS THE PICTURE

The Educational Services of the West (Servicios Educativos de Occidente, SEDOC) was formed in 1977 as an organization funded and directed by the Mexican Provincial Company of Jesús, the Mexican Jesuit brotherhood. Devoted to popular education, the organizers defined their goals as "contribut[ing] critically and actively with the popular process in the transformation of persons and social structures that create obstacles to the integral development of man and society as a whole" (SEDOC 1986, 1).

The Jesuit organization fostered a politicized vision of the "preferential option for the poor" by building on the conceptions of the rights of the poor and the state's responsibilities advocated in liberation theology. SEDOC workers were also influenced by Paolo Freire's vision of popular education, and his argument that the consciousness of the poor must be raised through radical education (Freire 1970). Freire emphasized that participation by the poor in consciousness raising would give them the tools to become a force to democratize society. SEDOC committed to this vision throughout its popular organizing work, accompanying it with strategies to educate the poor to further their participation in social struggle.

The Jesuit-run organization employed teams of Jesuit fathers, students, and laypersons to work in local projects in order to "try to develop a critical consciousness and transform unjust structures" (SEDOC 1989, 5). In 1985, SEDOC brought together several independent neighborhood groups in northern Guadalajara, creating the organization Intercolonias. In 1989, SEDOC initiated a similar project on Cerro del Cuatro. Padre David Velasco, a SEDOC organizer, worked extensively with the UCI from the late 1980s into 1993.

The Jesuits provided the UCI with extensive resources, including significant funding. Even before UCI's formal creation, SEDOC assigned several paid organizers to work with the union. Once neighborhood leaders emerged, SEDOC paid them the minimum wage to both ensure that they had free time for organizing and foster a sense of professionalism. Other material benefits followed, including an office replete with furniture, computer, telephone, and fax. SEDOC continued to pay the UCI's bills for a number of years and was its primary source of funds.

Second, the Jesuits brought a wealth of organizing experience and skills from a long history of popular education and community organizing in Latin America. Additionally, SEDOC workers incorporated periods of reflection, training, and workshops to further the mission of popular education.

The Jesuits also brought the legitimacy intrinsic to religious affiliation. Roderic Camp stresses the legitimacy the Catholic Church has in the eyes of the Mexican people. This is based not only on the predominance of Catholicism, as evidenced by the 85 percent of the population who are members of the Church, but also from it "being one of the most autonomous institutions in the society, operating outside the control of the state despite severe constitutional restrictions" (Camp 1993, 57).

This assessment of the Church's autonomy may be a bit misleading. Other authors have commented on how the Church has aided systemic stability (Riding 1989; Tangeman 1995). Regardless of the political implications of the Church hierarchy's role, the Church supplies an important moral basis for identity formation and community unification. Such moral force added further legitimacy to the actions of popular church workers, who offered distinct contrast to clientelist authority structures on Cerro del Cuatro. Agustín Martínez, a UCI leader, commented on the utility of working under the veneer of religious sanction when he discussed Padre David's role: "He had a lot of weight; a lot of ability to get people together. The people trusted him a lot. People have a lot of faith in priests; they have a lot more legitimacy than a leader or a neighbor. It [Padre David's presence] was something key to the organization."

Padre David's legitimacy was matched by his great energy, and UCI members and organizers felt great affection for him. He had also made personal connections in other opposition groups during his years with SEDOC, which increased UCI's ability to make connections beyond its neighborhoods. His networks included powerful government officials in some key ministries. Tito described Padre David's (and, by extension, SEDOC's) influence: "I think it was to give the organization more of a push, for all his capacity, his analysis, and his studies, and I think for the time he had, because he worked in many different things, he nourished the organization. He was also kind of paternal to the organization."

Most importantly, it was the Jesuit organization that unified the initially separate colonia groups, bringing residents of several neighborhoods together to form a wider union representing more of the hill.

The UCI was born at a moment with great potential for change in the long-standing urban political process of clientelism. Debt crisis pressures had simultaneously limited the patronage pool and increased demand stemming from urban growth. The reduction of patronage offered a series of possibilities for residents on Cerro del Cuatro. One was to continue to hew closely to the PRI, with the hope that whatever patronage was available would indeed be forthcoming to loyal clients. Many Cerro del Cuatro residents continued to follow this path.

Another possibility emerged when Jesuits nurtured an alternative view of justice that contrasted with the increasingly empty rhetoric of revolutionary inclusion. Liberation theology influenced some Cerro del Cuatro residents to think about their rights in ways that brought them, conceptually and organizationally, closer to many groups active in Mexico's democratization movement. Clientelism generates exchange of political support by the less powerful for various social goods by more powerful members of society. Liberation theology, in contrast, argues that the rights of citizens cannot be denied to anyone in God's kingdom. This new way of thinking was reinforced with exposure to SEDOC's own network of organizations devoted to social change. As the UCI's relationship with SEDOC blossomed, its political landscape widened, and the organization took on larger roles in the local drive to democratization.

4

MOBILIZING FOR BASIC NEEDS

This chapter examines the UCI's early years. The SEDOC's unification of the UCI offers a clear example of how groups within civil society work together to effect social change. The unification demonstrated SEDOC's popular education strategy, and how the organization targeted the improvement of urban services on Cerro del Cuatro to elicit support and recruit members. Although SEDOC's mission of wider political change was articulated early on, UCI members' actions gave priority to their own long-standing needs.

Once SEDOC had united the separate colonia groups under the UCI, organizing work began. In addition to turning to the CEBs, SEDOC's paid organizers sought out and cultivated local leaders, particularly those who had been vocal about their dissatisfaction with services, and they urged these people to reach out to their own communities in order bring residents together as small groups within the union. By focusing on neighborhood needs, the UCI won wide popular support and was able to achieve notable victories.

The pressure of living without water, electricity, and sewers increased as the population on Cerro del Cuatro grew, and to obtain those services, the UCI built on earlier efforts that had been organized by the CEBs. The PRI remained the predominant neighborhood political force, yet frustrated residents increasingly looked to the CEBs and the incipient UCI for leadership. As the colonia groups consolidated under the UCI, a long agenda of material needs determined the group's activity.

Simultaneous with its work on urban services, the UCI became involved in varied political issues, contradicting the trajectory of neighborhood organizations, as the clientelism literature usually describes it. The UCI confronted neighborhood brokers and other manifestations of PRI power rather than negotiating with and deferring to them. From its inception, the organization identified the field of struggle as being beyond the local and basic needs of its constituents. The UCI, under SEDOC's influence, forged important contacts with other opposition organizations of similar and different backgrounds. SEDOC was largely responsible for urging the UCI to enter into a different kind of political activity from that being pursued by other neighborhood organizations. SEDOC's goal of playing a role in the democratization of Mexico manifested in its efforts to push the groups it worked with toward analysis and action went beyond local concerns and material needs.

The co-existence of these very different political goals—the demand for basic services and democratization of Mexico's political system—provides an example of the political education in which SEDOC engaged. SEDOC was intent on teaching UCI members how their poverty had roots in the PRI's corruption and that national economic distress was linked to the party's turn from neoliberalism to populism. Many of the UCI leaders and members were willing students, having suffered the price of that corruption in their own households.

During UCI's early years, the focus on basic needs was facilitated by reaching out to other groups, by unification of separate groups, and by forging varying relationships with the state. President Carlos Salinas's Solidaridad program engendered some divergence in aims between municipal PRI power holders and those in the federal government. This split provided resources on which the UCI and SEDOC could draw. SEDOC's efforts to push the UCI along a non-clientelist path occurred at a propitious moment of state change. SEDOC's and UCI's early successes in working with the state and obtaining urban services generated support for democratization efforts that brought the UCI beyond the local concerns of the colonia. Yet over the course of its life, the UCI would have to address the tension that existed between these two goals.

LUCHAMOS UNIDOS POR UNA VIDA DIGNA!
BASIC SERVICES AS CITIZEN RIGHTS

Before the formal creation of the UCI, SEDOC militants worked with some of the most coherently organized colonia groups to publish a newsletter, *Abriendo Camino,* that would continue to be issued until the SEDOC funding ended. With painstaking coaching by the Jesuits, the colonos from Nueva Santa María began learning to articulate their demands. Content was written by SEDOC and UCI organizers, and it ranged from descriptions of actions to lists of accomplishments. The newsletter also relied on comic strips to illustrate the UCI's

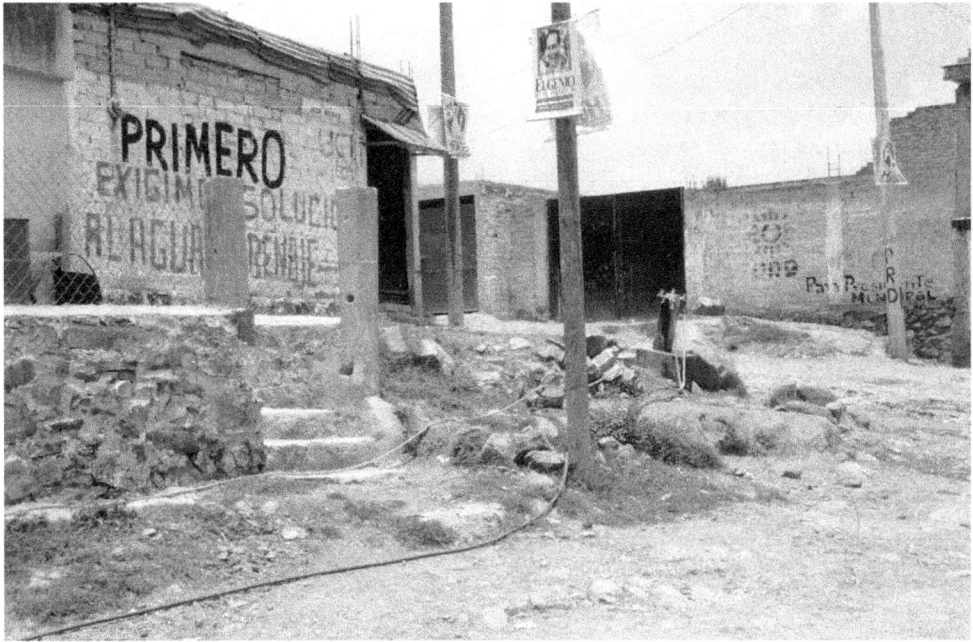

FIG. 7   A UCI-installed hydrant, supplying water to households on several blocks. Cerro del Cuatro, 1994

struggles. The publication served as a UCI recruiting tool and a way to distribute information throughout Cerro del Cuatro.

In its very first issues, the newsletter reported on the gravest concerns of the residents: the illegality of their landholdings and the provision of sorely lacking urban services. The September 1989 newsletter detailed at length residents' unsatisfying negotiations with the Commission for the Regularization of Land Tenure (Comisión Reguladora de la Tenencia de la Tierra, CORETT), a federal agency. Cerro del Cuatro residents had been asking CORETT for assistance for over a decade. That article reported that the residents had been shuffled from one federal agency to another in search of information on how to legalize their land. In one meeting with CORETT, a delegation from Colonia Santa María was told that it should meet with a delegation from the National Fund for Low-Income Housing (Fondo Nacional para la Habitación Popular, FONHAPO) at an unspecified future date, and that FONHAPO representatives would conduct a local census as the first step to regularization. Despite the runaround and the unclear timing for the next steps, the Santa María group empowered a thirteen-member commission to act on the neighborhood's behalf and to "report on

FIG. 8   Near the top of Cerro del Cuatro, 1994

the problems of the colonia [in order] to defend our rights, in a clean and honest way" (Grupo Santa María 1989a, 1).

The November 1989 issue of the newsletter returned to the issue of regularization in both a comic strip and a column asking, "Who Is the Real Owner of the Colonia Nueva Santa María?" The players identified included federal agencies, small property owners, and the indigenous community who "defends its rights, with titles given them by the viceroyalty" during Mexico's colonial period (Grupo Santa María 1989b, 2). In later issues, the newsletter detailed efforts the colonos pursued to obtain electricity and water, complaints about the lack of sewers, and community plans to build a park.

In 1990, with SEDOC organizers urging the various colonia groups to recognize their common grievances, the newsletter authors began to document the groups' coalescence. In April, delegations from Colonia Santa María had visited groups in seven other colonias on the hill to share information on the work they were doing and to discuss how a united effort might serve their needs more efficiently. SEDOC organizers compiled a preliminary budget, which was reviewed and discussed by their colleagues.

On June 3, 1990, neighborhood CEBs and colonia groups that had partisan origins united to form the UCI. As Hermano Javier, a UCI leader, explained: "In 1990, the UCI was formally created out of small groups in the colonias. They came out of the CEBs, which had been coordinated by Jesuits and missionaries.

FIG. 9   Another Cerro del Cuatro street, 1994

The UCI was born of these groups and others, to ask for services. We began to mobilize for land titles and services."

On August 12, 1990, on the nearby campus of ITESO, Guadalajara's Jesuit university, the newly united neighborhood groups celebrated the birth of the UCI in a formal constitution ceremony during which the organization defined its goals:

1. regularization of all property on Cerro del Cuatro,
2. provision of all public services to the area,
3. recognition by government agencies of the organization as an independent representative of the area,
4. achieving social justice and alleviation of misery,
5. respect for the human rights of the area's residents, and democracy in all spheres of society. (UCI–Cerro del Cuatro 1990)

The UCI coined the slogan "Luchamos Unidos por una Vida Digna" (we struggle united for a dignified life). A dignified life required the satisfaction of

FIG. 10   The UCI holds a meeting, planning for a demonstration, 1994

the infrastructural needs that had plagued Cerro del Cuatro for more than fifteen years. Pursuing a dignified life for residents also meant participating in non-clientelist politics and reaching out to the wider Mexican political sphere.

From the UCI's inception, the SEDOC team forged the members into a broad opposition front, exposing them to wider political issues than those previously confronted within the neighborhoods and nurturing a sense that they were involved in national politics. SEDOC consistently identified its role as cultivating popular organizations to take a place among the growing opposition to the PRI. In a planning document predating the UCI, the Jesuits' mission statement demonstrated the intentions that organizations they fostered would pursue political aims well beyond those of obtaining basic needs: "To consolidate and strengthen the independent popular movement, through its [SEDOC's] organizations. . . . To support the consolidation of the independent popular movement, from each and every one of its projects, and create closer relations between them and the support centers, in order to form a common front . . . to link ourselves with wide social movements, with whose planning and goals we are aligned" (SEDOC 1986, 14).

The goals set by the newly united colonia groups focused on addressing local needs, as had been demonstrated by issues of the newsletter that had been

FIG. 11   The UCI office, 1994

published before the UCI formed. Prior to unification, the neighborhood groups' actions were designed around neighborhood defense and obtaining urban services. The former efforts were evident in neighbors' successful halting of government attempts to dislodge residents (see Chapter 3). The struggle to gain urban services was especially visible in Buenos Aires and Nueva Santa María, the two earliest active colonias. The Buenos Aires group increased water deliveries and began to attack the control of that delivery by PRI broker and neighborhood leader Elisa Cantero. It also built an outdoor communal laundry with the financial aid of a Catholic charity and successfully exerted pressure on the municipal government to build an elementary school. The Nueva Santa María neighborhood group was less successful in their struggle to obtain water, but it helped residents collectively "borrow" electricity from overhead power lines and nearby transformers, and it successfully petitioned for street paving, which, although limited, facilitated another important gain: the extension of bus service to the community.

The newsletter further confirmed residents' focus on the provision of basic needs. Early newsletter authors wrote about the UCI's work on land regularization, church building, and organization building. Conspicuous by its absence was discussion of national concerns, which only began after unification, and as

SEDOC pushed residents to accompany them in making contacts with other organizations. After the UCI was founded, SEDOC's influence was apparent in the consistent focus in the newsletter and group meetings of broader political issues.

ORGANIZATIONAL STRUCTURE

The UCI and other popular groups SEDOC had organized were embedded in a structure that reveals SEDOC's domination over the UCI (Chart 1). At the pinnacle was the Mexican Province of the Society of Jesus. Although the Jesuit hierarchy did not direct SEDOC or the UCI on a daily basis, its position as the main funding agency and the predominant Jesuit authority made its power paramount. In its documents, SEDOC referred to itself as an organization subject to Jesuit authority (SEDOC 1986, 1). SEDOC organized groups like the UCI and Inter-colonias, sought money from the Jesuit hierarchy and other sources, and forged and maintained a wide array of local and national contacts in Mexico's democratization movement (Regalado 1986). SEDOC members pursued research intended to strengthen and coalesce the urban popular movement, and it staffed the SEDOC team (Equipo SEDOC), which organized the colonia groups and recruited and mobilized residents. The team also designed strategy, devised and coordinated training workshops, and made connections with other organizations. It also participated actively in all contacts with the government. These paid organizers possessed extensive experience in popular education and community organization.

The SEDOC team consisted of Padre David Velasco and, initially, three laypersons: Juan Diego Ortiz, Cecilia Saucedo, and Miguel Ángel Juárez Medina. Juan Diego and Cecilia were PRD militants, and in 1992, Juan Diego left SEDOC to work full time for the party. Cecilia's brother was an important PRD leader, Mario Saucedo, who later lost the 1994 Jalisco governor's race. Cecilia left SEDOC in 1993 to start a family.

Miguel Ángel, known to all as Tito, had worked in social change efforts for many years before joining SEDOC. He traced his interest in social justice to his childhood experiences in nearby colonia Polanco. While Tito was growing up, Polanco was at Guadalajara's periphery, and residents had to fight many battles for urban services and to secure the titles to their property. Tito participated in these struggles by joining CEBs and also the young adults' wing of the popular organization in Polanco. Tito joined the SEDOC team coordinating the UCI in 1991, and by 1994, he was the sole remaining member still working with the UCI.

Mexican Province of the Society of Jesus
(Provincia Mexicana de la Compañía de Jesús)
⇓
SEDOC
⇓
SEDOC Team (Equipo SEDOC)
⇓
UCI
⇓
Base Development Team (Equipo Promotor de Base)
Work and Area Commissions
Colonia Groups

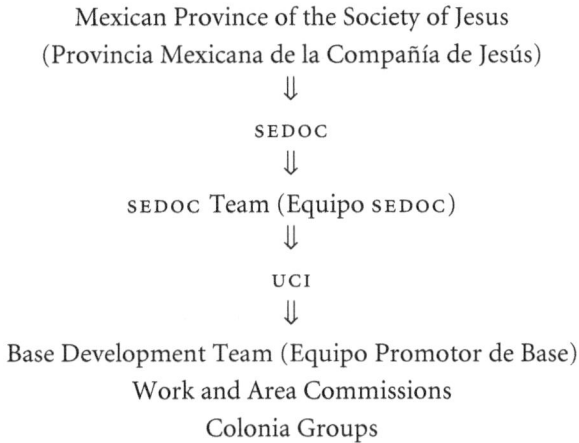

Chart 1. UCI/SEDOC organizational chart, 1989–93

Tito was known across the city and was well respected by NGO members and others for his long history of organizing and trenchant political analysis. Tito had a presence on the hill for many years since he continued to work voluntarily once SEDOC funding ended. His influence was extensive because his experiences in Colonia Polanco informed his work on Cerro del Cuatro and because he consistently attended the small-group meetings of the UCI rank and file, often substituting for the UCI leaders when they could not attend. Once SEDOC could no longer pay him, he had to search for ways to support his family.

The UCI itself was the wide organizational umbrella formed by SEDOC and joined by Cerro del Cuatro residents. The UCI's leaders emerged from neighborhood CEBs and other organizational activity. SEDOC played an important role in recognizing and nurturing leadership qualities. These leaders were the communications conduit to those above and below them in the SEDOC/UCI hierarchy. They created the work and area commissions when confronted by both longstanding and temporary political issues. The leaders were also the coordinators of the colonia groups, which organized by neighborhood in accordance with laws governing *juntas de vecinos* (neighborhood organizations). Under the UCI was the Base Development Team (*equipo promotor de base*), the development team for the community.

To increase the SEDOC team coordinators' sense of professionalism and give them more time to devote to organizing, SEDOC paid each of them the minimum salary. They also received extensive training through formal workshops on organizing and on the functioning of the Mexican political system. This was an important supplement to the informal learning that occurred through their contacts with SEDOC personnel. In 1990, the coordinators included Ana Mondragón, Carmen Castañeda, Javier Cruz (better known as Hermano Javier), Ester Torres, and four others. By 1994, the coordinator's team had shrunk and now included only Ana, Carmen, Hermano Javier, and Agustín Martínez, who had joined the group in 1991.

Ana, a mother of three, worked with the UCI from its inception until 1999. A tough-speaking, relentless worker, she coordinated a group in Buenos Aires even before the UCI's formal creation. Ana's interest in political action developed when she joined a CEB after moving to Cerro del Cuatro in 1983. She helped her neighbors defend themselves against the attempt to dislodge them in 1986, and she then worked with Jesuit student Ricardo Herrera in the late 1980s, organizing supporters and petitioning for the laundry facility and other needed services in Buenos Aires. Ana saw the material needs of the colonia as the spur to her and others' work. Ana's husband, Jorge, supported her involvement with the UCI, and her three children often accompanied her on her organizing rounds. When their oldest son became a firefighter and started a family of his own, he and his father subdivided the lot and built a separate small house. The middle child, another son, continued to live with the parents, working with Jorge as a carpenter. Their youngest child, a daughter, trained to become a nurse. Ana continued to stay active in the neighborhood, and she was attending a woman's group in 2004. Ana also began running a small *taqueria* (taco shop) out of the front room of their house.

Carmen Castañeda, a mother of five, worked with the UCI from its nascency until 1999. A longtime resident of Cerro del Cuatro, she too began her political involvement by joining a CEB in her colonia. A coordinator of a base group in Nueva Santa María, Carmen's first political action came during the protest against the government's attempt to destroy houses and dislodge residents from a section of Nueva Santa María in 1984. Despite the responsibilities of young children, Carmen took on the heavy workload required by the base development team, all the while maintaining great empathy and a sense of humor. Her husband ran his own auto mechanic business, which eventually employed several of their sons. The care of Carmen's youngest daughter, Carmelita, was shared by all during group meetings in 1994. By 2004, Carmen had left the UCI but continued to work in the community through her local church. We laughed about this in 2004, as that church's former priest had been an ally of local PRI power holders and had used the pulpit to condemn UCI leaders, including Carmen.

Hermano Javier Cruz is a baker and father of two. He bakes his wares in a circular oven he built on his lot in Colonia Francisco I. Madero. For decades, he has walked the hill selling his products from a large straw basket tied to a converted bicycle, followed incessantly by his changing retinue of flea-ridden dogs. He greets all those he meets with a boisterous *"Hermano"* (brother) or *"Hermana"* (sister), and in response, almost everyone calls him Hermano. He is always ready with calming words or a joke at tense moments. After being orphaned at 9, he lived on the streets, and he learned his trade from bakers, who took him in after seeing him trying to keep warm beside their bakery every night. After his move to Cerro del Cuatro in 1983, his wife started to attend CEB meetings. Hermano also participated in these meetings and joined the Madero colonia group, which would form part of the UCI. He also later led one of the Madero neighborhood groups. Almost illiterate when he began working with the UCI, Hermano Javier worked hard to develop his reading and writing skills, as well as his ability to analyze local and national issues. A man of great gentleness, Hermano Javier referred to his wife and daughter as *mi reina* (my queen) and his son, as *mi rey* (my king). By 2004, years of pushing his cart around the hill had taken its toll, and he was forced to hire a neighborhood boy to accompany him on his rounds. Hermano's son Javier refused to take his schoolwork seriously, while his daughter María was planning to enter a local university. His pride in his daughter was mixed with anxiety he and his wife felt over impending tuition payments.

Frustrated and disgusted with the clientelist politics practiced by the PRI, Agustín Martínez joined the UCI in 1991 and soon rose to a leadership position as coordinator of a colonia group in Guayabitos. A father of two, he had moved to Guadalajara from Mexico City and in 1986, he arrived in Cerro del Cuatro where he built his own home. After feeling exploited in his factory job, he started his own small clothing business and peddled his goods in a large warehouse area in Guadalajara. In 1995, he was beset by personal tragedy when his wife died after giving birth to a developmentally disabled child. Agustín's family responsibilities then forced him to withdraw from active organizing work with the UCI and move away from the hill. However, in 2004, having remarried, he returned and was seeking work.

Ana, Carmen, Hermano Javier, and Agustín are deeply religious, and they trace much of their commitment to aid others to their faith, although they all hold strong political beliefs as well. Except for Agustín, all began working in colonia groups before SEDOC arrived, and all continued working as leaders of the base development team after SEDOC's departure. As leaders, they met weekly for planning, decision making, information sharing, and more frequently for working on specific tasks. The coordinators of the colonia groups also met weekly with their groups to share information, air grievances, and plan action.

The UCI recruited colonia residents into commissions and work areas that began by initially supporting the struggle for urban services but which evolved into entities focused on other efforts, including communications, housing, and organizing. Eventually, in response to the interests of group leaders and SEDOC organizers, subgroups that pursued human rights, "militant spirituality," and popular health also emerged. In these work groups, the residents planned further strategy, made contacts with government functionaries, and solicited participation from their neighbors. These groups collaborated with other groups, such as university students, seeking counsel in the area of health care, building a unified popular voice, and denouncing human rights violations.

The organizational structure built around SEDOC was designed to assign work, communicate needs and information, and represent the desires of the organization's members. Ideally, the SEDOC team was to meet for planning and evaluation sessions, then communicate the results to the base development team. In turn, the base coordinators were to bring these plans to their colonia groups for discussion. Again ideally, the colonia groups would express their interests and needs and so guide the UCI's actions from below. Complaints of deficient services, for example, quickly transformed into work plans, with commissions formed from the colonia groups and the development team. These smaller groups decided how to pursue their goals, what government functionaries to contact, and how to publicize their needs in the media.

The hierarchical structure revealed SEDOC's perception that Cerro del Cuatro residents required direction and control from outside. SEDOC's control of its popular organizations was also revealed in a consistent pattern of language use. SEDOC members would refer to the UCI and other groups as "our projects" or as entities that "belonged to SEDOC." Using a "culture of poverty" analysis, UCI members were assessed as individuals with "low" or "marginal" levels of culture, which posed obstacles to organizing and self-direction. Thus, these apparently paternalistic views did not belie SEDOC's commitment to democratic participation in the popular movement but rather were a reflection of a belief that the community was simply not yet ready to act on its own, without external direction.

The structure allowed SEDOC to facilitate participation within the UCI, while leaders and members were undergoing a training process akin to resocialization. SEDOC did not specify a finite period of control and direction, which further demonstrates that there was a perception that it would take quite some time before the UCI could be responsible for its own organizational needs. For example, SEDOC did not give full control to Intercolonias, an organization they founded in 1985, until they were forced to do so in 1993. This is evidence that SEDOC was prepared to stay at the UCI's helm for a long period. Despite its grounding in the democratic visions offered by liberation theology and theories of popular education, SEDOC designed a hierarchy that revealed its perception of Cerro del Cuatro residents as requiring direction and training from those with greater education, privilege, and status.

SEDOC trained the base group leaders in areas such as group management, the impact of neoliberal economics on the poor, governmental structure, and constitutional rights. This instruction was useful for political analysis of how to obtain and press advantage against a state characterized by growing conflicts between local, state, and federal entities. Additionally, the training helped the UCI deal with agencies whose mandates often shifted. SEDOC organizers also coached UCI leaders for their meetings with officials, accompanying them to the office of the powerful.

Little of this training was made available to the members of the colonia groups. Organizing and educating the base became the task of UCI leaders. The selective availability of training and workshops produced trained and politicized leaders, but it created a gulf between leaders' and members' political perspectives. Close contact between the SEDOC organizers and UCI leaders resulted in leaders usually endorsing the Jesuits' policy decisions, including those that proposed extra-local political action. The formal hierarchy was reinforced by close contacts between base group leaders, uniformly poor, limited in education, and possessing deep religious beliefs, and the SEDOC organizers, all of whom possessed higher levels of education, came from more middle-class backgrounds, and worked for a religious organization. Differences in status, class, education, and legitimacy bolstered the hierarchy established by SEDOC and endangered its professed values of democratic participation. The close contact between SEDOC and UCI leaders also opened a gap between those leaders and UCI members. This gap was to cause problems in the future.

The UCI gained great support during its early years because of the resources, direction, and aid given by SEDOC. At the height of UCI participation (late 1991), approximately twenty-five small groups met weekly, each of which averaged about fifty participants. When the UCI called general assemblies on the hill they were able to turn out audiences of more than two thousand people, and in excess of four hundred joined the marches on government offices. This support was gained by giving priority to the material needs of the urban poor of Cerro del Cuatro.

SELF-HELP SERVICE PROVISION

PRI militants promised Cerro del Cuatro residents the delivery of urban services when they sold lots to the newcomers. Fifteen years later, most of the promises remained unfulfilled. For example, residents of three colonias, Nueva Santa María, Buenos Aires, and Francisco I. Madero, had long been dependent on sporadic water delivery by Tlaquepaque municipal trucks. Although this was allegedly a free service, actual delivery was assured only by paying tips to drivers and dispatchers, and local PRI leaders scheduled the deliveries, so delivery was contingent on demonstrated support for the ruling party. Those not enjoying local PRI leaders' favor, such as UCI supporters, had to rely on private entre-preneurs who sold water of dubious quality from large vats kept on their trucks. In both cases, residents stored the water in a variety of receptacles, including oil drums and large plastic storage tanks on the house roofs.

Immediately after it formed, the UCI petitioned for water services in Nueva Santa María. Led by Carmen Castañeda, local residents repeatedly visited the Tlaquepaque Department of Public Works. María Andrés Andrés, a UCI member living in Nueva Santa María, recalled that "we went three times to Public Works, and they denied the permission. At the end, after three times, the official said, 'Put it in. But it's your own problem.' . . . He said, 'We won't do anything in writing, only in words—but put it in.' So we said okay. But we were fearful about who would come to stop us. But thanks to God, nothing happened."

Carmen and others investigated the fees and recruited interested residents. Each block elected a captain in charge of labor recruitment and fee collection. UCI members organized residents into work crews, dug trenches through their streets, set plastic pipe to carry the water, and built *hidrantes,* communally shared faucets mounted either on wooden or concrete pedestals. UCI members then attached long lengths of hose to the faucets, so that one hydrant could serve an entire block of houses.

After installing the infrastructure, UCI members had to find a water source. The municipality had provided water to PRI-affiliated neighborhoods, and so they went there. Despite the PRI leaders' objections, the UCI tapped into those water lines and ran the water to Colonia Nueva Santa María. Doña Alicia Escalante Torres, one of the block captains, explained how PRI leaders resisted:

> Those who don't support the PRI don't get anything. And to us, they put up obstacles. They said, "No, you can't take it from here." And we said, "What do you mean, no? Water is for everybody, everybody is

paying for it. We're paying for it with our taxes, and everybody has the right." And they said, "No, no!" And we said, "Yes!" And we put it in. And they said they'd take it out, but they didn't, and so we put more in. We finished with bloody hands, with blisters . . . and when we left, with the stream of water from the hoses, many people came to see, because they still didn't believe it. And afterwards, everyone wanted water!

By installing their own infrastructure, the Nueva Santa María residents were able to bring water to fifteen blocks that had previously been dependent on the water trucks. Similar projects yielded water hydrants for eight blocks in Francisco I. Madero and eight more in Buenos Aires.

The UCI's efforts to gain services were not limited to self-installation. They also circumvented PRI neighborhood groups by going directly to various municipal, state, and federal agencies in search of infrastructure. By mid-1991, a year after its formation, the UCI reported important successes in obtaining services for the colonias in which it worked. In La Mezquitera, work had begun on a water and sewer project. Garbage pickup had also increased, and the public services agency had installed street lighting on eight streets.

In Guayabitos, one of several promised water cisterns had been delivered. Posts for electric lines had been installed throughout the colonia, the first step for legal electrification. In Buenos Aires, residents built a network of water hydrants, although the PRI leader in the area battled the UCI for control of the water. A handful of streets in Buenos Aires had been paved as well, which allowed bus routes to expand to previously unreachable areas.

In Loma Linda, a colonia whose organized residents joined the UCI in the summer of 1991, members working with UCI leaders from other colonias had also installed a network of water hydrants, and they had received titles to their lots. Tlaquepaque and Guadalajara had each argued that the other was responsible for Loma Linda; UCI members forced the resolution of negotiations over which municipality was responsible for further service delivery. With the decision made, residents more effectively targeted Tlaquepaque officials to resolve their problems. In Nueva Santa María and Francisco I. Madero, UCI members installed water hydrants and continued to investigate which federal agency could legally resolve their land tenure problems.

In addition to these concrete service gains, negotiations continued on land regularization, electricity, increased access to water, and sewer infrastructure. UCI members had also successfully negotiated for two parcels of land, one in Buenos Aires and one in Francisco I. Madero, on which they built structures for meetings and storage. Donating labor and materials, the organization helped build a full service parish in Nueva Santa María, while in Buenos Aires, members built a small church, used as a satellite facility.

These successes, along with continued recruitment and organizing work, led to organizational growth. New UCI groups became active in Loma Linda, Guayabitos, Buenos Aires, and Nueva Santa María, and more people joined the groups already active in each colonia. In addition, a UCI group formed in Santa Anita, a small settlement in the municipality of Tlaquepaque.

With its successes, the UCI also started to move slowly into other work areas. It recruited local builders to hold construction workshops, while UCI leaders themselves held workshops on organizing. SEDOC organizers and the UCI leaders began talking about other work areas in which the UCI could serve the community. Organizers, leaders, and members brought up ideas such as human-rights training and support, forming youth groups, and self-help medical training. Nevertheless, the work that elicited the most popular support continued to be the struggle to obtain urban services.

The UCI's work dramatically improved residents' quality of life. Its success also meant that the participants came to recognize that independent organizing could supply a fruitful alternative to clientelism.

THE REGULARIZATION STRUGGLE, PART 1

Cerro del Cuatro residents always bitterly denied the label of land invaders that some government officials used to describe them. Rather than invaders, the residents considered themselves victims of the corrupt practices of the CROC, a PRI-controlled union. CROC members sold lots to many of the residents, with promises that such sales were legal and that urban services would soon follow. These land traffickers even provided certificates of ownership. The certificates turned out to be false, as did the promise of services. The several attempts to dislodge Cerro residents from their homes in the mid-1980s and their inability to obtain legal title caused great insecurity. Even though many residents recognized that the dense settlement of the hill made removing them nearly impossible, rumors that they would be displaced continued to plague them into 1994.

The lack of land titles had important legal implications, as Ana Mondragón noted, "I want to sell half the lot, and I can't sell it, because the whole hill is under dispute. I can't sell it because my land title isn't valid. No one [could challenge my ownership now], because it would damage the image of the system.

But legally, we can't sell. And if you can't sell what is yours, you don't have the rights they say you do." Leaders complained that their efforts in increasing the quality and quantity of urban services had had the perverse effect of stimulating land trafficking by CROC members (del Castillo 1993). Despite the condemnation by the UCI, the landowners, and even government functionaries, the CROC militants continued to sell lots illegally. During 1994, CROC members set up a stand to sell lots in the valley between Cerro del Cuatro and Cerro Tesoro, and unwitting buyers, hoping to escape the high cost of housing in Guadalajara, fell prey. From the farthest reaches of the Cerro del Cuatro settlement, where Avenida 8 de Julio narrowed to a path barely passable by cars, one could overlook the *techos azules,* or the blue tarpaulin roofs, of the new settlers' homes below. For the UCI leaders, securing land rights was a key strategy for several reasons. First, control over land sales in Cerro del Cuatro was one of the main sources of the CROC's local power, and regularization would undermine that. Second, UCI leaders understood that once the land was regularized, the government would be forced to provide urban services. If the government recognized the residents' right to live on the hill, leaders reasoned, wouldn't it then have to recognize the right to services? Third, the leaders also understood that their demands for urban infrastructure would have greater moral force once the residents held the land legally. For these reasons, the fight for regularization was an important part of the UCI's political struggle.

The effort in Nueva Santa María, one of the first areas settled on Cerro del Cuatro, is a good example of the UCI's struggle for regularization of property rights. The land title dispute had a long and complicated history, dating from the colonia's founding, that involved a number of actors: the original communal landholders (in what had been the village Santa María Tequepexpan), private property owners, new settlers, two different federal regularization agencies, several state and *municipio* governments, the UCI, the CROC, and some PRI-affiliated neighborhood organizations (López Rangel 1987). The UCI advocated federal expropriation of the entire Cerro del Cuatro area in order to centralize the problem and keep the multiple parties with contradictory interests out of the negotiation. Expropriation would facilitate regularization and would be the best, most comprehensive, and most rapid solution.

Despite repeated visits to the Palacio de Gobierno and to different federal regularization agencies, the UCI leaders were unsuccessful in determining who had the power to regularize the area. This led to discussions between the UCI and the then-federal Secretary of Social Development Luis Donaldo Colosio, who would later be the PRI presidential candidate until he was assassinated in

1994. Colosio, as a significant national figure in the PRI, was well out of the reach of the UCI as a negotiating partner, but SEDOC organizer Padre David Velasco had longstanding ties with Carlos Rojas, national coordinator of the Solidaridad program. With this connection, SEDOC was able to entice Colosio to the hill to talk. UCI leaders and members recounted the tale of Colosio sitting on an over-turned bucket in the dust of an open lot, listening to group members. In the summer of 1992, Colosio broke the logjam by deciding that CORETT would be the responsible agency. Despite the advance that decision represented, the CORETT's bureaucratic process slowed the negotiations with the UCI.

CORETT charged for the regularization of the land titles. Using a rate applied to areas with complete public services, a fee was assessed based on the size of the lot. Even though the agency offered to extend credit to the residents, they protested the fees since Nueva Santa María did not enjoy full urban services, on the one hand, and those that did exist were the fruit of the UCI's labor, on the other. UCI members charged that these high fee assessments in effect penalized them for their work on behalf of their community, and they demanded that the federal agency charge at a level appropriate to the conditions of the area when the residents bought their lots. Given the poverty of the residents, the UCI also requested that residents be allowed an extended time to pay the fees. The agency refused to reduce the rate it charged, but it did extend the payment time from one to three years. And for many years, little change occurred. Regularization remained one of the most difficult goals to achieve on Cerro del Cuatro. The UCI was most successful at obtaining secure land titles and other services when it could count on various state agencies working on its behalf. The connections with SEDOC provided the UCI with access to state actors. But SEDOC and UCI were most successful in marshalling state resources during moments of changing clientelism.

CHANGING CLIENTELISM AND NEW OPPORTUNITIES

Supported by local power blocs embedded in the country's corporatist structure, the Mexican government was highly centralized, with the president holding overwhelming power to set policy (Cornelius and Craig 1991; Camp 1993). Despite the state's efforts to maintain dominance, the foundation began to crack in the late 1980s and 1990s, when the federal government's neoliberal policies weakened the local power blocs. Economic and political crises simultaneously damaged the PRI's hegemony, pushing the state and the party to institute various reforms. The shrinking of the government sector reduced patronage resources to levels far below what local power brokers were accustomed to deploying. The party's delegitimation, the reforms, and the shrinking patronage resulted in electoral losses at the local level.

Rather than bolster local power holders, the federal government attempted to regain popular support by building a new foundation. President Carlos Salinas de Gortari's unsuccessful early efforts to reconstruct the corporatist system by replacing the PRI mass organizations with three "movements" was resisted fiercely by the organizations' militants (Teichman 1995). Nevertheless, Salinas's removal of thirteen governors demonstrated his willingness to sacrifice vulnerable local power holders to maintain overall PRI hegemony (Eisenstadt 2004, 104). As further electoral reforms that he had proposed in 1993 and 1994 were approved, the power of the local blocs continued to erode.

The main policy instrument for recapturing popular support was the National Solidarity Program (Programa Nacional de Solidaridad, PRONASOL), which President Salinas created immediately upon taking office in December 1988. Years of economic policy harming the poor and the middle class had diminished the PRI's support, forcing Salinas's hand. Years before, when writing his doctoral dissertation at Harvard, he had pondered how to reinvigorate PRI hegemony. Writing about the faltering relationship between the Mexican government and rural communities, Salinas suggested launching "a concerted effort by the PRI-government apparatus to promote the emergence of a new generation of leaders at the community level who could serve as more effective interlocutors between citizens and the state" (Cornelius, Craig, and Fox 1994, 6).

It was not merely new leadership that the PRI sought. The urban political challenges that emerged throughout the 1980s required a state response. Denise Dresser argued that "PRONASOL was created as a discretionary fund designed to construct new patronage networks with low-income groups across the country, especially those with electoral weight" (1994, 147). She quotes an "ex-member of Salinas' team at the Ministry of Budget and Planning," who acknowledged that Solidaridad was created to respond to the new urban politics. "The intention behind PRONASOL is to create, through public works and services, a new urban base for the Mexican state. By the end of the 1980s, the social bases of the Mexican state were unraveling. We were confronted with an unfamiliar urban scenario that we had to organize politically" (official quoted by Dresser 1994, 148).

Originally housed within the Ministry of Budget and Planning, Solidaridad became the umbrella under which new programs were created, and existing programs were moved. When Salinas created the Social Development Ministry (SEDESOL) in 1992, the increasing importance of the Solidaridad programs became even more evident. Solidaridad programs were the centerpiece of the new ministry, which was led by the president of the PRI's executive committee (and later presidential candidate), Luis Donaldo Colosio. The heightened profile was matched by increased spending, as the program's budget nearly quadrupled in four years, rising from US$680 million in 1989 to US$2.5 billion by 1993.[1]

Throughout Salinas's term in office (1988–1994), the government trumpeted Solidaridad's potential and its accomplishments using extensive advertising campaigns and annual "Solidarity weeks." During the public relations blitz of those weeks, Salinas traveled throughout the country, delivering speeches lauding the program and receiving thanks from participants in planned cere-monies. By the final excursion of his presidency, the government was boasting that 250,000 Solidaridad committees had worked in over 98 percent of the country's municipios, accomplishing 500,000 projects that ranged from infra-structure building, to school remodeling, to legalization of individual families' landholdings (Ballinas 1994).

Yet Solidaridad's significance was not rooted only in its service delivery. Because government functionaries hoped to revive popular support for the gov-ernment, the program's institutional goals evolved rapidly. Democratizing the urban community, according to Solidaridad managers, was crucial to Mexico's transition to democracy, and they and Salinas touted the program as the structure through which state-society relations were to be re-created.

The Solidaridad program was initially defined as a comprehensive attempt to attack root causes of poverty: "It is fundamental to emphasize that Solidaridad does not attempt to be a palliative for extreme poverty, in which wide sectors of the Mexican population find themselves immersed; what it is attempting is to attack the structural causes of poverty" (Presidencia de la República 1992, 15). The state, recognizing its negligence in responding to growing inequality, would address popular needs through the Solidaridad program.

The objectives were expanded beyond battling poverty when the govern-ment announced that Solidaridad's goals included social justice (SEDESOL 1993a; 1993b). Government publications emphasized that clientelist politics had both delayed the arrival of democracy and perpetuated poverty. In contrast, Solidaridad would follow principles of community respect and democratic participation, and it would facilitate the transition from "clientelism, hierarchy, paternalism, and political conditionality" (SEDESOL 1993b, 8). The next step

---

1. Although some of this growth reflects transfers of program budgets moved from other min-istries, the increase is still dramatic.

was to create a new democratic political culture, to be rooted in "participation," "ties of commitment between organization members," "solidary attitudes," "democratic practices in decision making," and "autonomy" (SEDESOL 1993b). By working together in organized committees, the poor would come to share these values. The benefits to the community from the Solidaridad program would then far surpass the finite public works projects.

Thus, the intentions of the Solidaridad program evolved from addressing poverty to the creation of a new political culture. The rhetoric surrounding the *comités de solidaridad* (solidarity committees) themselves transformed. From initially depicting them as instruments to alleviate poverty, they came to be portrayed as carriers of a new democratic culture, and, ultimately, as the new expression of the organized urban poor. By working with Solidaridad, the urban poor would find avenues of representation and participation in the newly democratizing Mexico, and they would be part of the restructuring of state-society relations. "Through the Comités de Solidaridad, the impoverished groups of our country have won the opening of pathways of coordination and communication for the communities, with new responsive and practical forms in their relations with the government, making decisions and resolving problems democratically" (SEDESOL 1993a).

Not surprisingly, critics found that Solidaridad's real-life practices contradicted its lofty goals. Municipal presidents charged that Solidaridad discriminated against non-priísta municipios. In addition, some opposition politicians charged that local PRI organizations used Solidaridad resources as patronage goods, selectively dispensing them during election campaigns. Both academics and politicians pointed out that Solidaridad was used to strengthen the PRI's electoral campaigns, with the program devoting more attention to areas where the opposition was strong (Correa 1991; Corro 1991; Molinar Horcasitas and Weldon 1994; Ward 1994; Dresser 1994).

In Dresser's view, Solidaridad incorporated dissident social reformers into its projects in order to forge state ties with noncorporate social groups. In this way, Solidaridad programs strengthened both the presidency and the PRI, if not its corporate sectors (Dresser 1991). Similarly, Jonathan Fox (1994a) emphasized that participants still worked through governmental channels, petitioned within predetermined constraints, and carefully avoided public criticism of the government. Contrary to the pronouncements by Solidaridad officials, grassroots communities participated only in implementing projects, not in making decisions.

The threat to local power made the local authorities use Solidaridad's resources in ways that were quite distinct from how it was used by federal officials. Locally,

Solidaridad resources were used as patronage to bolster entrenched power. The federal interest in building new structures of representation to support the government led it to sometimes challenge existing power holders. Solidaridad often bypassed local PRI corporatist organizations in its attempt to present a new political face and maintain centralized power. But local power holders were more interested in the immediate problem of how to hold on to the reins of power, even if their efforts defied the federal mandate. Because the federal program was administered by federal, state, and municipal officials, Solidarity became an area of contestation, containing within it seeds of conflict between the centralized government and the local powers upon which it relied. On Cerro del Cuatro, the conflict became open when local power holders battled federal officials over how the programs resources would be distributed. The divergent interests in resource allocation created new opportunities for the UCI.

TWO SOLIDARITIES CLASH: THE ELECTRIFICATION PROJECT

In September 1990, the municipality of Tlaquepaque announced that they would bring electricity to Colonia Buenos Aires as the first phase of an electrification project for the entire hill. UCI members reacted skeptically to the announcement, because they had heard such promises before; the timing coincided with local election campaigns; and the announcement was made by the municipal Solidaridad coordinator, who was also a leader in the Tlaquepaque PRI. During a general meeting, the Solidaridad coordinator quoted a per-household installation cost of 207,000 pesos. The federal government, through Solidaridad, committed to paying a quarter of the costs, the state government would pay another quarter, and the residents themselves would pay half.

Ana Mondragón described this meeting: "An official from Solidaridad in Tlaquepaque came, and gave the cost for the entire project . . . Of this, they were going to collect a quarter from the colonia [and they announced the amount to the residents]. And the people applauded . . . At that moment, I remember [SEDOC organizer] Juan Diego, who had accompanied me, turned to me and said, 'How? How are we going to pay that?'"

UCI leaders returned to their office after the meeting and discussed the proposed project costs with their SEDOC mentors. Ana recalled that with a quick assessment of resident numbers in the affected neighborhoods, "We discovered and proved a fraud. We obtained data about how much the work would cost, and we found out that they [the municipality] would collect double [the amount that the residents were supposed to be paying]. And the struggle to prove that they were charging too much lasted for fifteen months."

In October, the UCI denounced the overcharges. By their estimation, it would cost 94,000 pesos to install electricity per household, not the quoted 207,000 pesos. UCI members worked with a federal land regularization agency to conduct a census in Buenos Aires, which counted 2,058 lots in the colonia. A Tlaquepaque functionary then requoted the installation fee at 100,000 pesos per household, that is, each household would pay 50,000 pesos, its 50 percent share of the cost. The functionary promised that the electricity would be in place by the following May. Despite this development, the municipal Solidaridad apparatus, PRI neighborhood leaders, and the municipal treasury continued to collect the higher fee from residents. When UCI coordinators suggested that residents postpone payments until these officials reduced the assessed fees to their proper levels, PRI municipal officials charged that the UCI was delaying installation of the service.

The controversy meant that the promise of electrification went unfulfilled. To add insult to injury, the control of the work was turned over to local comités de solidaridad in May 1991. These committees were run by neighborhood PRI leaders, which increased the UCI's concerns about fraud. These were the same priístas who had sold land fraudulently, had collected money for various public works that remained uninstalled, and had given access to water only to their followers. UCI leaders said they felt like billiard balls, as they repeatedly bounced between municipal offices, the Jalisco public works department, the Solidaridad offices, and the Federal Institute of Electricity. Throughout the period, officials from the Tlaquepaque Public Works offices, from the CROC, and from another PRI organization continued to quote different costs to the residents.

Unknown to Tlaquepaque municipal officials, the UCI's connection to SEDOC brought good relations with the federal Solidarity delegate Francisco Mora. Padre David Velasco knew the director of the national Solidarity program, Carlos Rojas, and this contact facilitated a connection with Mora. Mora and his team gave UCI members untainted figures on the costs of the public works.

In November 1991, after repeated attempts to meet jointly with all the agencies involved with the electrification program, the UCI finally sat down with representatives from the federal Solidaridad program, from the local Solidaridad committees, and from the municipality. They discussed how to come to an agreement on the census count and the per-household installation cost. By December, a figure of 120,000 pesos per household had been set, and the work was on its way. The Tlaquepaque authorities admitted they had overcharged residents and began returning some of the money to those who had already paid. It was not until elections neared, however, that Tlaquepaque officials admitted their "error," and the Tlaquepaque president congratulated Ana Mondragón, admitting the UCI had won.

The success in Colonia Buenas Aires had required several forms of aid from SEDOC. First, the Tlaquepaque officials would never have been sufficiently challenged without the accurate cost estimates provided by federal Solidaridad workers. SEDOC organizers proved crucial to obtaining this information. That data and further collaboration with the federal government in the census count also provided UCI some immediate legitimacy as a community voice, which was visible not only in evoking popular support but also in eventually forcing Tlaquepaque politicians to meet and to rescind the fees they had quoted. The struggle in Buenos Aires also demonstrated schisms between local and federal political actors. SEDOC was able to capitalize on its connections to take advantage of the division between the different power holders. Finally, the fight had required both research skills to locate needed information and a clear map of the maze of municipal, state, and federal bureaucrats with whom the UCI was forced to negotiate. In that, SEDOC proved invaluable, accompanying UCI leaders and members to meetings, and coaching them in advance. Meeting with the bureaucrats was an ongoing training exercise for UCI leaders and members. Many commented that this struggle for electrification provided important instruction on how to work with bureaucrats without becoming intimidated.

The fifteen-month campaign was a triumph for the UCI. The organization successfully confronted the PRI and convinced municipal authorities to significantly reduce the costs of the service delivery to Buenos Aires and to set a just price for the rest of the hill. In addition, the UCI continued to press for installation of electricity, which may have met with even longer delays without UCI's watchdog role. UCI's reputation as a forthright and successful defender of the interests of Cerro del Cuatro residents grew.

The electrification campaign demonstrates the complex relationship the UCI had with the state. Local PRI powers, especially those linked to the CROC, tried to seize control of a substantial portion of the Solidaridad budget and linked the promised service to the area's support for the PRI. Thus, the CROC tried to kill two birds with one stone: lining their pockets by padding the costs while also winning electoral support in exchange for their promises. Later interactions with the comités de solidaridad further showed how the UCI, with SEDOC's help, interacted with a state divided by those interests that were struggling to maintain local power and those focused on rebuilding centralized power. Both in the confrontation with Solidaridad and in the self-help method of infrastructure installation, the popular organization gained support by addressing the long-unaddressed material needs of the poor residents.

THE UCI AND THE COMITÉS DE SOLIDARIDAD

Given their experiences with the Solidaridad committees and the CROC's links to the municipal Solidaridad program, the UCI leaders were skeptical about the program's claims of nonpartisanship and respect for non-PRI organizations. UCI leaders interpreted Solidaridad's organizing of colonia residents as an attempt to maintain patron-client relations under the guise of community participation. The Solidaridad committee organizing process confirmed their beliefs. It began with either small groups of residents petitioning for aid from local Solidaridad offices or Solidaridad promoters visiting local communities and publicizing the program's potential benefits. Solidaridad workers would then invite residents to a general assembly where the organizing process was explained. The community would select their committee leaders and hold a preliminary discussion to prioritize needs. After the committee formed, leaders fulfilled various duties: writing formal proposals for the desired project, collecting residents' contribution for their share of expenses, finding and negotiating with contractors, and overseeing the work (author interview with a SEDESOL organizing team).

This model notwithstanding, when local PRI groups became linked to Solidaridad, they used these allegedly nonpartisan activities to maintain local clientelist relations. In communities with preexisting PRI neighborhood groups, the PRI leaders often became the new committee leaders. Whether they were imposed by higher authorities, selected through open elections, or chosen as a result of their control of the community, PRI domination was reinforced by local PRI leaders' control over the new resources.

Such was the case on Cerro del Cuatro. Although the electricity fraud was the most egregious example of Solidaridad's links to the local PRI, the party's links to people on the hill were widespread. UCI leaders and members consistently identified Solidaridad projects on Cerro del Cuatro with local PRI leaders.[2]

In response to PRI domination of the committees, the UCI declared its skepticism about the Solidaridad program, and its May 1991 newsletter warned

---

2. Local PRI leaders' link to Solidaridad was not anomalous. On the other side of Cerro del Cuatro, eight out of the nine Solidaridad committee presidents that I interviewed were also local PRI leaders.

that residents were likely be manipulated and that the availability of resources would spark conflict among contending PRI groups:

> !!Comités de Solidaridad: The Same Corrupt People!!
> A few months ago PRONASOL's publicity campaign arrived. The commercials on television left us feeling that everything is very beautiful, and they tried to convince us that it is a "new way of working" or that [we will be] "united to progress." . . . A most complicated fight can be foreseen in Nueva Santa María, where priísta groups, one from the CROC and the other from the CNC, will fight a war for a comité de solidaridad. Both are without real popular support, given that they are led by persons who trafficked in lots during the establishment of the colonia and who now want to control the comité for water and sewers.

As the 1991 elections neared, the UCI tried to convince their constituents that Solidaridad was more about PRI electioneering than about popular representation:

> As we said in the May newsletter, the COMITÉS DE SOLIDARIDAD remain in the same corrupt hands of the traditional PRI leaders who do not represent the true interests of the colonos of Cerro del Cuatro. Even more, these leaders are remarkable for their swindles and corruption. All of this coincides with the initiation of the 1991 electoral campaign. Announcements of public services [are now being made], even though we have been haggling over them for ten years. (UCI–Cerro del Cuatro 1990–94 [June 1991], original emphasis)

Even after the elections, the UCI kept the heat on the Solidaridad program on Cerro del Cuatro:

> Now in an agency with which the UCI has always had good relations, various engineers are telling us that we must form a comité de solidaridad to finish the water and sewer works. In interviews with SEDESOL functionaries like Colosio, Rojas, Navarro, Mora Anaya, and others, all of them said that THAT A COMITE DE SOLIDARIDAD WAS NOT A CONDITION to finish the works. Why don't the functionaries come to an agreement, leaving off fights between federal and state [agencies] and resolve the problems that the UCI has demonstrated? The deeper

problem is that neither the state nor the federal functionaries want to admit that 1993 is not an election year, and that is why they have not done anything to resolve the work that has been pending since 1990. (UCI–Cerro del Cuatro 1990–94 [June 1993], original emphasis)

When I interviewed him, the chief Solidaridad official on Cerro del Cuatro, Luis Fuentes, grudgingly acknowledged the validity of UCI's critique that the program's resources were tied to the PRI. Without confirming PRI domination of the Solidaridad committees on Cerro del Cuatro, he told me "neighborhood leaders" often carry out Solidaridad work.

> There has been a consent [about leadership] within the community for more than ten years. Leaders have emerged from the community, and they are part of preexisting organizations. These organizations keep their eyes open, and when comités are established, some of these people identified with political groups become presidents of the committees or members. Why? Because the people chose them for their work, maybe, for the good work that they have done. But [community leaders' entry into committees] gives us access. It permits access because these people can block [the access] also. . . . Sometimes, maybe, something that escapes our control, is that the same organizations get ready earlier, and say come on, let's move in there and put so-and-so in. There have been cases like this, but we can't directly control this, because we don't want to provoke a confrontation in the community when we arrive.

Fuentes asked to see my questionnaire beforehand, and he also called his boss at the central SEDESOL office in Guadalajara to ask permission to grant the interview, because several of the issues I wanted to discuss were "hot." I had already had a cordial conversation with his boss, and so he gave Fuentes permission to answer any questions. Nevertheless, Fuentes chose his words extremely carefully when he talked about Solidaridad connections with local power.

Fuente's boss had been more relaxed during our conversation and like his subordinate, he claimed that Solidaridad's work had no connection to the elections. Juan Manuel Clema Godínez, a coordinator of Comité de Solidaridad projects in Jalisco, assured me that "Here in Jalisco, [this kind of behavior] has been prohibited by the delegate. There have been cases where people have been fired, when it has been proven that they took electoral action. At least here, it does not occur. We don't expect anything in return, absolutely nothing. We expect to serve, we are public servants. Understanding that the people have needs, have paid taxes, and this creates an obligation for us to serve them." The SEDESOL official admitted, however, that some of the constellations of power in which Solidaridad worked complicated its efforts:

> Sometimes the municipio presidents jump the norms, the rules, and promote the creation of committees, sometimes democratically, and other times, by designation. "You're going to have a committee here, you'll have one here, you'll have another one here." To extend their own power. When it is by designation by the municipio president or sometimes by the federal deputy, things change, and conflict starts. The natural leaders of the society fight with the imposed leaders [the government] and great arguments ensue, and sometimes the work has to be suspended. But yes, we do work in part with the associations of colonos or vecinos or the barrio groups.

The preestablished organizations about which Fuentes talked in cautious code, and the associations of vecinos or barrio groups that his boss mentioned, were controlled by the PRI. The UCI's interpretation that local power blocs were able to take advantage of Solidaridad resources despite federal SEDESOL's expressed intentions to break with the old structures was, at least partly, acknowledged by SEDESOL officials.

Solidaridad was never reticent about claiming credit for the services they brought to Cerro del Cuatro. In October 1993, Solidaridad established an office prominently located on Avenida 8 de Julio. By early 1994, Solidaridad had brought electricity to part of Cerro del Cuatro (in the scandal-plagued effort described earlier), had paved a few streets, had renovated several schools, and given grants to schoolchildren, and the program was preparing more projects.

Compared to the work on the eastern side of the hill, Solidaridad provided minimal resources to the western sections of Cerro del Cuatro, where the UCI had a presence. In the 1994 Approved Investment Budget for Jalisco, the federal Solidaridad program for public works in the colonias allocated approximately 448,712 pesos to the western side. These projects included pipes for potable water, sewers, and pavement (PRONASOL 1994). This sum had to be matched by the state or the municipio, in addition to the share paid by the residents who would receive the services.[3] On the eastern side of Cerro del Cuatro, Alfredo Barba's CROC forces dominated the Solidaridad committees. The investment budget allocated close to a million-and-a-half pesos for infrastructure work, including waterlines, sewers, pavement, and electricity. In addition to these urban services, additional projects were planned to install more potable water systems and sewers, although the cost for these projects was not specified in complementary budget documents. Both sides of the hill had nearly equivalent services, but compared to the western flank, the eastern side was much less densely settled. It was, however, more firmly under CROC control and lacked an independent alternative like the UCI. Here the struggles over Solidaridad funds engendered internecine battles, with the CROC triumphing over the other PRI sectors.

UCI leaders acknowledged that some Solidaridad projects might be directed more honorably than the ones controlled by the CROC. But the UCI leaders still believed Solidaridad benefits would come to the colonias only in exchange for their political support. In general, the UCI leaders and members believed that the Solidaridad program offered them no more than the services they deserved, and often less. First, Cerro del Cuatro residents were required to pay a portion of the costs of any project from which they benefited. Thus, they paid double, as it was their taxes that funded the various governments' contributions. Second, the Solidaridad program built infrastructure of shoddy quality or that was unconnected to other service networks, thus not completely fulfilling residents' needs. In addition, this infrastructure was as haphazardly placed as other patronal contributions, with a street paved for several blocks, beginning and ending abruptly. The logic of the placement of Solidaridad public works, in the opinion of the UCI members, followed the logic of municipio works: it rewarded and placated loyal communities. Finally, the timing of Solidaridad projects was consistently suspect, with a great deal of activity occurring near elections. The electoral link continued during my initial years of fieldwork.

The early years of the UCI reveal much about that organization's attempt to resist clientelism, as well as about how civil society organizations work together with each other and with the state. The very relationship between SEDOC and the UCI contradicts much of the literature on clientelism and its focus on the isolation of neighborhood organizations. As the intensive involvement of SEDOC

---

3. Because of matching-funds requisites, as well as filtration through local power, the amount the federal government invested in the area does not always translate into concrete work projects in the colonias.

demonstrates, the UCI was anything but isolated. SEDOC brought the UCI into contact with a set of extra-local actors. Moreover, the UCI did not act deferentially in its response to the dominant single-party state. Finally, although UCI's strategic focus during its early years was on satisfying basic needs, those efforts were presented in a language of rights as opposed to a language of clientelist exchange. SEDOC's use and transmission of this language was the first step in its strategy to work for democratization. SEDOC's interest in democratization helped a new language of contention emerge at the colonia level.

The relationship between these two civil society organizations helped impede the clientelist efforts of both federal and local state actors and achieved notable successes in addressing the needs of long-suffering Cerro del Cuatro residents. However, civil society's divided character was apparent even within the successful SEDOC-UCI relationship. First, with the power and legitimacy of the Jesuit order behind it, SEDOC stood firmly at the top of the internal hierarchy. Nevertheless, this stratified organizational structure was rational, given the disparate levels of experience and resources and the differences in class, status, and education that existed between the members of SEDOC and the members of the UCI.

Despite the hierarchical features of the SEDOC-UCI relationship, it bore substantial fruit. SEDOC facilitated the UCI leaders' entrée to centralized state actors and offered important resources and expertise in its battles with local state actors. The electrification campaign demonstrated both advantages. Yet even during this successful period, the organizational hierarchy is evidence of the stratification of civil society and the implications that division had for unity. Unity held while the interests of the poor were foremost strategically in the efforts of both organizations, but a breakdown came as SEDOC asserted its own interests over those of the UCI.

5

ELECTORAL STRATEGY AND THE
DIMINUTION OF POPULAR SUPPORT

The UCI, under SEDOC's influence, reoriented its priorities from urban-services needs to a concern for national democratization. The change became evident when the UCI ran candidates for political office in both the 1991 and 1992 elections. SEDOC's intellectual and political interests and the opportunities created by a political juncture were the impetus for the UCI's focus on democratization.

I further argue that it was during this period that SEDOC's domination manifested problems for the popular organization. These problems were revealed in two ways. First, the structure of the organization reinforced differences between organizers and UCI members on hierarchies of class and status and made it impossible for critique about the changed focus to filter up from below. Second, the promoters' nurturing of the leaders created a gap between these two segments of the organization and the organization's base. Such a gap further diminished alternatives for members to contest the direction of their organization.

ELECTIONS: UCI-PRD

The 1989 formation of the Party of the Democratic Revolution (Partido de la Revolución Democrática, PRD) coalesced the small leftist parties and urban social movements that had run as the National Democratic Front or FDN in the 1988 elections (Bruhn 1997). Its origins resulted in the new party being plagued by factionalism. The nascent PRD struggled to find strategies that would expand the party and exploit the groundswell of anger displayed after the 1988 presidential election, which was generally interpreted to have been stolen by the PRI through voter fraud. To build on its foundation of social movement support, the PRD solicited popular organizations to run candidates using its formal registration as a political party. Although it approached popular organizations that had no PRD activists, the party particularly saw organizations with which it shared some base or leadership as fertile ground to build alliances (Bruhn 1997; Eisentadt 2004).

The UCI was one of these. Its successes had demonstrated the viability of creating alternatives to PRI neighborhood groups. The PRD, as a perceived alternative to the corrupt PRI, enjoyed some support in the community, and PRD members had attended the UCI's formal constitution ceremony. More importantly, several of the SEDOC team were also PRD militants. At their urging, the PRD first approached SEDOC and then the UCI, offering the latter a chance to compete in the state convention to select nominees for state and municipal offices.

The close relationship between the team members and the PRD effectively sealed the deal between the party and the UCI. A 1991 SEDOC document had identified dangers in electioneering—such as the possibility that their popular organizations would dissolve into the party or that electoral efforts in the very large District 18 that included Cerro del Cuatro might be beyond the UCI's capabilities. Nevertheless, SEDOC organizers revised their goals "to push a policy of alliances that will help the real construction of the party . . . to promote cadres for positions of popular election . . . to take on electoral processes as educational, reflecting, and politicizing processes, not merely for pragmatic electoral ends" (SEDOC 1991, 2).

These sorts of statements reflected SEDOC's commitment to push into the electoral sphere. The organizers aligned their popular education strategies and theological motivations with their party ambitions, and they discussed how their Christian commitment and values were confirmed by their participation with the new party. Although SEDOC organizers feared that politicians might use the party and its allied social organizations for personal ends, they felt that their Christian inspiration would enrich partisan political militance (SEDOC 1991).

Guadalajara possessed other electoral alternatives that were also deeply influenced by religion. The National Action Party (Partido Acción Nacional, PAN) was founded in 1939 by middle-class Catholic activists responding to the dominance of the anti-clerical National Revolutionary Party, the forerunner of the PRI. The PRD was joined by the PAN in denouncing the 1988 electoral fraud, but its efforts to strengthen the party largely revolved around conservative middle-class discontent (Tangeman 1995). In large part because of their own political choices, but also because of the opposition of the progressive Church, the PAN had little presence on Cerro del Cuatro until the election of 2000.

The PRD proposed that the UCI run a candidate for federal deputy (a position roughly equivalent to a U.S. congressperson) in District 18, which includes Cerro del Cuatro and Santa Anita, another area where SEDOC promoted popular organization. The SEDOC team and UCI leaders discussed the idea and then brought it to the colonia groups, where members approved the action. At the convention, the UCI won the right to run its candidate in the August 1991 elections. Jesús Padilla, a UCI stalwart, began a campaign to challenge Alfredo Barba Hernández, the PRI candidate, who was the former municipal president of Tlaquepaque and a CROC strongman.

With the Jesuit team strongly supporting the effort, members embarked on electioneering duties. In its May 1991 newsletter, the UCI announced the decision to participate in the campaign, with a candidate running as representatives of UCI under the PRD banner. The Union offered this rationale to the Cerro residents:

> In the UCI, we have analyzed the political situation, and the importance of participating in the next elections, and we have analyzed the different parties, and have seen that we identify most with the PRD. Because of the necessity to struggle to gain spaces for authentic popular representation, we have seen that we must take advantage of its [the PRD's] registration as a political party, and we have decided to participate in the next elections with our own candidate from the UCI, who is Jesús Padilla, knowing his past as an honest worker and his training as a participant in the CEBS. We want him because he will represent our political interests as the UCI while the great directions of the whole country are being defined. The Chamber of Deputies, where NAFTA will be discussed, which will define the future of Mexico as a sovereign or dominated nation. (UCI–Cerro del Cuatro 1990–94 [May 1991])

The UCI launched its candidate as a member of the PRD's national political campaign. The strategy was notable since it took on national political issues that were well beyond the daily needs of the colonias. The Union's electoral work was notable also for the absence of a rationale linking a UCI presence in the Chamber of Deputies to patronage benefits for local community members. The UCI's anti-clientelist stance precluded it from arguing that winning office would bring material improvements to the community, despite the efforts the Union had expended to win those benefits under PRI domination.

As the campaign continued, UCI members painted murals and passed out fliers. They also talked to residents about the importance of participating in the election and voting for the PRD, and they launched walking tours of the hill, using a portable PA system to propagandize. The small-group agendas began to highlight election work, with SEDOC organizers and UCI leaders exhorting the base to support the candidate and get out the vote. The UCI used its newsletter to promote Padilla's candidacy and to remind Cerro residents about Alfredo Barba's history. Barba was a candidate about whom the residents of Cerro del Cuatro knew a great deal, one who had largely ignored their needs. Indeed, he had never been reticent about insulting Cerro residents. In various open confrontations with UCI members, he had called them tattered, shabby land invaders. When UCI members petitioned Barba for aid as the president of Tlaquepaque, he responded: "Who told you to live on the hill? I am not the father of your children to resolve your problems" (UCI–Cerro del Cuatro 1990–94 [June 1991]; author interviews).

The UCI did its best to remind residents of Barba's attitudes, and about the electricity fraud he had presided over during his municipal presidency (see Chapter 4). The activity of PRI neighborhood groups headed by CROC affiliates loyal to Barba also provided daily reminders of PRI corruption. The UCI leveled charges that the PRI's propaganda murals were painted by Tlaquepaque municipal workers, and so citizens' taxes were paying for the work. As the election neared, PRI candidates promised they would help Cerro del Cuatro by regularizing the entire hill. In response, the UCI reminded residents that regularization could only be achieved by the designated federal agencies, not by individual politicians. Here, too, the UCI tried to remain faithful to their anti-clientelist position by refusing to counter the PRI's promises with some of their own.

The UCI lost the election. The large size of District 18, which extends well outside of the Guadalajara Metropolitan Zone, principally accounts for the loss. The UCI was unknown beyond Cerro del Cuatro and Santa Anita, and the PRD did not campaign for Padilla, because the party's weakness in the Guadalajara Metropolitan Zone limited the resources and efforts on behalf of the their candidates. The UCI leaders and the Jesuit team had recognized early on that winning the deputy seat was close to impossible.

UCI members had not fooled themselves into thinking the election would be clean. Afterward, the UCI denounced a number of "irregularities" by the PRI, including the failure to deliver voter credentials to some registered voters and the removal from electoral rolls of the names of others. In addition, the UCI complained that a heavy, and illegal, presence of PRI representatives at the polling places had intimidated voters. The polling officials were almost all priístas, and they had allowed noncredentialed voters to vote, while annulling many PRD and PAN votes. Election officials had also changed the locations of the polling places to confuse voters. Despite these criticisms, the contention that the UCI would have won a free election was noticeably absent.

Given their limited objectives, the UCI and the PRD did quite poorly. Recognizing the impossibility of winning the deputy's seat, they had hoped to displace the third largest political force in Tlaquepaque, the Cardenista Front for National Reconstruction Party (Partido del Frente Cardenista de Reconstrucción Nacional, PFCRN). They failed to reach this modest goal. Despite the overwhelming defeat, little critique was articulated at the time regarding the decision to participate in elections.

Instead, SEDOC organizers and the UCI began preparing almost immediately for the 1992 local elections. The UCI again ran a candidate, Gloria Tepete, for the Tlaquepaque municipal president, and again lost the election by a large margin. They also failed to attain the more realistic goal of representation on the town council, which could have been won with a mere 4 percent share of the votes cast. This election marked the end of a formal affiliation with the PRD, and the end of running UCI candidates for elected office. However, it was just the beginning of the controversy over SEDOC's strategy of affiliating with the PRD and participating in elections. Before discussing the strategy's impact on the Union, it is worth considering why SEDOC and the UCI made this choice.

THE ELECTIONEERING STRATEGY

Why did SEDOC decide to change the UCI strategy? Why, rather than follow the local agenda that had won support and genuine gains for the UCI, did it begin to run candidates for office in pursuit of nationwide democratization? In retrospect, the decision to join a two-year-old party that had been unable to effectively challenge the hegemonic party during the demonstrably fraudulent 1988 election seems like a huge, and incomprehensible, tactical mistake.

The context in which SEDOC worked helps provide some answers. First, the Jesuits have a long history of working with the Left in Latin America. Second, many popular organizations across Mexico accepted the PRD's invitation to run for office. Third, the Jesuits made a consciously pragmatic decision to support the PRD over the electoral alternatives of the corrupt PRI and the highly conservative PAN. Finally, the Jesuits in SEDOC had studied a number of theories of social change, but their intellectual background had a distinctly

Gramscian flavor that led them to make decisions that, in their view, would nurture the emergence of organic intellectuals.

The Jesuits and the Left in Latin America

The Jesuits were by no means always a progressive element in the Latin American Catholic Church. In Mexico in the eighteenth century, for example, the order profited immensely by using unpaid indigenous agricultural labor, and before Mexican Independence, it continued to accumulate wealth and political power by forging connections with the emerging upper class (Tangeman 1995, 21). The Jesuits' social action during much of the twentieth century was limited to the order's social-action programs in middle-class and elite schools. However, even before the advent of liberation theology, the Jesuits had had an important influence over middle-class leftist radicals. Both Fidel Castro and Abimael Guzmán, the founder of Peru's Sendero Luminoso, studied with Jesuits. With the founding of liberation theology, the order undertook a novel politicized effort to work with poor communities.

Liberation theology endowed the Jesuits with a solid foundation on which to base their political work. The identification of the "preferential option for the poor," the central theme of liberation theology, drove an active search for freedom from oppressive social conditions. Jorge Castañeda (1993) documents the contribution of the Catholic Church to what he considered the "second coming" of the revolutionary left in Latin America. In this role, the Church, generally, and Jesuits, more specifically, played important roles in both armed and civil resistance. Many of El Salvador's armed cadres and opposition intellectuals, for example, "had established connections with the Society of Jesús, ranging from simple friendship to membership in the order" (Castañeda 1993, 99). The Jesuit University of Central America in El Salvador was long an important actor in the civil opposition in that country, and it paid for its activism during the massacre of 1989.

As did other members of the progressive Church, Jesuit priests and affiliated laypeople also played important roles in organizing peasants, urban communities, and labor throughout the continent (Castañeda 1993). The Church actively recruited for the Brazilian Worker's Party in rural areas, and in Nicaragua, the Catholic Church contributed to the insurrection against Somoza. In Peru, Father Gustavo Gutiérrez helped other priests push the left-leaning popular church even further to the left. In Colombia, the Jesuits have been key actors not only in working in grassroots organizing with the poor but also in institutional politics as advisers and technical experts for leftist partisans (Castañeda 1993, 99). Jesuits have also played important roles in urban and rural organizing in Venezuela (Levine 1992).

The Mexican case is mixed, as conservative elements of the Church have remained very powerful (Tangeman 1994). Yet since the mid-1970s, CEBs in Mexico expanded rapidly to become an important part of the popular organizing field. At the same time, "the Jesuits had modified the order's conception of their role in society, and . . . they tilted toward the 'option of the poor,' often organizing CEBs (Castañeda 1993, 212). Mexican Jesuits have also played important roles in the creation of nongovernmental organizations denouncing national human rights abuses. In 1986, Jesuit priests established the Miguel Agustín Pro Juárez Human Rights Center, which has been at the forefront of condemnation of human rights abuses of indigenous peoples and opposition political parties (Tangeman 1995, 72). In several Mexican Jesuit seminaries, students are expected to work with popular organizations as part of their pastoral work (author interviews). Thus, the Jesuit participation on the left is, if anything, to be expected. Still, why did SEDOC choose to participate in the elections?

The PRD's Struggle for Consolidation

In 1991, the PRD tried to capitalize on the popular mobilization that had previously supported the opposition coalition candidate, Cuauhtémoc Cárdenas. The PRD, analyzing its recent popular appeal, felt that the best way to win elected office was to take advantage of popular organizational infrastructure and personalities. Rent by factional difficulties, with limited campaign funds, and targeted by the PRI government through its preferential dispensing of Solidaridad funds, the PRD's ability to participate in the 1991 elections was constrained. Using pre-established popular bases and organizations seemed its best chance.

Many popular organizations ran their candidates under the PRD banner, but this diverted attention away from other elements of their agendas.[1] Despite the negative results of this strategy for these organizations, at the time, the choice appeared to be a viable one given the widespread desire to challenge the authoritarian PRI state. On Cerro del Cuatro, the experiences with a corrupt

---

1. I am grateful to Dr. Juan Manuel Ramírez Sáiz for pointing out the wide acceptance of the PRD's 1991 offer to run social movement candidates and the subsequent problems faced by many popular organizations (personal communication with author; see also Bruhn 1997).

PRI highlighted the need for an electoral alternative. In the context of SEDOC's progressive political and theological orientation, the conservative PAN did not provide that alternative.

The PRI and the Growing Strength of the PAN

SEDOC had long identified itself as speaking for and organizing the urban popular movement. In its 1986 planning documents and statutes, SEDOC used imprecise language, defining its mission as being to "help the independent popular movement to promote democratic processes that favor a change of power" (SEDOC 1986, 14). By 1991, SEDOC's partisan commitment had grown to the extent that the organization's mission statement specified the need to "promote a real articulation between social organizations and the PRD" (SEDOC 1991, 2).

SEDOC made a clear choice in its battle against a corrupt one-party state. In the wake of the 1988 electoral fraud, it recognized that broad political change would be impossible as long as the PRI held the reins of power, and this fueled SEDOC's continuing interest in pushing "its" popular organizations beyond local struggles and into national politics.

The alliance with the PRD was a strategic decision made in order to exert popular leverage against the state, but the growing strength of the PAN (Partido Accíon Nacional, or National Action Party) in Jalisco also influenced the decision. Indeed, the Jesuits joined the electoral struggle in response to the PAN's growing strength because the PAN had long been allied with some of the most conservative elements of the Catholic Church. In its early years, the party counted among its ranks a large segment who saw the party as "the Christian alternative to the Mexican Revolution" (La Botz 1995, 59). Although the party moderated some of its fierce conservatism as the Church itself became more liberal, liberation theology and the preferential option for the poor certainly contradicted the PAN's ideological and policy stance. In addition, the increasing parallels between the pro-business economic policies advocated by the PAN but put into action by the PRI convinced SEDOC that a PAN government would provide little economic relief. If anything, SEDOC workers expected that were it to win, the PAN would impose even greater control over civil society than the PRI had done. PAN-affiliated clergy in Guadalajara were quite critical of liberation theology, in general, and, specifically, of Jesuit efforts to organize the urban poor. If the order was to participate in elections, it was clear that the PRD was its only option.

The Jesuits Meet the Ghost of Gramsci

The SEDOC members had studied theories of social change along with liberation theology, and they juxtaposed both against the reality of Mexico's politics
and economy. They were convinced that the organized poor were not ready to
emerge as an independent opposition, and they believed that their role was to
help develop a popular politics and political culture that the poor could share,
thus aiding them to more fully participate in a struggle against the PRI. Both
the Jesuits' efforts to create a new political vision, and the role they played in
the struggle, emerged from a Gramscian view of social change.[2]

Gramsci believed that organic intellectuals could challenge capitalist hegemony by creating a popular politics and culture. The essence of the organic
intellectual is the "active participation in practical life, as constructor, organizer, 'permanent persuader,' and not just [as] a simple orator" (Gramsci 1971,
10). Gramsci believed that intellectuals could emerge from and represent the
proletariat, and so "provide the dynamic connecting link between theory and
practice, the intellectual and the spontaneous, the political and the social"
(Gramsci 1971, 223). Organic intellectuals have a duty to those they lead and
represent to make "coherent the principles and the problems raised by the
masses in their practical activity" (Gramsci 1971, 330).

The Jesuits in SEDOC took Gramsci's organizing lessons seriously. For the
urban poor to emerge as a fully participating and independent force, leadership
and organizations indigenous to their ranks had to be created. Given the
patronage, co-optation, and corruption endemic in Mexican politics, the Jesuits
believed that there would be a long wait before the poor could emerge as a
united and self-conscious political actor, but their studies of Gramsci also
revealed strategies to hasten just that.

The Jesuits recognized themselves among the ranks of the traditional intellectuals, whom Gramsci had described as maintaining capitalist hegemony.[3] Yet
Gramsci also believed that the traditional intellectuals could have a revolutionary
function. The Jesuits found Gramsci's discussion of the importance of opposition intellectuals suggestive: "Innovation cannot come from the mass, at least at
the beginning, except through the mediation of an élite for whom the conception
implicit in human activity has already become to a certain degree a coherent

---

2. This section is based on discussions with Jesuit students in Guadalajara about their studies,
and SEDOC training documents that discuss Gramsci's contributions to organizing.

3. It would have been difficult to avoid such a realization, given that Gramsci clearly identified
Latin American clergy as traditional intellectuals (1971, 22).

and systematic ever-present awareness and a precise and decisive will" (Gramsci 1971, 335).[4]

The Jesuits' role, then, was to become Gramsci's elites, substituting a Christian-influenced liberation for the goal of revolution. In this position, the Jesuits would entice the organic intellectuals from the ranks of the urban poor. Using the unifying vision of liberation theology to supply an ideological foundation for social change, the Jesuits hoped to build a coherent and organized opposition. Because of their religious legitimacy, they gained access to the poor, and began creating new political organizations rooted in Bible studies and the framework of the CEBS.

Despite his criticism of the Catholic Church[5] as an intellectual basis of authoritarianism, Gramsci could have been writing about the CEBS when he said: "Critical understanding of self takes place therefore through a struggle of political 'hegemonies' and of opposing directions, first in the ethical field and then in that of politics proper, in order to arrive at the working out at a higher level of one's own conception of reality" (Gramsci 1971, 333).

SEDOC organizers saw the CEBS and the UCI as the site where the poor could begin to address the ethical foundations of a struggle for social justice. Through Bible study, pre-political thought and action would build on a new interpretation of the life of Christ, and then transform into more coherent political thought and action. The Jesuits believed their job was to help organize and train cadres of leaders who were to become the organic intellectuals.

Gramscian theory was also marshaled to help guide the Jesuits in deciding to work in the electoral arena. "What matters" about the party, according to Gramsci, "is the function, which is directive and organizational, i.e., educative, i.e., intellectual" (Gramsci 1971, 16). SEDOC found in Gramsci's work a rationale for joining their popular education orientation to electioneering activity. The PRD was seen as one more resource upon which SEDOC could draw to challenge Mexico's political and economic inequalities and to further direct, organize, and educate the urban poor. Those SEDOC workers who were also party militants felt that the PRD could be used to achieve the organization's expressed goal of popular education and the "creation of the new man." Their argument found a

4. Gramsci's translators, Quintin Hoare and Geoffrey Nowell Smith, write that the organic intellectuals derived the critical self-consciousness necessary for militance from elite intellectuals, the "revolutionary vanguard of a social class in constant contact with its political and intellectual base" (Gramsci 1971, 334n).

5. The Jesuit's affinity for Gramscian theory is a bit ironic, given Gramsci's castigation of the Catholic Church, in general, and the Jesuits, specifically, as carriers of a traditional but especially authoritarian and reactionary hegemony (1971, 331–33).

theoretical home in Gramsci's view that the revolutionary party was a site where the efforts of organic intellectuals and the changing traditional intellectuals could be joined. This would politicize the organic and wean the traditional intellectuals from their hegemony-serving ways (Gramsci 1971, 16). Thus, the elites and organic intellectuals would emerge in common effort.

The dissemination of liberation theology, the focus on training for political and expressive purposes, the reliance on the Bible as a foundation for social justice, all followed a strategy aimed at nurturing the emergence of organic intellectuals. The Jesuits welded this ideological position to Paolo Freire's strategies of popular education, democratizing knowledge as a step toward wider democratization.

This context makes it easier to understand the choice to pursue electoral office. Pragmatic political opportunities led SEDOC to weld theological and theoretical tools to popular education strategies in their work with the urban poor. Eventually, the Jesuits' analysis of the political opportunities led SEDOC to drive the Union of Independent Settlers into the electoral arena. Yet the SEDOC team members applied its method unevenly. They spent extensive amounts of time training those they saw as likely leaders, while offering less attention to the UCI's base. SEDOC's interpretation of theory and methodology was to separate the SEDOC organizers from the UCI's base, and the UCI's base from its leaders. This separation became apparent after the elections.

THE ELECTION AFTERMATH: UNHAPPY MEMBERS

Although UCI members agreed to accept the electioneering strategy, discontent followed each election loss. One obvious sign of dissatisfaction came during the campaigns, when the lack of base participation was noted. UCI members were dismayed at the energy that was spent on the campaigns, energy that otherwise might have been devoted to the area's still dramatic infrastructure needs. Many felt that the PRD alliance belied the organization's independence and also effectively ended any potential for negotiation with the PRI. However, SEDOC's organizational structure made it difficult for UCI members to challenge the decisions made by SEDOC and accepted by the UCI leaders.

Two members of the Union, Ana Ramírez and Carmen Montoya, criticized the UCI after the elections. They had been active members in the Buenos Aires group, and they increased their involvement after Padre David Velasco and other SEDOC workers united the UCI. These two women worked intensely, and they delighted in the gains the Union made. Yet they disagreed with participating in the elections, and they left the UCI because of that. Ana said, "I started to see that the group was inclined to one party, and I didn't like it. I felt manipulated by a party— that it violated my liberty. I felt psychologically managed, so I refused to do the election work." Carmen concurred: "I really like political work, but I like to remain independent. Really there were a lot of us who wanted to remain independent. But there were key persons who pushed more.... The decision to participate in the PRD was a decision of the directors, not of the people." Ana's and Carmen's departure indicated some strong dissatisfaction with the direction the UCI had taken.

Another indication of the lack of base support for participating in elections can be found in SEDOC's complaints and internal evaluations of the process. After the second defeat, in a letter advocating increased links between the PRD and the UCI, SEDOC organizer Juan Diego Ortiz noted the lack of active work in support of the candidate. Although UCI leaders had agreed that their principal responsibility would be to strengthen their efforts during the second campaign, Juan Diego complained that "in some of UCI's weekly meetings, the topic of the election was not even touched on, or else it was done as a point in the agenda, without giving it the attention it merited . . . [which indicates that] . . . we could not awaken interest among the base" (Ortiz 1992). He is referring to the colonia group meetings, where UCI members' presence was strongest. The lack of interest in discussing the election work is a good indication of members' disinterest in the campaign. Yet the lack of discussion about the strategy of aligning with the PRD to run candidates also tells us that the members were uncomfortable about criticizing the hierarchy or that there was little space available to do so.

Despite the relative quiet within the meetings, UCI leaders recognized that the base was dissatisfied with the participation in the elections, as is shown in another part of the internal critique, which hinted that the base did not support the effort: "First, the people of the UCI have to assimilate the policy; later we could take the path to the PRD.... The electoral participation must be considered as one more activity of the UCI, rather than keeping it separate" (SEDOC 1992a, 6).

While Juan Diego felt that the UCI was insufficiently committed to partisan politics, UCI members felt that those efforts had been imposed on them. Indeed, the comments of formerly loyal members and the nonparticipation noted by the SEDOC team offer substantial evidence that the base did not favor running candidates on a PRD slate. Part of the dissatisfaction arose because campaigns for urban services no longer had the same vigor as before, and in some cases, they were completely suspended. SEDOC documents confirm that election work supplanted other organizational work. "During the period, there was practically no social organization; everything was dedicated to the issue of the elections. . . . During the electoral work, much of the service work was side-lined. Only one general mobilization about the land question was planned" (SEDOC 1992b, 6–7).

If SEDOC organizers—those most invested in the partisan alliance—recognized that UCI's work had been concentrated too heavily on the elections, the members' were even more convinced. UCI leaders were forced to explain their participation in the elections. Many of the explanations discussed the UCI's independence from the PRD, an indication of the discomfort among the membership over the issue. Three newsletter excerpts were typical of the UCI leaders' defense: "We were in agreement with the PRD on many things, and we participated electorally with this party. The UCI did not lose its independence and the relationship between the UCI and the PRD is one of mutual respect" (UCI–Cerro del Cuatro 1990–94 [December 1991]). This comment was followed later by a more forceful state-ment. "The UCI does not belong to the PRD or any other political party. It is independent. Some of its members do belong to the PRD. There is an ALLIANCE between a social organization and a political party" (UCI–Cerro del Cuatro 1990–94 [January–February 1992], emphasis in the original). A third newsletter claimed, "We say that we are independent because we do not depend on any political party or on the government. The government and the parties would like to have us under their control because we are bothersome and uncontrollable" (UCI–Cerro del Cuatro 1990–94 [May 1992]).

It became clear that the alliance hurt the Union of Independent Settlers much more than it had helped. UCI leaders all agreed that the elections had contributed to a loss of support. Their analysis, however, came too late. Agustín Martínez put it very clearly: "We didn't know how to explain this participation in the elections with the PRD, to say we could participate with a political party in the elections and still be independent. This was the problem with the process: it happened very rapidly, and the people left."

Agustín felt that the electioneering was insufficiently explained to the member-ship, despite it having been discussed with the colonia groups prior to the PRD convention. The members reacted in ways that, to Agustín, showed that they neither understood nor supported the decisions. "They were afraid. They thought, 'We were part of an independent social organization. Why this change?'"

Other UCI leaders were equally convinced of the error. Ana Mondragón acknowledged that the UCI had lost support: "During the struggle for services, the colonia meetings attracted one hundred to one hundred fifty people, every week. And in 1989 and 1990, there came the struggle for the electricity. And we had some success. Then in 1991, we saw that it would be advantageous to support those of the PRD who had worked with us. So in 1991 came the elections and the distribution of the campaign propaganda with the UCI and the PRD, and all that, and the meetings dropped to twenty-five people."

Ana believed that this drop-off in participation was partly because of the UCI's successes in winning services, which eased the community's grievances and, consequently, lessened commitment to the organization. But she also felt the UCI's electioneering had been a mistake and something that further diminished popular support.

Hermano Javier also attributed the loss of support for the UCI to the involvement in the elections. "The people crumbled, the support left, because they thought UCI would continue being part of the PRD, and it wouldn't be an independent UCI–Cerro del Cuatro, no? And we worked hard to convince the people that the UCI is the UCI."

Similarly, Ana Mondragón felt that after the elections, government functionaries saw the UCI as *perredistas,* that is, PRD supporters. This perspective diminished the access to officials that mobilization had won: "During the campaign, they marked us as part of the PRD, and they are priístas. . . . Tlaquepaque talks a lot about helping us, but they don't do anything because they think we are perredistas."

Ex-UCI members Ana Ramírez and Carmen Montoya agreed with Ana Mondragón's analysis. They felt that the UCI suffered from the electioneering strategy because it became identified with the PRD, which hurt the residents in talks with the government. Carmen noted, "The credibility of UCI was damaged after the elections because the government was no longer willing to work with us. So, the UCI has been less able to obtain services since 1992, and it lost supporters."

These various comments demonstrate that the anti-clientelist stand of UCI members did not neatly translate into supporting other parties. The avoidance of party identification was attractive to many, as these interview excerpts show:

> When we went to demand the water, they asked us who we were, from what party, and we told them, "No, we don't belong to any party. We are alone. We are independent. No one sent us." —Doña Elisa Quintero Palafox

> [The UCI] helps us in everything, and it is not a party. It doesn't have any interest—because a party has a single interest, that you vote for it. They look out for the welfare of people, and more than anything, they seek a dignified life. —Martina Jiménez

> The UCI is an organization that helps the community [and] that doesn't belong to any party. Because many people ask, "What party is the UCI?" But, no, we don't belong to any party. —Elvira Novarro de Toro

For others, their own analysis of power on the hill came into play. Members who remained loyal to the UCI were largely disinterested in the electoral path, or they worried about how the strategy would be interpreted by other partisans. Some felt that electoral contestation was useless in an area so dominated by the PRI, as Francisco I. Madero resident Marta Luisa Rodríguez mentioned: "No party helps us. If you vote for the PAN, the PRI wins. If you vote for the PRD, the PRI wins. Vote for whomever, and the PRI always wins."

Others identified partisan affiliation as intrinsic to the clientelism that they had come to oppose:

> There are other people who say, "We'll vote for those wretched people, because they give us milk, they give us tortillas." And things continue the same, and worse. —Gloria Tovar

> We are supposed to join the party so that they will arrange for all of our services. But we don't want to join with them to do this. —Doña Clara

Members' fears that PRI government functionaries would identify the UCI with the PRD does not imply that they desired to build clientelist relations with that party. None of the UCI members with whom I talked were willing to enter into a relationship in which votes for the PRI were exchanged for urban services. Yet the UCI members still saw the exercise of their voting rights as one of the political tools that they could use in their struggles, along with protest and confrontation. If government officials were to identify the UCI as an arm of the PRD (as members and leaders alike felt they did), the UCI would lose a potent tool.

SEDOC workers understandably chose to push the UCI into electoral participation. The Jesuit history with the Left, the opportunities offered by the PRD in the context of a strong PRI and a strengthening PAN, and members' strong connections to the PRD are all good reasons. Yet what explains the UCI leaders misinterpreting their constituency? The status of leaders and members differed only within the Union; outside of it, they were neighbors, equally poor with little formal education. Why did the leaders fail to recognize their neighbors' reluctance to campaign? The separation of UCI's leaders from the base supplies much of the answer.

CLOSE RELATIONS AND INCREASING DISTANCE

In his work on U.S. community organizations, Gary Delgado noted that the gap in "political education" privileged (external) organizers over (internal) leaders in setting policy directions and making decisions. After recognizing this gap, organizations began to address this problem with extensive leadership training programs, which focused largely on skills rather than on wider political analysis (Delgado 1986, 226).

SEDOC and the UCI confronted similar problems. In response, the SEDOC team worked intensively with UCI leaders to train them in skills such as media work, negotiating with government functionaries, recruitment, and meeting facilitation. Training also included discussions of national political economy and the benefits of broad alliances. Workshops focused on the requisites of democracy, the intersection of faith and democracy, historical abuses of the PRI, and social, political, and economic alternatives to the Mexican system. The Jesuits tried to close the "political education gap" by adding political analysis to the toolbox available to the UCI leaders. This was an integral element of the Jesuits' attempts to form organic intellectuals.

The SEDOC team members were largely self-congratulatory in their evaluations of their training efforts. In numerous comments, they agreed that the training of the UCI leaders had been one of the greatest advances made. The following quote is typical: "The training of cadres has been such that SEDOC workers no longer have to accompany them in their negotiations with functionaries" (SEDOC 1992a, 8).

Yet even in the positive evaluations, clues appeared that the training differentiated the leaders from the base. SEDOC organizers admitted that despite their focus on educating the leaders, little effort had been expended to educate the base (SEDOC 1992a, 12). They recognized that they had not reached their goal of sufficiently educating base members to negotiate with functionaries on their own: "This result was obtained in only some negotiations, and only some from the base dared to do so" (SEDOC 1992a, 9). The organizers especially recognized that the base's failure to understand the relationship between the UCI and the PRD was the result of insufficient education: "Most of the people have had trouble grasping this; you could say that those who understood it best were the base development team" (SEDOC 1992d, 8).

Although the gap between organizers and leaders, of which Delgado warned, was avoided, the close association between UCI leaders and the SEDOC team resulted in a political gap between the base and the leaders. UCI leaders benefited from their consistent contact with the organizers by attaining a wide set of skills. One result was that the leaders came to agree that wide political change was a more important goal than the satisfaction of local needs. Agustín Martínez responded to a question about UCI's functions:

> The most important work? It is the raising of the people's consciousness. That they have to defend themselves, to know their rights. Teaching them how to work for others. For me, the gains in the regularization and all of this is secondary, because if the people aren't more conscious, they wouldn't gain this second area. The main gain is in the consciousness of the people.

Hermano Javier felt similarly about the UCI's most important contribution to Cerro del Cuatro residents: "The UCI tries to make the people conscious that they have to participate, to make them aware that they can participate in the government, to be a spokesman for the people. To make them know that the government has to give services to the people, to the citizens, and not the reverse."

For Tito, the urban services work was largely the vehicle for other kinds of education and change:[6] "But this is the means. For me, and for some other folks, this is not the end of the struggle, to obtain the services. It's rather a means to make the people conscious that nobody can be for them what they can be, and do, for themselves. To make them conscious that with struggle, they can get more than the government says it is authorized to give. For me, this is the most important."

These comments reveal that SEDOC's popular education efforts endowed the UCI leaders with a wider political perspective, a national rather than local reference, and the desire to participate in wide political-change efforts aimed at democratizing Mexico. Yet this interest also differentiated the leaders from the base.

When I asked people in the base about the most important work that the UCI pursued, without exception, the first answer was "obtaining services." At times, various members suggested the higher importance of one service over another—the sewers were especially important to some residents, followed by water and electricity. But members' first response always mentioned services. When pressed, subsequent answers identified creating an interest for each other among the community, "awakening" and "defending" people in the

---

6. Tito was one of SEDOC's paid organizers and not a UCI leader. I include his comments here because of their coherence and because his background and work in Colonia Polanco was so similar to the lives of those on Cerro del Cuatro.

community, and preparing residents to speak with those in higher positions of power. Even those answers, however, identified services as the subjects about which they wanted to speak with the powerful.

Similarly, when I asked about the UCI's most important successes, obtaining services and regularization topped every member's list. Uniting people in the community was the second most common answer. But the reason for uniting people was often to obtain the services. The failures of the UCI, in contrast, had to do with the inability to convince more community residents to participate and take responsibility for satisfying their needs. Finally, when I asked members, they often knew little about non-service-related UCI projects, such as the organization's work on human rights, alternative health, or building relationships with other organizations. Few people in the base talked about democracy or national political change, although with prompting several members mentioned their increased knowledge of the government and the human rights that they had asserted through the struggle. Long-standing members of the base answered questions about the UCI's contributions in this way:

> The most important is that they help us put in the electricity, the water, this is the most important, they look out for us, to help us, in many ways. We've gained a lot from the UCI. Like the electricity, and the [land] regularization. —Doña Clara

> UCI struggles for the services for the colonia. This is the most important for us. Everything that there is here—the electricity, water, the laundry area—all are gains by the UCI. —Doña Elisa

> [The UCI's most important work concerns] water and sewers—getting them to the houses. The sewers are indispensable, as is water for each house. —Doña Julia

When I asked leaders about the UCI's successes, they consistently demonstrated their concern for mobilizing the community. They identified their most important work as organizing and "awakening" the people, increasing their political consciousness, and teaching people to work for the good of the community. They identified all facets of their work as equally important. In their answers, their only comment regarding urban services had to do with the research they pursued. For the leaders, the UCI's most important successes revolved around their consciousness-raising efforts, the evidence of fraud they had uncovered, and the organization of the community. Indeed, even the language with which members and leaders referred to the uci differed. Members were more likely to say that the uci helped them greatly, rather than to use proprietary language about the organization. In contrast, the leaders talked about the uci as the "people," "the organization," or even as "us."

Thus, the perceptions of leaders and base regarding uci's role and contribution differ significantly. The base members were consistently more interested in improving their quality of life through urban services provision, while the leaders were more interested in contributing to the building of a Mexican democracy. Yet the interviews revealed few differences between leaders and members in class, background, household makeup, and previous political experience. The fundamental difference was the increased exposure the leaders had had to sedoc organizers, which included political training. Consequently, the leaders had embraced the Jesuits' political project.

The leaders themselves willingly acknowledged the important role the organizers had played in their political thinking. They spoke glowingly of the training they underwent and the close relationships that they enjoyed. Both had greatly increased the leaders' capacity to organize and to think about political issues in broader terms. Yet the close relations and training also created a strong alignment between organizers and leaders. Ana Mondragón's comment is telling: "And because we were new, and we said they had helped us do so many things, we had to support them [in the election efforts]."

Although the connection to the sedoc team led uci leaders to support it, the differential levels of training between base and leadership created a distance between the two segments, so that the likelihood of leaders hearing base critiques of organizers' policy shrank. The status differences between organizers and base reinforced the likelihood that sedoc programmatic desires would be heard over those of the uci base. The ability of poor working-class people to criticize the middle-class, educated, politically experienced, and religiously affiliated sedoc organizers was very limited.

The organizational structure, in which sedoc made decisions in consultation with uci leaders also created constraints. In theory, the organizational structure was designed to nurture discussion, policy, and critique from below within the colonia-level groups. Yet the hierarchical structure, when combined with the status and class differences, was sure to supply further barriers.

The decline in support confirms base members' perceptions that the uci's most important work was its efforts to obtain urban services. It appears that the decline was caused by both the involvement in elections and the success in obtaining services. Several SEDOC organizers and UCI leaders noted that some participants left after they gained access to water or electricity (de la Peña 1991),[7] but these same organizers and leaders also criticized the involvement in the elections. At the height of UCI participation, in late 1991, between two and five groups were active in each of the seven colonias, and the UCI consistently mobilized approximately two thousand supporters. By mid-1992, after the election failures, the UCI's mobilizing capacity had diminished to about eight-hundred supporters. If the base members were unable to get the message across to the leaders and organizers that they did not support the involvement in elections, it became clear as they voted with their feet.

In their pursuit of social change, the organizers pondered their roles as organizers of and advocates for the urban poor. SEDOC workers were impelled to help alleviate the material needs of the poor on Cerro del Cuatro, but their highest priority was to create an organization that would contribute to a national opposition movement based in poor neighborhoods. The organizers always tried to widen political thinking on the hill, so that the poor residents would recognize that the injustice they suffered was a consequence of national problems, not merely of the local abuse of power.

The organizers felt the best way to contribute to a wider opposition was through partisan work even though the base did not support that. Cerro del Cuatro residents certainly became interested in political issues and participated in wide opposition efforts, but when SEDOC organizers imposed their vision of national political change, giving priority to this goal at the expense of the base members' struggle for services, it diminished the UCI's hard-won popular support.

The electoral experience reveals some of the strata of civil society. SEDOC yielded to its own self-defined political priorities rather than pursue the agenda of the poor. The means—urban-service provision—was jettisoned in favor of a more direct attempt to reach the end—democratization. The process of agenda change and shifted priorities forces us to look with some skepticism at the extent to which self-avowed civil society organizations may aid the poor. Indeed, SEDOC's domination of the UCI, its rigid hierarchy, and the substituted priorities demonstrate the class and status stratification in civil society.

The Jesuit workers' decisions were a product of their desire for social justice and their religious and academic training. SEDOC's direction of the popular organization reflected a perspective on political change not necessarily shared by the UCI's rank and file. Notwithstanding SEDOC's good intentions, the

---

7. This trajectory follows a well-established pattern (Nelson 1979).

organizers' activity posed the dilemma that a privileged sector in an extremely class- and status-stratified society offered the ideas and the training about democratization. Gramsci wrote, "For organic intellectuals to become a critical force in class struggle, however, traditional social cleavages, cultural divisions, and political tensions between different strata would have to be broken down" (1971, 224).

The SEDOC team's privileged status limited this breakdown. Their more secure access to resources reinforced important cleavages, rather than erasing them. Even though Jesuit organizers entered the community to get to know the social reality of the poor, many of them still knew it from the outside, from positions of relative power, and from temporary vantage points. Adding to the differences in class, experiences, and resources was the stratification by status that is intrinsic to the Jesuits' religious authority and legitimacy. The SEDOC team's greater knowledge, organizing experience, and the legitimacy of their religious status, as well as their material resources, kept UCI members from openly questioning the Jesuits' direction.

Further, the team's interpretation of Gramsci presented problems. First, the vision is basically a paternalist one, emphasizing the elite's greater capabilities to plan and understand struggle. The necessity of having elites to nurture organic intellectuals clearly indicates a perspective that political consciousness itself is differentially available, with those higher on other hierarchies possessing a higher consciousness. Second, the conception of how popular opposition was to be built focused on aligning the organizers with the popular leaders, creating great political and ideological distance between them and the rank and file. Leaders' belief in the Jesuits' expertise and policy-making skill made it even harder for undercurrents of dissent to arise from the base and be heard.

The choice to pursue a strategy that involved partisan politics and election-eering did more than reveal important class and status fractures. The connection to the Jesuit civil society organization had given the UCI the ability to insert a wedge between contending elements of the state, but the shift in strategy away from urban-services provision cast doubt on whether the UCI could maintain that leverage.

Other urban movements express an array of anti-clientelist sentiments, some of which integrate more successfully with electoral politics. Luis Hernández and Jonathan Fox write, "For urban social movements, winning the city or town hall meant gaining access to resources, both to deliver public services and to reinforce political legitimacy" (1994b, 184). This willingness to address citizen needs by participating in electoral campaigns is consistent with the transition

from clientelism to citizenship (Fox 1994). Popular politics during this transition has multiple possibilities, including social movements taking office and
negotiating with candidates in ways that emphasize the carrot of exchange
rather than the stick of state or party punishment.

Robert Gay (2006) further addresses the range of possible state-neighborhood
movement relationships in his investigation of how a favela leader negotiated
with contending parties, effectively forcing a bidding war for the bloc of votes
he controlled. This process of negotiation contrasted with the electoral campaign
run by the UCI under the PRD banner. That campaign employed a rhetoric of
national democratization and harshly criticized the PRI for its lies and clientelist
distribution of resources. This put the UCI in a position of having to abstain
from clientelist politics and precluded making promises to its supporters about
further material improvements in Cerro del Cuatro.

An anti-clientelist stance made sense given the corrupt manner in which
patronage had traditionally been distributed and the PRI's declining resources
after the implementation of neoliberal policies. The electoral competition,
however, was not a well-thought-out strategy given the PRD's weakness in
Guadalajara. The absence of clientelist promises suggested a new way to go
about politics, but it may also have suggested the inability of a PRD office-
holder to deliver the goods sought by the members of the UCI. Without paying
attention to local needs, the appeal of a rhetoric about national democratization was insufficient to gain support. Indeed, it evoked a rational fear that if the
UCI were to affiliate with a weak party, its own independent capacity to pressure
the dominant party in nonelection years was lessened.

SEDOC's contribution to the politicization and training of the poor on
Cerro del Cuatro was undeniable. Notwithstanding that contribution, the outcome of the SEDOC-driven strategy to engage in electioneering was a loss of
base support for the UCI. SEDOC and the UCI might have weathered this storm,
however, if the partisan choices had not incurred the wrath of the upper tiers
of the Jesuit hierarchy. The impact of the SEDOC strategy was shortly to bring
even greater problems for the UCI.

6

FROM CRISIS TO SURVIVAL

SEDOC played an important role in uniting neighborhood groups on Cerro del Cuatro. With its substantial support, the UCI became a force to be reckoned with. SEDOC and the UCI demonstrated both their ability to work together and the force they wielded to make demands on an unresponsive government.

Despite achieving important gains that added to the quality of life for area residents, fissures appeared between the organizations. SEDOC gave priority to its democratization agenda over the material needs of the Cerro del Cuatro residents. The organizers were so blinded by their partisan interests that they continued to argue for affiliation with the PRD even after the elections had proven disastrous for the UCI. This continuing error demonstrated divergent perceptions, based in a stratification of power and privilege. As time wore on, the errors of this policy became increasingly apparent to the UCI leaders, who were left with the problem of how to return to work that would elicit base support when they did not have full control over their organization. The resolution of this problem was hastened by organizational crisis.

The crisis developed as a direct result of SEDOC's strategy to participate in elections. Because of the close link between SEDOC and the PRD, the Jesuit provincial authority forced SEDOC to close and leave the urban organizing field. As SEDOC withdrew, UCI leaders were forced to step forward to take over true direction of the neighborhood organization. UCI leaders faced dual dilemmas: How could the organization survive when funding, training, and direction were withdrawn? How could they regain popular support without jettisoning the democratization work that had become important to them?

MISPERCEPTIONS AND COSTS

SEDOC organizers recognized that the electoral strategy had not captured the UCI's rank-and-file interest. In an internal critique, some organizers expressed their doubts about maintaining relations with the PRD. They saw that the effort "had diluted the dynamic of the social organization in the party and the campaign" (SEDOC 1991, 1). Despite this recognition, SEDOC continued to "urge a policy of alliances that have as [shared] criteria the real construction of the party . . . [and] . . . the simultaneous push to provide the training and consciousness raising for the social organization and electoral partisan [participation] . . . to push the relation and assert the importance of the alliance between the PRD and members of the urban popular movement, workers, and campesinos" (SEDOC 1991, 1–2).

Even after both electoral defeats, several organizers felt that close alignment with the PRD was necessary to reach their goal of building the UCI into an organization equaling other members of the urban popular opposition. The internal critique focused mainly on the conduct of the electoral campaign rather than on the decision to participate. SEDOC remained convinced of the need for their popular organizations to ally with the PRD. What had been missing was greater preparation and explanation. Even while recognizing that the base had not participated sufficiently in the campaign, SEDOC argued that it had achieved its goal:

> Pushing the articulation between the social movement—as an expression of the organized civil society—and the party was successful. The advances are clear, the majority of the members of the UCI feel themselves to be perredistas. The past electoral experiences gave to the base and the leadership of the UCI a specific partisan identity. . . . Those of us who have promoted the party have the sufficient sensibility and necessary tact to know how to convey and induce this political-partisan consciousness in the people. (SEDOC 1992a, 13)

This self-congratulatory analysis clearly indicates that SEDOC organizers had not read the UCI constituency correctly. SEDOC also stated its rationale for partisan work based on the desire to create a wide opposition: "The politicization of the citizenry and of civil society in our country is an imperative that we must continue promoting. . . . For the cause of the democratizing movement in the country, the PRD, despite its great limitations, is the most viable project in political and electoral terms that can push the country toward a democratic transition" (SEDOC 1992a, 13).

My interview with Juan Diego Ortiz provided further evidence that SEDOC organizers had made a misjudgment in their choice of electoral strategy. Ortiz, as a SEDOC organizer, relentlessly pushed the UCI to ally with the PRD, and after leaving SEDOC, he worked as a PRD militant. In our conversation, Juan Diego articulated his perception that it was not the strategy that was problematic:

> From my point of view, the alliance with the PRD, rather than having been an error, lacked a deepening of the relationship. But the UCI people were new to the process of popular organization. UCI members needed more politicization and political consistency . . . a vision that went beyond their local needs. They needed to recognize that local fights are not against just local targets but against a national system and party and [that they] should be furthering attempts to build a new system and an alternative. . . . It didn't appear to me that there was much future in a social struggle within just a few colonias without a national struggle with political alliances.

Thus, the Jesuit organization failed to correctly gauge the reactions of the urban poor to its partisan strategy. The vast differences between SEDOC workers and UCI base members help explain this perceptual gap. However, the multi-layered structure of the Jesuit organization was also a factor, as it created a distance between decision makers and the base that made it difficult for SEDOC to hear critique. The structure also reinforced the status and class differences. Poor, poorly educated residents of a peripheral neighborhood found it extremely difficult to criticize well-educated, middle-class organizers affiliated with a Jesuit organization.

Although the SEDOC organizers who worked with the UCI were largely convinced of the need for partisan affiliation, the extent of that affiliation lagged behind their counterparts in Intercolonias, one of SEDOC's other popular organizations. Intercolonias had committed itself even more strongly to the PRD and pressured their UCI counterparts to follow their lead. The arguments within SEDOC about what partisan identification meant, and how extensive it should be, grew quite vociferous. Padre David, a SEDOC team member assigned to work with the UCI, had never supported the strategy but had remained silent during the electoral campaigns. As the conflict grew more bitter, David expressed his opposition to partisan affiliation more openly. Bad feelings grew rapidly between SEDOC's Intercolonias organizers and those of the UCI.

Through the spring and summer of 1992, SEDOC meetings became increasingly vicious. Intercolonias organizers, continuing to push UCI organizers to take a firmer partisan stance, cast doubts on the UCI's anti-clientelist commitment. Intercolonias organizers also accused UCI organizers of being unsophisticated and captive to traditional deferential politics. Ironically, the links to government officials that Padre David and the UCI had exploited to win electrification were criticized during these arguments. By September 1992, the SEDOC team directing UCI was, in turn, accusing the Intercolonias workers of "fighting dirty," intransigence, and general meanness (SEDOC 1992c). The crisis had grown so absorbing that in a workshop addressing these and other issues, one of the solutions offered was euthanasia, affording the organization a "Christian burial" (SEDOC 1992c).

The SEDOC September meeting passed without agreements about how to mend intra-group relations. It was suggested that the Mexican Province of the Society of Jesús, the Jesuit order's national authority, decide what course the group should follow. SEDOC workers did not have to wait long for the provincial authorities' answer.

SEDOC WITHDRAWS

At the end of October, the Mexican Province leader, Padre José Morales Orozco, expressed the belief that SEDOC had erred in forging close ties with the PRD. SEDOC had subordinated its goals to that of the PRD, and this, Padre Morales said, was unacceptable. Throughout the Jesuit order, according to Padre Morales, SEDOC was seen as an instrument of the PRD. The authorities feared that the partisan organizers would not separate themselves from the Jesuit organization and instead continue to force it along an electoral path. The conflict, according to the authorities, "in place of strengthening the urban popular movement in the Guadalajara Metropolitan Zone has fractured it with intra-party struggles" (Guzmán Anell 1992, 3).

There was only one way out, Padre Morales concluded: "Starting in November 1992, the regional projects of the Northeast and the South of the Guadalajara Metropolitan Zone will begin the process of the terminal phase. By November

1993, this process will be ended, and SEDOC will separate from all of its obligations with the promoters and with the organizations" (Guzmán Anell 1992, 4).[1]

The decision was met with a flurry of activity. SEDOC and UCI workers alike were anxious for their personal and organizational futures, and they faced a multitude of transitional tasks. Worries over budgets preoccupied UCI and Intercolonias members. SEDOC's day-to-day direction would terminate in 1993, and financing would then last only for a fixed period, after which time the popular organizations would be responsible for obtaining their own funding.

As 1993 began, SEDOC's impending departure was foremost on the minds of the SEDOC team members and the Intercolonias and UCI leaders they directed. SEDOC director José Teódulo Guzmán Anell attempted to calm some fears. In a letter addressed to friends and acquaintances, he tried to explain the causes and consequences of SEDOC's withdrawal, putting the best face possible on the issue. Guzmán Anell reminded readers that the organizing methodology always intended the eventual separation of SEDOC from its popular organizations. Without the removal of the Jesuit organization, leaving the base developers to work on their own, it would be impossible to evaluate the gains of the popular organizing project. Guzmán Anell also raised the specter of the Jesuit order's declining resources as a partial rationale for SEDOC's departure. He barely touched on the electoral strategy, admitting only that some of the reason to "disincorporate" from the popular projects "was our own political immaturity to coherently manage the relationship between the social organizations and the political-partisan militancy of their members" (Guzmán Anell 1993). The planned 1993 separation of the UCI would proceed with assurances that the Jesuits would aid in the search for resources. UCI's work in the meantime was to create funding proposals.

Throughout the spring and summer of 1993, the SEDOC team and UCI leaders worked together to design a UCI budget. Some budgetary issues resolved themselves when two of the four paid team members left the Jesuit organization to follow their own directions. Juan Diego Ortiz joined the PRD as a full-time organizer. Ceci Saucedo left soon also.

The greatest personnel blow to the UCI came in August 1993, when Padre David Velasco left Guadalajara to pursue graduate studies in Chile. On my arrival at the UCI office in early 1994, the pain of Padre David's departure was

---

1. In addition to SEDOC's partisan squabbles, the provincial authority itself had some financial problems that added to their rationale to divert human and capital resources away from SEDOC.

still fresh. David had for years been a constant and central presence on Cerro del Cuatro. Leaders and members alike talked of his friendship as much as they talked about his political role. For many, his departure was the worst aspect of SEDOC's withdrawal, and UCI leaders felt they had been orphaned. Although SEDOC's imminent departure had been foreseen for well over a year, and the SEDOC team had already lost the valuable participation of Juan Diego and Ceci, David's departure was the most dramatic indication that the UCI was on its own. In November 1993, SEDOC's direction of the UCI ceased, and the Union was forced to become independent. It did not take long for various state entities to recognize that the UCI had entered a new stage.

SEDESOL GOES FISHING

The arrival of a new federal SEDESOL delegate, Oscar Navarro Gárate, occurred contemporaneously with SEDOC's departure, and it signaled a change in the relationship between the UCI and the state.[2] Navarro Gárate was less interested in helping the UCI than his predecessor had been. Compared to Francisco Mora, Navarro had a much colder personal style. UCI leaders warmly remembered Mora, in part, because he had allowed SEDESOL staff to help them research how to regularize the lots on Cerro del Cuatro. They also spoke of his visit to the organization with his then-boss, Luis Donaldo Colosio, and their lack of pretensions as they talked to UCI leaders on the hill. With Padre David's departure, his personal ties to SEDESOL functionaries could no longer be utilized to access the agency's resources.

Earlier, the conflict between the two Solidaridad programs, one loyal to federal power and the other to municipal power, had been exploited by the UCI. The local program was dominated by the Tlaquepaque CROC and staffed by the local PRI power brokers. The federal group, focused on centralizing power regardless of the impact on the local PRI, provided the UCI with useful opportunities. The change in the federal delegate disrupted the relationship facilitated by the personal connection between Padre David and Francisco Mora and eliminated the possibility that federal Solidaridad workers would be a resource for the UCI. Governmental relationships appeared increasingly likely to pose only two possibilities: be an enemy of local CROC/Solidaridad or be absorbed

2. SEDESOL, Mexico's social development secretariat, was the parent entity for the Solidaridad program.

by federal Solidaridad. The second alternative loomed as Ester Torres Munguia, a UCI leader, became involved with Solidaridad.

Ester, like other UCI leaders, had worked with local groups since before the UCI was officially formed. Because of its relative proximity to the city, her colonia, La Mezquitera, enjoyed many urban services long before the rest of the hill. During much of 1992 and 1993, Ester worked as the UCI human-rights coordinator, which took her all over the hill. She was well liked by many UCI members, but her work in other colonias elicited some jealousy from certain UCI leaders.

In September 1993, Navarro Gárate advised the UCI leaders that Solidaridad was planning a multitude of projects for Cerro del Cuatro, and out of respect for independent popular organizations, he wanted the work to proceed with openness and dialogue. Ester remembered the meeting:

> Navarro said, "We want all of us to be together on what the goals of the program will be, to talk about it, to see what you all want, and to see what we can do. He who wants to participate in the struggle to improve the colonia will be well received and welcome, regardless of what party or organization you come from." My God! I didn't believe what I was hearing. Later he said, "We're going to outfit the Cerro with all that is necessary: markets, schools, everything. We're going to arrange for the [legal] title to the land." It seemed like a utopia to me. . . . And it kind of scared me. Before, when we asked for things, they responded that there was no money. And now he says that there is sufficient money, and everything will be done, and he is saying, "Señora, all of you count."

The Solidaridad work was to begin with street paving. The UCI immediately opposed the plan because it was to start without completing the long-unfinished sewer project. Because street paving was relatively easy, and much quicker to complete than other public works, the government had previously used such work to provide the facade of service. Piecemeal paving projects where there were no sewers merely gave the sewage a smoother surface on which to flow but failed to address sanitation and health problems. Additionally, without an underlying sewer system to channel runoff, street paving often lasted only two rainy seasons, after which even the façade of change was destroyed.

The UCI objections appeared to have some impact. Ester remembered that a few weeks later, "They called a big meeting, where they said that the decision whether to work on the pavement or the sewers would be made. So I called

Tito, and told him there was going to be a big meeting. 'What do you think?' And he said, 'Go ahead and go. But don't get too close to them.'"

At the neighborhood meeting, a conflict immediately erupted between federal SEDESOL workers and their municipal counterparts, who were controlled by Tlaquepaque politician Alfredo Barba and his CROC militants. The CROC group tried to control the proceedings and install a local leader, Elisa Cantero, as president of the local committee. Appealing to the meeting participants to take control of the meeting, the federal workers pushed Cantero away from the podium. The participants agreed that they did not want the local priísta, who was tainted by corrupt dealings in land and services, to head up the committee. Yet no one else volunteered. Then, according to Ester, "something strange occurred that we had never planned for in the UCI and that we never thought might happen."

> When they [the meeting participants] were asked who should head up the work, they mentioned me. And I said, "I can't." And they said, "You can." And I said, "I can't. I belong to an independent organization, and I don't want to get involved in these kinds of things." And then the people said, "No Ester. We nominated you." And I didn't know how to manage the situation. When I wanted to refuse the position, they [the federal Solidaridad workers] said, "Señora, how is it possible that you always are so critical of this person [Cantero] and what she does, and now when you have the possibility of winning a space, you turn it down?"

When Ester brought her dilemma to Tito, he advised her to accept the position but renounce it in December. This strategy would keep the resources out of the hands of the CROC, at least temporarily. Tito expected that, given government bureaucracy, not much would occur in the next two months. He also calculated that because 1994 was an election year, Solidaridad would delay some of the actual work so that it would make more of an impact closer to the elections.

But the Solidaridad workers moved quickly. They soon told Ester that she must sign a document authorizing the release of a large sum of money to the just-formed committee. According to the Solidaridad staff, Ester had to sign immediately, or the money would return to the federal agency and not be spent locally.

Ester questioned signing the paper because the issue of paving the streets before installing the sewers had not been resolved during the earlier contentious assembly. The Solidaridad officials pressured her and assured her that protecting the budget came first. When project engineers were sent to talk to Ester, they told her that these scheduling for paving and sewer installation was better dealt with by those with technical knowledge. Under pressure, Ester signed. Ester remembers that the pace of the work accelerated:

> And the time for signing for the money came, with the heavy machinery on its heels, and Cantero's people angry and trying to obstruct the work, and the police were around to placate her and her people. And then Ana comes and says, "Ester, Tito called and told you to get out of there." And with all that was going on, I said, "I can't right now. I'm afraid." And I said, "On the contrary, you all come here, and help me." And later Tito and Sofía came with long faces and asked what happened. Tito asked me, "Do you want to file a police complaint?" And I answered, "What can I denounce? Things are happening so fast, I'm not sure what's going on." And Tito continued to say, "Get out of there!" And I said, "How? My signature is now on the promissory note, and I'm afraid someone will steal all this money, and I will be held responsible!" And this scared me. I had no idea how to manage so much. And I told Tito that I was between the rock and a hard place. And Tito said I was going to have to decide between the UCI and Solidaridad.

Ester felt obligated to continue with the Solidaridad project. Although she tried to stay in close contact with her colleagues, their relationships suffered. "When I came to the meetings, they kept quiet. They didn't want to talk about many things because they thought I might be a spy. Finally, they told me I could no longer attend the UCI meetings."

The troubling interpersonal issues were complicated by the fact that the UCI offices had been built as a second floor on Ester's house, although with a separate entrance. Additionally, Ester's daughter had worked as the UCI's secretary before SEDOC's departure cut that position, so she also knew many of the details about the organization. My field notes, recording a leaders' meeting in mid-March 1994, reveal their anxiety over the situation:

> Ana enters and starts talking about the office, and what kind of UCI information Ester and her daughter are bringing to Solidaridad. The discussion proceeds with a lot of tension.
> Tito: "We must get clear on this week. We'll have to talk to her."

Javier tries to calm his friends. They should talk to her, he agrees, but "there is no reason to worry ourselves."

Agustín disagrees. "This is a grave problem. She's a person with a lot of information about how we work, who we are, about who supports us, with what, with whom we are involved."

Carmen agrees that she also feels threatened.

Socorro says: "She has a lot of information, and she can take copies of information in the archives that are important to us. It can give them ways to attack us."

Carmen elaborates on Socorro's fears. "The archive has some information that is not public. It's not very secret, but she knows a lot about us."

Ana says, "A women from the Solidaridad committees said Ester had brought copies of documents from here." Ana, too, wants the issue to be resolved soon and believes it's important to find out what happened to create a schism.

Socorro continues: "With the office information, they can divide us, defame us, call us misinformed, and say that we are misinforming the public."

Tito tries to calm some fears: "Little harm can be done with the documents we have here."

Sophia, a UCI adviser, also urges the leaders to think more calmly. "What kind of support do you have that would be so destructive if it were public? Sure, you should be careful with the documents, but the real information is up here." She points to her head.

The issue continued to plague the UCI throughout much of 1994. For the leaders, Ester's departure posed a triple threat. First, they were losing a valuable leader, and the conflict reflected poorly on the rest of the leadership. Members did not understand what had happened among their leaders. When I interviewed the membership, the level of anxiety was apparent in the way I was pumped for information about Ester's departure.

Second, the leaders felt insecure. Discussion arose time and again about the need to find new office space. What had seemed advantageous—saving money by not buying a new lot, and Ester's consistent presence—was redefined as a problem. UCI leaders' new perceptions of Ester led them to think that their hold on the office was endangered. Even after Ester turned in her key, the leaders installed a new lock on the door. When Ester made no claim to what could be interpreted as her property, their fears diminished somewhat, but they were stirred anew when Ester's daughter, now needing to find a new job, went to work for SEDESOL in a clerical position.

Finally, recalling that the UCI base had not differentiated between the Union and the PRD during the election debacles, Ana, Agustín, Carmen, and Tito all worried about a similar potential confusion about UCI's relationship with the government now that a highly visible leader was working with Solidaridad.

Although their anxiety convinced the leaders that they needed to talk with Ester, that never occurred, despite asking several intermediaries to talk to her on the UCI leaders' behalf. One of the young missionaries from Espíritu Santo who worked on Cerro del Cuatro did talk with Ester, but he never reported back to the UCI, and so no way was found to reopen communication.[3]

Eventually the leaders' tension diminished, but certain events aggravated their concerns. One was the publication in a local newspaper of a letter signed by Guadalajara Solidaridad committee presidents, thanking President Salinas for his largesse in creating the program that had benefited their communities. Ester's signature on the letter brought anger and alarm. Ester assured me that she had never given permission to have her name affixed to the letter. She additionally told me of other public relations efforts the Solidaridad workers unsuccessfully tried to impose on her. At one point, the governor came to Cerro del Cuatro to celebrate the inauguration of a new bus line. When Solidaridad workers asked her to hug Governor Rivera Aceves in thanks, with the intention of catching the moment on film, she blistered the air with her refusal.

Indeed, Ester renounced her position as committee president as soon as she was sure she would not be held liable for the funds. She continued to work in social-change efforts, becoming a staff person at an organization devoted to aiding street children. She remained deeply hurt by all that had transpired. When Ester reflected on the events, she thought it was a clear case of manipulation by Solidaridad, which had exploited the opportunity that appeared when her supporters demanded that she lead the committee. In a strategy to divide the UCI, the Solidaridad workers had then forced her to ally with them by quickly imposing a responsibility on her that she could not refuse.

In their calmer moments, the UCI leaders also saw Solidaridad behind the rift, which occurred at a time when the UCI leaders felt quite vulnerable. The recent departures of both Padre David and the friendly SEDESOL delegate

---

3. At the end of 1994, each party asked me to convey information to the other. I tried to do so while walking the tightrope of researcher ethics. I was able to tell Ester and the UCI leaders that neither wished the other ill, but I was not able to heal the communications breach.

Mora Naya, coupled with the impending loss of the remaining SEDOC financing, created a siege mentality, and so Ester's action was more readily interpreted as a betrayal rather than a mistake.

It is unclear whether the Solidaridad workers engineered the conflict between Ester and her colleagues, but it is certainly consistent with strategies used by government or party agencies to divide or channel opposition. Although the federal SEDESOL workers in this case initially stood firm against the potential for abuse by local PRI authorities, their actions also divided those involved in local independent political organizing. The federal officials demonstrated an interest in creating new sources of support for the central government. Without SEDOC, and amid the new perception of the UCI as PRD supporters, however, federal Solidaridad workers no longer respected UCI's independence. The temporary coaxing of Ester into their ranks demonstrated a changed relationship. Federal Solidaridad tried to make the UCI dependent on the government, knowing that this would limit militant dissent. The UCI's leverage, gained by playing one state power off against another, had diminished with SEDOC's departure.

SOLIDARIDAD ON THE STREETS

SEDESOL and Solidaridad increased their activity on Cerro del Cuatro throughout 1994.[4] Solidaridad organizers became exceptionally active, enticing Cerro del Cuatro residents to participate in all sorts of programs, providing social goods above and beyond those formally defined within the program.[5] In addition to providing urban infrastructure, school remodeling, and grants to pay children's school costs, Solidaridad began sending water trucks around the hill, from which customers could fill whatever containers they owned.

Solidaridad also began to offer food aid. During an interview I conducted in Spring 1994 with Nueva Santa María resident and UCI member Alicia Escalante Torres, a knock came on the door. A young woman from a Solidaridad group asked to talk to Alicia and offered her coupons for free tortillas. Doña Alicia, a UCI stalwart, took the coupons, happy to consume whatever resources the government wanted to make available even though she had absolutely no

---

4. This increased activity is consistent with critiques that the organizations targeted urban areas interpreted as susceptible to the carrots of clientelist exchange (Dresser 1994; Molinar Horcasitas and Weldon 1994).

5. See Bailey and Boone 1994 for an extensive list of Solidaridad programs.

intention of voting for the PRI. Alicia explained that Solidaridad's heightened profile was due to the upcoming August elections and that the government was just manipulating the residents with public works installation and free tortillas: "'They're helping me now.' Many people will think this way. Apart from the presents, others threaten them, like those of the committees, who say, 'If you don't vote, we'll stop the work. We'll take away the tortilla card.' And they'll start a new work in June to impress the people, and so, the PRI will win the elections in August."

The Solidaridad workers intensified their attempts to organize committees on Cerro del Cuatro as the elections neared. During one afternoon meeting, an unknowing Solidaridad worker knocked on the UCI office door, inviting the leaders to a block meeting. This elicited much hilarity, and Tito finally noted, "Their new strategy is to have meetings by streets. Now they are trying to go more local. It is easier to be convinced by a neighbor who to vote for than by someone who comes from elsewhere. They are doing the fine work now, the fine tuning, putting it on a personal level."

As summer proceeded, more projects appeared on Cerro del Cuatro. On Avenida 8 de Julio, for example, street paving and sewer work began, only three-quarters of a mile from the UCI office. Several of the pounded-earth streets were bulldozed and leveled after having been pockmarked and treacherous for years. The work, according to UCI members, was happening because of the proximate elections.

Although the Solidaridad committees represented new governmental strategies to work with the poor, not all previous strategies were abandoned. UCI leaders told me of SEDESOL efforts to integrate the UCI within its ranks.[6] The new SEDESOL delegate, Navarro Gárate, used old strategies in his dealings with the UCI. Agustín Martínez remembered how the new official dangled bait in front of the colonos:

> When Navarro Gárate came here to the Cerro . . . he wanted to train part of the UCI—he wanted to make it part of his team. He offered us a salary, those of us who are in the UCI, to work with him, to become UCI-Solidaridad.
> JS: What were your responses?

6. These efforts are similar to others described in Vélez-Ibáñez 1983, Cornelius 1975, and Eckstein 1988.

AM: We rejected him, we'd become their servants [if we accepted].
What we want is for them to work for the colonos, and not the colonos
for them.
JS: And what were their reactions?
AM: To close down talks. Now they don't want to know about UCI
because UCI isn't a Solidaridad committee.

Hermano Javier remembered other attempts to associate the UCI with
SEDESOL: "They've wanted the support of the UCI, but we haven't given it to
them, because it doesn't suit the UCI. One attempt was by an official who came
from Guanajuato, from SEDESOL. He wanted UCI to help them . . . painting
murals that said "UCI-SEDESOL, United to Win." To try and spread Solidaridad
through the UCI. We said no, if they wanted to do these murals, they would
have to do it with their people."

Ana Mondragón also remembered several more individually targeted attempts
by SEDESOL functionaries. "Later, the Solidaridad team from the Federal District
came, and they asked us to work with them. And the same people came to
Hermano Javier and offered him a Panaderia Digna [laughs]. They offered him 60
million pesos for a Panaderia Digna (and other perks).[7] And Hermano answered
it would be more dignified if he weren't with Solidaridad."

UCI's interactions with Solidaridad demonstrated a complicated organizational environment. At times, the state used a multitude of resources to maintain traditional clientelism. At other times, different state entities were at odds
about how to work with independent organizations. As the UCI became more
vulnerable, Solidaridad resources were used in a very different way, one that
injured the UCI. Importantly, the government functionaries from the different
Solidaridad groups recognized the UCI's dramatic material needs more than had
SEDOC. Solidaridad's work on the hill consistently targeted basic needs, whether
infrastructure or the ownership of a bakery. Even as their rhetoric changed
from transforming political culture to favoring democratization, Solidaridad
functionaries recognized that to be successful, urban service projects had to be
the medium to attract popular support. SEDOC, in contrast, had moved toward
the abstraction of democracy, prioritizing work that pushed UCI into a role
that did not match the interests of its constituents.

7. A Panadería Digna (dignified bakery) appears to be improvised on the Escuela Digna, a program that which renovated schools in working-class and poor colonias.

The UCI leaders were unwilling to retreat from all efforts linked to democratization even though SEDOC's tutelage had diverted their work from the basic needs of the Cerro del Cuatro residents. The leadership painfully recognized the errors of following SEDOC's electoral aspirations, yet they had learned the anti-clientelist lesson well. Local work brought local benefits, but systemic PRI corruption could only be altered through a national effort. The 1994 elections offered new possibilities for limiting PRI domination. Civic organizations across Mexico saw opportunities to build on the anger expressed by the Zapatistas and their supporters by channeling it into efforts to drive the PRI from office.

The Foro Callejero was one of the tactics pursued by Guadalajara's democratization movement.[8] Carefully articulated as nonpartisan, the idea was to increase voter turnout and so foment change. UCI leaders built on the foundations laid by regional get-out-the-vote coalitions by trying to convince their base of the necessity to voting.

THE DEMOCRACY WORKSHOP

The Foro Callejero attracted UCI supporters from across the hill. This get-out-the-vote event continued to influence UCI members long after the dust settled and the devil had departed. Three weeks later, at the weekly meeting of UCI leaders, Tito distributed videos of the event. Each UCI leader bought a copy to use in democracy workshops in the neighborhood groups that they coordinated.

Later in June, Agustín Martínez scheduled such a workshop for his group. The television at Doña Clara's house, where the weekly meeting was held, did not work with the VCR Agustín brought from the UCI office. He and I went off in search of a television that would work, and we returned with a mammoth set offered by a neighbor. While Agustín and I wrestled with the TV and various cables, the group members, fifteen women and several of their children, circled their chairs and buckets in the packed dirt of Doña Clara's open yard, discussing the potential of holding a weekly raffle to raise money for a communal sewing machine. A couple of weeks earlier, the group suggested offering a workshop on production sewing as a way that the women might supplement family income. At this meeting, the group members discussed what food items to include in the raffle prize, how to sell tickets, and how quickly they might be able to buy

8. See Chapter 1.

the sewing machine. The raffle discussion halted when Agustín and I finally got the vcr connected and running.

Agustín started the video, an edited version of the Foro Callejero, interrupting it immediately following the footage of living conditions on the hill. "What did we see?" he asked. Teasing comments were interspersed by comments like: "sewage," "pure filth," "garbage," and "the sewer is still not there." Agustín continued: "The mcj came to help make the area more unified. Is it a good thing that these groups care about us?"

Doña Luisa, a heavy-set forty-one-year-old woman and a long-time resident of the community, replied: "Yes. Others don't care; we should be happy for those who do come. They can tell others what we lack here, what help we need." Other group members brought up a myriad of local complaints, including the lack of garbage collection, the presence of a man who sold bad bottled water, and the low water pressure in the hoses that run from the uci-installed water hydrants.

Agustín refocused the discussion. "Think about why they are struggling. For what is mcj struggling?" He answered his own question. "For democracy. What is democracy for us? For you all? Does it exist here?" The homeowner, Doña Clara, a tiny woman who worked as a domestic servant for a middle-class family in the city, answered: "There is no democracy here, because there are no services."

Agustín pressed the point: "What is democracy?" A response came: "A person independent of whatever thing." Agustín continued to guide the discussion. "When we, as citizens, elect a representative we can trust, and choose who will represent us, when services are given for the benefit of all citizens. We saw many things in the video that we are accustomed to in our daily life. We have a lot of problems. How can we create a democracy, so as responsible citizens we can resolve problems? How do they receive us when we visit [officials in] the government?"

Doña Gloria, the matriarch of a family that was building a house nearby, bitingly contributed, "Like they are doing us a favor." Agustín played off her clearly expressed contempt and asked, "Why are they there?" Doña Gloria quickly replied, "Because we put them there."

"Exactly. They are public servants. The government has one party here, one system. Does this system function well, nationally and on the hill? Does it fulfill citizen needs? Are we going to stay here with these badly done services, or build a real democracy? In this time of elections, we have a great responsibility. What are we going to do in this election, to demand a change, to build a real democracy?"

Agustín ended the workshop by saying, "This is the material that was given to us to think about. What is democracy? What do we do about the serious problems in the colonia? What are we committed to do in the elections? We have a chance for a change." As the women agreed, Agustín reminded them their greatest responsibility is to vote for a change in government, one that would result in true representation.

The democracy workshop over, the discussion returned to the logistics of the raffle, and ongoing problems with water and land-tenure negotiations. When an argument ensued about how often the raffle should be conducted, Agustín expressed his position forcefully, then agreed to the opposing opinion held by most of the group. But he made a point: "See, this is democracy, when we can disagree, but then decide for the good of all." The meeting wound down, and the UCI members returned to their homes and duties while Agustín and I returned the mammoth TV to its owner.

The democratization movement continued to create tension for the UCI. Although Agustín pursued the theme of democratization with his neighborhood group, he framed democratization as a tool to address local needs. The needs themselves had greater prominence, as the discussion of the raffle shows.

The new kind of democratization work was the result of new relationships that UCI had forged with other organizations as SEDOC withdrew. The Foro Callejero event, and the video that was produced for use as a popular education tool, provides proof of this new relationship. The UCI continued to work in a wide political environment, but using local political needs and lenses more consistently than it had since its first years. The Foro itself, and the democracy workshop, demonstrated the UCI's recognition that appeals to democracy had to be grounded in the material experience of Cerro del Cuatro. It was no accident that NGO spokespersons drew attention in speeches and videos to the poverty of Cerro del Cuatro residents, and the poor conditions under which they lived. Nor was it accidental that during their efforts to get their members to vote, UCI leaders explicitly addressed the basic material needs that had been unsatisfied on the hill. The leaders recognized that the abstractions of democratization pushed by SEDOC had left UCI members unconvinced. The unwillingness to link democratization and urban services in earlier campaigns had cost UCI supporters, and the leaders were determined to participate in the democratic movement without repeating previous errors. This approach contrasted dramatically with the campaigns under SEDOC, when the insistence on an anti-clientelist stance prohibited any linking of material outcomes to electoral campaigns.

The nonpartisan nature of the Foro Callejero and the subsequent workshops also helped UCI leaders evade the label of "PRD supporters." The effort was strictly focused on getting out the vote as a democratic exercise, and any recommendations for whom UCI members should vote were omitted. The UCI was also to play an important role in another nonpartisan effort, this time in defense of the vote.[9]

UN JUEGO LIMPIO: THE UCI HELPS THE
ALIANZA CÍVICA OBSERVE THE ELECTIONS

In Spring 1994, more than three hundred and fifty nongovernmental organizations, civic groups, human-rights groups, and popular organizations formed the Alianza Cívica (Civic Alliance) to observe the coming elections (Regalado 1994; Olvera 2001). The Alianza stressed its nonpartisan profile: "The Alianza has not been created to favor a certain candidate or to oppose the regime; our work is strictly nonpartisan and nongovernmental" (Alianza Cívica 1994, 2).

Protestations of nonpartisanship notwithstanding, the very existence of the Alianza testified to its deep-rooted mistrust of the PRI. The Alianza's motto, "a clean game" (*un juego limpio*), expressed that well-earned mistrust. The PRI had long maintained power by defrauding the electorate and manipulating voters. The most flagrant recent national example of a long-standing tradition came during the 1988 elections, when vote-counting computers mysteriously broke down as presidential-aspirant Cuauhtémoc Cárdenas was winning, only to come back on line three days later to reveal that Carlos Salinas was the winner. The early 1990s were punctuated by charges of stolen federal, gubernatorial, and local elections.

The Alianza was created to contest these sorts of PRI abuses. In Jalisco, the organizer of the Foro Callejero, MCJ, and a popular education organization, the Mexican Institute for Community Development (Instituto Mexicano para el Desarrollo Comunitario, IMDEC), led the Alianza. The strategy was to recruit students, workers, popular-group members, and others to serve as poll watchers. The Alianza trained each poll watcher according to Federal Electoral Institute (Instituto Federal Electoral, IFE) requirements. In addition to a civics lessons, training focused on what kind of "irregularities" poll observers should watch for and the recourses they would have when faced with a problem.

After consulting with the neighborhood groups, the UCI leadership agreed to take charge of poll watching on Cerro del Cuatro. In early July, I joined Tito, Agustín, and others affiliated with the UCI at a daylong seminar. We joined about thrity-five other people, each a representative of an organization that had

---

9. It is important not to overemphasize the nonpartisan nature of the democratization movement in Mexico, which always had at least one specifically partisan intention: the toppling of the PRI.

committed to working with the Jalisco Alianza Cívica campaign. The representatives were to return to train their own community of observers. As part of the IFE requirements, each group that trained observers took their recruits through a regimented workshop, complete with video materials and scripted discussions. Tito and Agustín brought the information back to the UCI, which then recruited poll watchers. Ideally, the Alianza wanted three observers for each polling place: two IFE-accredited observers who would be present inside the polling place, and another unaccredited observer who would be a runner, taking results, problems, and requests to the UCI office, which was to serve as a main information center. The UCI had committed to covering fifty polling places in Tlaquepaque, so recruitment posed a challenge.

The UCI's initial mission was to train its members. Ana Mondragón and others helped organize a training seminar for observers at the Tepeyac parish, presided over by Padre Felipe. About twenty-five Cerro del Cuatro residents attended that workshop, and were eventually accredited by the IFE as Alianza observers. In July, the UCI organized a workshop given by Carlos Peralta of IMDEC. About thirty-five people attended this training session, which began with a videotape provided by the IFE, demonstrating its plush offices, extensive technology, and purported independence from the government. As the videotape continued, the words *Certeza, Objetividad, Independencia* (Certainty, Objectivity, Independence) flashed on the screen, eliciting snickers and remarks of disbelief from the viewers. When Peralta asked for comments after the videotape, most focused on the IFE's plush accommodations. Others doubted that the agency was truly independent, given that its director was a cabinet official. Carlos refocused the discussion on the interests of the Alianza Cívica, the definitions of voting violations, and the recourses the poll watchers would have when confronted with violations. My field notes demonstrate some of the trainees' concerns, and the problems the Alianza faced:

> The discussion led to the powers held by observers, and their inability to become involved in active challenges. According to Carlos, only the on-site party representatives can denounce violations at the moment of their occurrence. Further questions and answers focused on violations.
>
> "If someone comes in with a PRI t-shirt, should we report them? How do we prove it?"
>
> "With a camera, if you have one."
>
> "What about if someone volunteers to take in the votes, we have to be careful of that, don't we?"

"You must report that immediately, if that happens. That's one way a lot of fraud is committed."

Hermano asks: "What if the police patrols pass by a lot? Or if we see trucks or buses bringing people?"

Carlos answers: "Take down the license plates, so we can see if it happens with the same cars elsewhere. This is clearly illegal, when people are brought to vote for a particular candidate. It is sometimes hard to prove, but it is a crime."

Carlos continues quizzing people on the functions of the polling-place officials, and what other actions constitute violations of law: "If they try to run us off, this is a violation." "We have to be aware also of what is going on outside."

Carmen Castañeda comments: "It is illegal to pressure by giving a free breakfast or to give money."

A man tells about pressure imposed by local priístas, who ask residents to think carefully about the services that may or may not come to the colonia depending on the vote. Carlos says this is blackmail and a crime, although again difficult to document. A bag of groceries sits on the floor with a logo of the PRI slogan "*Bienestar para la familia*," received in a PRI giveaway on the hill earlier that morning.

The electoral law clearly limited the Alianza's abilities to challenge abuses. As nonpartisan observers, Alianza workers could only document violations and criticize them after the election. In addition, the kind of pressure identified as illegal composed part of the daily survival options of the poor Cerro del Cuatro residents. Although providing free food in a political campaign was illegal, the PRI was doing it on the hill that very morning. Household poverty forced even those who wanted to keep the PRI from stealing the election to take the free groceries. Finally, the limited resources of the fledgling operation forced it to rely on Alianza observers to record violations for later tally and charges. The Alianza recognized that proving allegations of impropriety would be difficult. It would prove even more so with the Alianza relying on poor people to bring tape recorders or cameras with which to record the misdeeds.

The Alianza Cívica trained over twenty-one thousand electoral observers nationwide, nine hundred of whom worked in Jalisco (Martínez and Arenda 1994; Alianza Cívica Jalisco 1994, 2). The UCI recruited and helped train enough observers to staff over thirty polling places. But as election day grew closer, the Alianza's organizational problems became more apparent. Many of

FIG. 12   UCI propaganda, 1994

the required credentials did not arrive until two days before the election, and some never came, reducing the number of observers eligible to guard polling places on Cerro del Cuatro.

Additionally, the Alianza had planned to supply each observer with manuals as a supplement to the earlier training. Most of these were not delivered to the UCI office until the credentials came. Without prompt delivery of the manuals, the Alianza's methodology, in which observers would fill out three daily reports to be picked up by coordinators, could not be followed. These problems were compounded by the government's strategy of advertising the location of polling places mere days before the election. Between not knowing where they would work, or how to fill out the reports, many of the observers were unprepared for the election-monitoring task.

I spent election day walking from polling place to polling place all over Cerro del Cuatro with Tito. Because of the late delivery of Alianza Cívica manuals explaining the process of observation, Tito had to coax a report from each observer when the plan had been to have a prepared statement ready before he arrived. The reports of irregularities mounted, and we witnessed many ourselves. In some polling places, voters were not allowed to vote; other places did not open on time or failed to count the ballots publicly. Consistent PRI presence was noted in almost all voting areas, carrying an explicitly intimidating message to the voters, and reinforcing threats that even the scant government aid would end if the colonia voted against the PRI.

FIG. 13   Tito, far left, wearing a white shirt, on the rounds for the Alianza Cívica on election day, July 1, 1994

The Alianza's report found Jalisco's District 18, which includes Cerro del Cuatro, had more irregularities and complaints than any other district in Guadalajara. We documented incidents where PRI militants had asked voters for whom they had voted, and the presence of PRI leaders and local Solidaridad committee officials in areas from which they were prohibited by law. The Alianza Cívica's state evaluation found similar activity throughout Jalisco. In general, the Jalisco Alianza Cívica found "clearly distinguishable patterns of anomalies" which cast doubt on "the quality of the election," and in its assessment, "the process can not be labeled clean, transparent, or democratic" (Alianza Cívica Jalisco 1994, 3, 9).

The Alianza's final national report also explicitly condemned the election, saying that it should not be considered legitimate, as there was consistent fraud throughout the nation. The report documented coercive measures, such as trading promised future benefits for votes, and threats to revoke services and eliminate jobs in the case of opposition voting. Rather than isolated acts, the Alianza saw these as a coherent and consistent PRI strategy.

These reports came as no surprise to the UCI. The leaders had recognized the inequities during the preelection process, and they had had little expectation

FIG. 14   Waiting outside a polling place on election day, July 1, 1994

that the PRI would lose the presidency. More important for UCI leaders was how the work with the Alianza Cívica had proceeded, and whether the UCI should work in this role again.

Despite problems with the process, the UCI embraced the exercise because it merged local and national concerns. Poll-watching activities fit within UCI members' desires to pursue local work, as they participated in their own neighborhoods. Supporters saw the UCI present and active in its observation role on election day, and in this way, the UCI continued to keep a high political profile on the hill itself.

The observation work allowed UCI an electoral role while avoiding explicit partisan affiliation. Rather than advocating the defeat of the PRI, and pushing another party's candidates, the UCI's role as election observers allowed it to take the high ground, protecting the local exercise of national rights. The implication was that if the elections were not corrupt, the PRI would have nothing to fear.

In addition, the workshops fulfilled popular-education interests of UCI leaders. Even if the Alianza Cívica project was flawed, it offered UCI members opportunities to make relatively abstract concepts of justice and democracy concrete, and demonstrate them as attainable goals that could be reached through local, nonpartisan efforts. Yet the nonpartisan work did not halt pressure on UCI to explicitly identify itself in partisan terms.

THE PUSH TO PARTISANSHIP

UCI leaders evaluated their election-observer experiences in the Alianza quite critically. Late delivery of the observer credentials, and the incomplete training left Agustín especially distressed. Tito's efforts to compile information was also hampered by the inadequacy of the Alianza Cívica's efforts on the hill. Additionally, the inability to do more than record violations so that complaints could be filed at the national level proved frustrating. UCI leaders and members coveted party representatives' ability to lodge protests and have greater power at the polling place. Yet Agustín and other poll watchers were disgusted that the on-site PRD representatives had lodged few protests, despite their greater power to do so. Finally, the UCI was unimpressed with the Alianza's power as a public forum to challenge the elections' legitimacy. UCI leaders saw little benefit in the Alianza's eventual condemnation of the elections.

Although the work with Alianza Cívica served UCI's leaders' political interests, both the efficiency of the observation process and the negligible outcome of the Alianza's challenges left questions about whether to repeat such efforts. Because early 1995 would bring municipio and federal elections, discussions continued regarding how to pursue democratization in the electoral field without engaging in overt partisan efforts. What was the value of election monitoring if follow-up bore little fruit? Again, the push to partisanship emerged, and again it came from UCI advisers.

The interest in electoral work coupled with the Alianza's ineffectiveness posed a dilemma. The Alianza was not likely to attain greater intervention powers, certainly not prior to the 1995 elections. Yet working as party-affiliated observers, in order to wield greater power to challenge abuses, meant once more risking partisan affiliation. Hermano Javier and Ana Mondragón had participated individually as party observers, but they argued against making an organizational commitment. UCI leaders' misgivings about the effectiveness of the Alianza work were compounded by a great reluctance to return to the PRD fold, especially after its poor national showing. How then could the UCI continue to participate in the democratization movement?

Padre Enrique Flota served as one member of the UCI's widely dispersed network of advisers, which had become more important after SEDOC's departure.

A man of vast political experience, Padre Flota was simultaneously an adviser to Mexico City's Asamblea de Barrios and to Bishop Samuel Ruiz of Chiapas.[10] He was also a PRD militant. As a PRD adviser, Padre Flota reacted impatiently to the UCI's concerns about demonstrating any link to the party. At a support group meeting in December, where the 1995 elections were a topic of discussion, Padre Flota saw partisan affiliation as the only possible answer to the ineffectiveness of the Alianza Cívica:

> From the experience of the past months, it's more important to work with the [party] representatives than with observers. The work with the Alianza was a disaster. But the [party] representatives can denounce the irregularities. So, for me, that is the way to enter. We should prioritize the work with the representatives and train them well. The question begins to get difficult in the party issues. One thing is that UCI, as such, doesn't have a party link—either with the PRD or the PAN. But we also should not overexaggerate this autonomy. The UCI has to maintain independence as the UCI, but it can help one party or another.

UCI leaders nevertheless remained unwilling to favor one party over another, and they decided to split the effort. Those who could not abide partisan work would once again be trained by the UCI and participate with the Alianza. Padre Flota would train those with partisan affinities to become party representatives for both the PRD and the PAN.

The shifting electoral landscape, in which the PAN had become a much more viable alternative than the PRD, further complicated the debate. And even Padre Flota was forced to adjust. Several Jesuit university students, without SEDOC ties, had decided to help rebuild the UCI by organizing new groups outside the Cerro del Cuatro area. Some members of these emerging UCI groups were affiliated with the PAN. These newly organized activists had not suffered the pains associated with partisanship that the UCI–Cerro del Cuatro had suffered. For them, the partisan road appeared unproblematic. The UCI leaders in Cerro del Cuatro were confronting enough troubles of their own, and they lacked the time and energy to try to talk the new groups out of affiliating with a party. Indeed, the contacts between the longstanding UCI and the new groups were minimal, outside of the coordinating of the observation.

10. On the Asamblea de Barrios, see Haber 2006.

When the Jesuit students aiding the nascent UCI groups in other neighbor-hoods voiced their requests to participate, these new groups favored affiliating with the PAN. The UCI decided to provide avenues for political participation through independent means, as well as two opposing partisan options.

As a PRD adviser, Padre Flota made his preferences clear, but he had to avoid shoving the PRD down the UCI's throat as his SEDOC predecessors had done. The UCI leaders were willing to listen to advice, especially from Padre Flota, whom they respected. They were, however, no longer willing to take direction. Padre Flota was forced to recognize that for many UCI followers, the Alianza Cívica observer role was not only still viable but also preferable to partisan affiliation. Even more, he was forced to recognize that many in the new UCI groups supported the PAN.

The decision-making process regarding the 1995 elections demonstrated a hard-won perspective in the UCI. After suffering the results of allowing SEDOC to force PRD affiliation, the UCI had become wary about pursuing efforts that would be misinterpreted by their members. These misgivings were forthrightly articulated.

The 1994 and 1995 elections brought new opportunities for the UCI to con-tinue on the path down which SEDOC had led them. The struggle to topple the PRI and democratize Mexico continued, but with novel strategies that widened the possibilities for participation, so that those who were wary of party affilia-tion could still have an active role. The UCI leaders now found ways to work on democratization that gave priority to Cerro del Cuatro and its material needs. Democratization, as the UCI leaders articulated it, had everything to do with addressing the basic needs of residents. It was not an abstraction. The new approach elicited some support from UCI members while satisfying their leaders' interests in political mobilization beyond the colonias.

The articulation of material needs, however, meant little without actual work to satisfy them. This, too, was a lesson the UCI leaders had learned from the earlier electoral experiences. With Solidaridad promising the installation of various kinds of urban infrastructure, government officials tried to steer the UCI towards the program's committees. Because of the presence of Solidaridad, but also because the organization had won concrete gains regarding regulariza-tion, UCI efforts focused on land tenure.

THE REGULARIZATION STRUGGLE, PART 2

The UCI's regularization efforts progressed slowly. On May 8, 1993, during a ceremony on the main patio of the Palacio de Gobierno, interim Governor of

Jalisco Carlos Rivera Aceves gave eighty titles to Nueva Santa María residents. The governor promised that by the following February, the government would deliver the rest of the titles to the thousands of families in Nueva Santa María who still lacked them.

UCI leader Socorro Meza took advantage of the opportunity to remind the governor that the ceremony would not resolve the problems on Cerro del Cuatro. Socorro praised the change in state policy, remembering that a decade previously the government had tried to violently dislodge the same residents from their homes, an effort that was halted only by a mass protest. Socorro also reminded the governor that he had promised to halt the illegal trafficking in land titles, but members of the CROC continued to sell lots under the protection of Alfredo Barba Hernández, former municipal president of Tlaquepaque, who was now a federal deputy. The governor answered that the complaints would be addressed. "You need no longer fear being dislodged or violent action such as occurred in the past," said the governor to the colonos, and he again promised to resolve all the land-tenure problems on Cerro del Cuatro.

The governor did not meet his self-imposed February 1994 deadline. The UCI called a press conference in March to denounce the governor's inaction. Leaders also decried the high fees assessed by the federal regularization agency, FONHAPO. The leaders were especially angry at the FONHAPO's unwillingness to accept the UCI as the representative of Nueva Santa María residents since it had earlier enjoyed a good working relationship with the agency during the census taking on the hill.

Unfortunately, the media were out covering an event expressing local support for the Chiapas rebellion. We sat for some time in a meeting room of a downtown hotel waiting for the press to arrive. Finally, a sympathetic local newspaper reporter dragged several of his colleagues in to talk with the UCI, and so a few newspaper and radio reports recounted the UCI's charges. FONHAPO responded the following day, and although it denied that it had acted in bad faith, it reduced the fees it was assessing for regularization, a longstanding UCI demand. Nevertheless, during the coming months, the agency would do little to deliver land titles to the residents.

In response, UCI leaders mobilized members for a mass turnout at a meeting with the governor's main aide.[11] The added pressure made the official more forthcoming, but little new information was given. He did confirm which notaries would be responsible for entering documents into the public files, and

11. For a description of this event, see Chapter 1.

he also again promised that the governor would attend to the matter expeditiously. Two different public meetings on the hill turned out over one hundred fifty UCI supporters to discuss the issue during the spring.

Efforts continued at a slow pace throughout the spring and summer. Residents came to the UCI office to complain about unclear or contradictory information, and UCI leaders and members of the colonia groups formed small commissions to talk to state and federal functionaries. The land titles dribbled in. Rather than delivering documents block by block, the regularization agency sent documents to those households who contacted them most consistently. Not coincidentally, the residents who got their documents were either affiliated with the UCI or the CROC.

By the beginning of November 1994, only half of the deeds promised eighteen months earlier had been delivered, and the government announced the closing of FONHAPO's regional office, a worrisome development. Without a local office, regularization would be even more difficult. The regularization agency would still exist to give credit to needy residents, but negotiating the document delivery would happen through at the Jalisco state housing agency. When the UCI and journalists contacted that agency, however, the employees had not been informed of the change.

UCI responded to FONHAPO's closing by again arguing for expropriation of Cerro del Cuatro. Earlier the governor and his staff had looked on the suggestion favorably, but now, Governor Rivera denied saying anything about the possibilities of expropriation, despite journalists' evidence to the contrary. By the end of 1994, the UCI was still searching for the official who would be able to answer the questions raised by the closing of the agency office.

After SEDOC's departure, the UCI was faced with a series of problems. How could they survive without SEDOC's direction, funding, and staffing? SEDOC's push to electoral politics had diminished popular support, which posed another dilemma: how could the UCI rebuild their base? The increased politicization of UCI leaders exacerbated this dilemma, as the leaders were unwilling to leave democratization work behind. Finally, simultaneous with the departure of SEDOC, Solidaridad increased clientelist efforts to win support on Cerro del Cuatro.

To rebuild the base, the UCI leaders shifted the focus of their work back to addressing basic services needs. The regularization fight demonstrates the UCI's persistent attempts to address the needs of Cerro del Cuatro residents. Because of the governor's promise to attend to the land tenure issues, the UCI felt that this battle was one they could win. After various mobilizations, progress was made, but the ponderous pace demonstrated that with SEDOC gone, the UCI had lost much of the leverage that it had previously enjoyed. Padre David's connections with SEDESOL and other SEDOC team members' government contacts, as well as their understanding of the organizing environment, gave the UCI entrée to the state apparatus. The UCI's independence now meant fewer resources, in particular, relatively poorer access to the government.

Changes in national politics, embodied in the Solidaridad program, also limited access to the state. Despite UCI leaders' renewed efforts, their ability to satisfy members' material needs was hampered. The UCI, with SEDOC, had been privileged to enjoy benefits won from the state without clientelist expectations. SEDOC's retreat resulted in greater clientelist efforts by the state, coupled with withdrawal of previous advantages.

The UCI leaders now understood that democratization work must be balanced by efforts aimed at fulfilling local needs. At the same time, they realized that their local efforts were insufficient to achieve national change, a goal that they had come to espouse almost as strongly as their mentors had. The 1994 campaign for a clean vote, exemplified in both the Foro Callejero and subsequent community workshops and in the national Alianza Cívica campaigns, provided opportunities for the UCI to pursue democratization without taking an explicitly partisan position.

At the end of 1994, UCI leaders continued to feel the pull of these diverging goals. They could not fail to recognize the greater importance of basic needs to their constituency. Indeed, even the greater efforts of Solidaridad to reimpose control demonstrated the attraction of satisfying basic needs. But UCI leaders' desire to participate in wider politics had not diminished. The retreat from partisan politics led the UCI to use rhetoric linking poverty alleviation to democratization, an approach different from the democratization work under SEDOC's direction. The rhetoric may or may not have convinced the UCI rank and file. Regardless of the efforts to pursue the two distinct goals, the UCI's diminished power to get the state to deliver material goods was clear to all.

The UCI's new vulnerability in relation to the state demonstrates the strata of civil society. The alliance of the urban poor with an organization with far greater resources, as well as a higher location on hierarchies of class and status, allowed the UCI to make important gains for their constituency. The removal of its powerful partner left it in a weakened negotiating position vis-à-vis the state and also made it subject to clientelist incursions. The rapid decline of its power questions how much progress UCI would have made without SEDOC's backing.

The electoral strategy itself also demonstrates SEDOC's greater power within the alliance. Any number of community-based organizations can find ways to withstand clientelism.[12] Without SEDOC, the UCI would have been able to build on the CEB and liberation-theology orientations to citizenship rather than clientelism's orientation to exchange in its dealings with the government. Yet the distinct lack of enthusiasm for partisan politics displayed by the UCI rank and file suggests that this strategy was one that the UCI leaders would not have pursued in SEDOC's absence.

The stratification of civil society does not mean that in alliances made with those higher up in social and economic hierarchies, subordinate members have no power. They can choose to disengage or to ally only temporarily and strategically. The experience with SEDOC convinced UCI to work only in temporary alliance with the Alianza Cívica, which was important both for that moment in the history of the UCI and for this book. The 1994 elections led to a possibility of interest convergence and common tactics. The UCI's critique of such work shows that the UCI's exertion of power was to carefully examine the viability of conducting such activity in the future. The UCI leaders' ability to withstand the entreaties of Padre Flota to wholeheartedly rejoin the PRD efforts demonstrate that the UCI's power in relation to more powerful groups and individuals was to assess strategies individually and temporarily, rather than fully endorse efforts suggested by others.

The UCI limped into 1995. It had lost a great deal of direction and financial support with SEDOC's departure. Additionally, state efforts to reimpose clientelism had increased. At the same time, the UCI was pushed to certain strategies by allies. The UCI's ability to withstand such efforts, survive, and still provide some material advance is, in this context, quite impressive.

12. See, for example, Gay 1994; Stokes 1995; and Eckstein 1988.

7

DEMOCRATIZATION AND CHANGING POLITICS

I left Guadalajara in early 1995, with the UCI having weathered one of the most difficult years of its existence. The organization had begun 1994 fearing the information that Ester might share with Solidaridad about the inner workings of the UCI. Although those worries proved baseless, Ester's departure hurt the leaders' images. They also continued to reel from the impact of the diminishing support from the Jesuit authority. As financial support disappeared, Tito's continued presence was no longer assured, as family pressures pushed him to look for other work. Also in these precarious moments, UCI leaders and members had to decide how to resolve the dilemma of how to play a role in democratization, while addressing still lacking urban services in the community of Cerro del Cuatro.

The last event before my departure was another meeting discussing the electoral observations in the upcoming regional elections. Beset with sadness at leaving my friends, I had trouble focusing on the meeting. Yet among my impressions of blessings, laughter, and hugs remains my memory of the UCI girding itself for another foray into a civil society coalition effort focused on democratization. On my long drive up to the United States, I kept wondering whether the UCI could surmount this ongoing dilemma of local needs and national participation.

From early 1995 to 2004, Guadalajara, the state of Jalisco, and the Republic of Mexico underwent massive political change. The epitome of Mexico's electoral democratization—the change in federal power holding—occurred in 2000 and again in 2006. Similarly, Jalisco has seen the election of three PAN governors since 1995. Cerro del Cuatro lies partly in the municipio of Guadalajara and partly in the municipio of Tlaquepaque, and both also experienced subsequent PAN candidate wins. In the 2003 elections, the PRI, newly transformed into the opposition, won back all the municipios surrounding Guadalajara, while the PAN held on to the city itself. Thus, if we are to define democratization as the ability for elections to occur in a genuine context of competition, Jalisco and Mexico have made important gains.

Because democratization was such an important focus for the UCI and its allies, each time I returned to Guadalajara, I sought to answer a series of questions. How had the success of formal democratization changed life on the hill? How had the UCI fared as it continued to negotiate a balance between the pursuit of basic needs and actions to promote democratization? The democratization movement suggested that years of economic devastation would indeed be addressed through a genuinely democratic political process. In 1999, the PRI was still in power at the federal level, and Vicente Fox Quesada, Mexico's first non-PRI president in 70 years, took office only in 2001, during my prior trips I made in those years, it was not yet possible to measure democratization at the national level. However, Jalisco, having been governed by the PAN since 1994, offered a case to evaluate the local situation to determine if the lives of the Cerro del Cuatro residents had been improved. By 2004, the national-level changes could also be assessed at the level of the hill and the UCI.

From its very inception, the UCI was part of national and regional political efforts. An important literature addressing the politics of the urban poor in Mexico found that neighborhood-level politics was consistently defined by clientelism, which fragmented local politics, isolated potential allies, and kept the focus only on local material needs (Cornelius 1975; Fagen and Tuohy 1972; Vélez-Ibáñez 1983; Eckstein 1989). In my earlier research, I had found important differences between that characterization and the political action of the UCI. Far from being isolated, the UCI had allies and advisers that worked in a broad range of Mexican political opposition. How had these alliances fared during the transition to formal democracy? How had formal democracy changed the political process in the poor urban neighborhoods I had studied?

I returned to Cerro del Cuatro in 1997, 1998, 2001, 2004, and 2006. Except for the briefer visits in 1997 and 2006, these trips were four-week intensive forays into the field. Although I had remained in contact with the UCI leaders in the intervening time, I had notified only Tito of my visit in 1997. I still remember that my delight at seeing my friends around the UCI office conference table matched their surprise at seeing me come through the door. Tito and I were greeted with a chorus of "¡Qué milagro!" During that meeting, I quickly learned about the leaders' personal situations, as well as about what had transpired in the neighborhood since my departure in early 1995.

Little change was visible in the streets, with no new pavement or sewers in place. At that meeting, the UCI leaders discussed the land-tenure struggle that continued to plague them. With the departure of FONHAPO, the route they had had to pursue with the state agency had yielded almost no success.[1] One of the important changes that the UCI members discussed was the virtual disappearance of PRI-linked neighborhood groups in the wake of the PAN's local and state electoral victories. The irony was that with the disappearance of these neighborhood groups, which had been the fondest hope of the UCI for years, there existed even fewer political channels through which the newly elected PAN officials could hear the complaints of citizens. The PAN had been unable to replace the PRI networks, or perhaps they were uninterested in doing so. The absence of other groups meant that the UCI was one of the few organizations demanding government attention on Cerro del Cuatro. Few officials were listening to the needs of Cerro del Cuatro residents.

In their personal lives, the UCI leaders had experienced mixed fortunes during my two-year absence. Tito had found decent-paying and fulfilling work in a Jesuit high school's service learning department. His wife was close to finishing a master's degree in theology, and she was looking forward to teaching full time. Their excitement over a new baby, Sofía, born in February 1997, was tempered when the child was diagnosed with a serious disability. Tito and Mercedes were still reeling from the news during my visit.

Carmen Castañeda's family was doing well, as was her husband's mechanic business. The business was so demanding, however, that she had limited her involvement with the UCI as her husband relied on her to handle the paperwork. Her family was growing and healthy, and Carmen was happy.

Ana Mondragón was also happy and pleased to see both Tito and me, although she blistered the air with curses at us for having been absent for so long. She continued to work with the UCI, while her family life made her increasingly content. She was delighted with her oldest son's marriage, and he and his family had built a small house on a section of Ana's lot. Her younger son was working as a carpenter, often with her husband, Jorge, and Ana was looking forward to grandchildren and watching her daughter enter high school.

Agustín Martínez was no longer involved with the UCI, and the other leaders discussed his family's experiences with great sympathy. His wife had died in 1995 after a difficult childbirth that also left his new daughter with great physical and developmental problems. His job security had suffered over the years as he

1. See Chapter 6.

struggled over his wife's death and his child's needs. Things appeared to brighten when his cousins offered him help with childcare for both his daughters.

Hermano Javier Cruz seemed unchanged. His good humor remained intact, and for him, the struggle continued as it had before. He was the leader who remained in the closest contact with Agustín, and Javier expressed sadness over his friend's difficulties. Tito was reluctant to stay for the political and organizational discussion as he felt he could no longer contribute, given the demands of his work and family. So, after catching up on the personal news and changes to the organization, we left. My 1997 trip included additional short visits to my friends in their homes.

I continued my research on changes in the UCI and Cerro del Cuatro during my subsequent trips, when I spoke not just with the UCI leaders and members but also with the NGO activists who work with the UCI.

On a May day in 2001, I met Tito at a busy bus stop and we rode up to Cerro del Cuatro. Bus riding in Guadalajara is always an adventure. A greater number of riders than seats, multiple abrupt stops and speedy starts, maneuvering in cramped spaces to allow people on or off, and potholed streets makes it a challenge to stay on one's feet. This bus ride was a bit easier than in years past, as Avenida 8 de Julio had been paved in late 1997, all the way to the Periferico, the urban highway that encircles the Guadalajara Metropolitan Zone.

We rode the bus to Colonia Francisco I. Madero, the last populated part of the hill. Down the hill more settlements continued to be established, as the telltale blue tarps covering recently built shanties revealed. As we began walking, we encountered Hermano Javier on his route, selling bread from his pushcart. We heard him deliver his pitch long before we saw him: "Bolillos, birrotes, galletitas" all in his piercing, deep vendor's voice. We talked for a short time about his family and the state of the UCI. Hermano then continued along his route after we promised to return to his house for a longer visit later that afternoon. We continued on our walk, examining what changes had come to the hill.

We covered a lot of ground, walking from Francisco I. Madero, the southernmost colonia of Cerro del Cuatro to Buenos Aires, which bordered the first colonia built on the hill. The neighborhoods on the hill did not appear very different from how I remembered them. A few more streets served as bus routes, paved with cobblestones and bordered by concrete curbs. As we watched a paving crew set the stones in compacted sand, Tito explained that this form of paving never lasted more than a couple of years. With torrential rains undeterred by sewers, the rains would steadily wash away the paving.

Boulders marked the landscape; some occupied empty lots, while others blocked streets. We saw several instances where men built bonfires, trying to heat up the huge rocks in order to make them easier to smash and remove. One large man, laboring with a sledgehammer on a boulder at least eight feet high and six feet in diameter, invited my aid after I took a picture of him. After a few swings, I agreed it was hard work, and Tito and I continued on our walk.

The streets were full of trash, and streams of sewage carved through the streets. Many streets were dotted with concrete sewer manholes, but they were either not connected to anything or they were "tapados"—stopped up. Tito, whose work had prevented him from visiting the hill for quite some time, agreed that it looked like a place frozen in time. Everywhere hydrants continued to provide much of the water supply, with hoses extending from single faucets to serve a full block, but more houses seemed to enjoy indoor water access. We also saw a trash truck passing, a rarity in previous years. When we asked a woman running after the truck, she said she had to catch it because it had not been by in two weeks.

Two new features caught my attention during that walk. Several more small stores dotted the area, including groceries and hardware stores. I also spotted much more graffiti, which Tito said was gang-related. Violence on the hill had increased greatly, and we noted the large number of adolescent boys hanging out. Tito mentioned that the gangs were more active in the afternoon and evenings.

We returned after a couple of hours to talk with Hermano, who had just arrived and was putting his cart away. He sent out for beer, and we sat in his house, still unfinished with sacks of concrete stacked in the patio, and began to chat. Hermano talked at length about the anniversary of the UCI that he had organized earlier that summer. At this time, he lost the support of the Espíritu Santo missionaries, due to what he called "professional jealousy." He did not want to hold the anniversary indoors at their church, which stood directly across the street from his house, as he said the UCI was born in the streets and worked in the streets. In addition, Hermano asked several Jesuits to come to the event, which created a problem with the missionaries. He went on at great length about how the missionaries were needlessly offended, made a big deal of nothing, even after he had asked for their participation. Since then, there had been little contact between Hermano Javier, the members of his UCI group, and their former supporters, the missionaries.

Hermano spoke about the absence of either material or advisory aid from any source, including groups that had previously helped the UCI. He had minimal contacts with outreach workers from the nearby Jesuit university, the ITESO. They wanted to help residents' organize savings accounts, which he discounted sarcastically, saying few of his neighbors had enough to pay bills, let alone save. His business, for example, only provided his family with enough to eat. Expressing a mixture of optimism and skepticism, he pulled out a copy of a blueprint that detailed a plan to begin hooking up the sewers that month.

Beyond the changes to the UCI, in 2001, Hermano Javier noted few changes on Cerro del Cuatro. My observations and other research efforts confirmed his position.

SERVICES ON THE HILL

Although there were few readily apparent differences in the neighborhoods in which I had worked, the 2000 census revealed some subtle changes. Residents' occupations had changed little, but the statistics on income suggested greater prosperity. Cerro del Cuatro workers continued to be split between the secondary (51 percent) and tertiary (45 percent) sectors. Those defining themselves as self-employed remained at 15 percent of the local workforce, while employees were 75 percent. Salaries appear to have increased, with only 6 percent earning below one minimum wage, 38 percent earning between one and two minimum salaries, 47 percent earning between two and five minimum salaries, and a new category not evident in 1990, 3 percent earning above five minimum salaries.

Assessment of increased wages, however, must be tempered by the recognition that minimum salary at the time these statistics were compiled was less than US$4 per day. Thus, even the highest earning 3 percent of Cerro del Cuatro workers earned approximately $20 per day, while most earned between $7 and $15. Second, the wage increases disappear when controlled for inflation. Mexican workers' wages lost value dramatically over the decades of neoliberal policy. In 1980, 1.82 minimum salaries bought a basic food basket; by 1990, it took 3.97 minimum salaries to purchase the same commodities, and by 2000 it took 6.94 minimum salaries (Mexican Labor News and Analysis 2004). Real wages sank over the course of my study, with 2004 wages still below those of 1980 (Polaski 2004).[2]

2. Unless otherwise specified, these statistics are drawn from 2000 census data compiled by INEGI. By the 2000 census, the assessments were measured by colonias, rather than the previously used AGEBS. The 2000 census results document little difference in housing makeup and did not record the composition of the flooring in households.

Water availability had increased since 1990. By 2000, 58 percent of homes enjoyed piped water, 20 percent had access to water on their property, 8 percent reported using "public" water (from hidrantes), and the remaining 14 percent continued to pay to have trucks deliver water. The lack of sewer connections, however, continued to pose great challenges. No houses were hooked up to sewers in 1994. By 2000, individual households fared better, but the community still suffered from the faulty resolution of sewage problems. In the 2000 census, 50 percent of houses were reported as being connected to sewers, while 31 percent reported having either septic tank or having "free-spilling" sewage. Because this category is aggregated, it is hard to understand. It is even harder to understand household access to sewers, as 18 percent report no access to sewers, which appears little different than the partial category of "free-spilling."

Many locales on the hill belied the statistics regarding sewer access. First, the dirt-packed streets continued to run with sewage, marked by the ever-changing streambeds that formed during each rainy season. Second, sewer manholes dot many of these same streets. The manholes were built into brick or concrete openings, yet streambeds flow to each side of the structures. Finally, at the bottom of the streets that intersect with Avenida 8 de Julio, small ponds collected the refuse from sewer runoff and rain.

Discussions with residents cleared up the mystery. As late as 2004, the sewers continued to be unconnected to a main collector underneath Avenida 8 de Julio leading away from the hill. Many of the installed sewer lines ran only for a block, or several blocks, and end abruptly. Without completion or connection to the main collector, the amount of drainage quickly overwhelmed the minimal infrastructure in place to service the hill. Despite the cheery statistics, sewage remained a major problem for Cerro del Cuatro residents.

The inconsistencies between my observations and the statistical data led me to pursue different methods of data collection. The abbreviated time for research led me back to old contacts, who provided extremely useful information but left me concerned about limited data. To answer questions about how material life had changed on Cerro del Cuatro, I devised an informal survey regarding household access to urban services. In 2001, I spent two weeks walking the neighborhoods that I had come to know earlier, asking both acquaintances and men and women I had never met about their recent history of obtaining urban services.

I spoke with people in eleven areas in four neighborhoods on Cerro del Cuatro. I purposefully spoke to people in areas that were solid backers of the UCI and in areas that were not. I sat down with Tito and others as I devised my strategy in order to make sure that I represented both allied and non-allied areas. Tito, who had been absent from organizing on the hill for several years, accompanied me on several of my walks. At times, when Cerro del Cuatro residents recognized Tito, they asked when they could expect more organizing efforts. This was especially the case when we encountered activists from the now much diminished UCI.

During this informal survey, I spoke to forty household heads. Most had lived on Cerro del Cuatro, in those same neighborhoods and homes, for a long time. Only two people with whom I spoke had lived there for fewer than four years; five others had lived on the hill between five and seven years; and everyone else, between ten and twenty years.

The access to services and who provided them was determined by neighborhood age and clientelist history. La Mezquitera, the oldest colonia on the hill, and the closest to downtown Guadalajara, was a long-time bastion of PRI neighborhood groups. That loyalty resulted in services in part financed by Solidaridad, the public works and public relations project of the Salinas de Gortari administration (1988–1994). Residents of that neighborhood responded that they possessed all urban services, although many complained of problems with the sewers and garbage collection, as trucks rarely came by. When asked who had provided these services, the consistent answers from La Mezquitera residents were: "the [previous] government," "the PRI," and "Solidaridad." When asked about street paving, there was some variety, with two household heads attributing it to the PAN. The responses regarding the street paving provided evidence of ongoing projects, the result of heavy rains that often dislodged the poor-quality paving stones, leaving streets in the same muddy, rutted condition in which I first saw them. In other colonias with poorer access to sewers, the paving lasted even less time.

Buenos Aires is located immediately south and up the hill from La Mezquitera. These residents, like those in La Mezquitera, have one of the longest histories on the hill. Sections of Buenos Aires were among the first organized into CEBs, and the residents were later strong supporters of the UCI. Like much of the hill, however, the PRI and the UCI contested for control of La Mezquitera. I spoke with people from areas supporting each group.

Residents from PRI-affiliated parts of Buenos Aires have lived there between ten and twenty years, and they reported that they had electricity, water, and sewers. Most reported (and it was evident) that their area had not been paved, even with more-or-less temporary stone pavers. Residents described the garbage pickup schedule as "irregular" and often occurring only once a month. Most residents attributed the delivery of services to the PRI and the PAN. Several with whom I spoke commented that their needs had been addressed slowly, and the transition in governments had not changed that. Others, however, claimed that the PAN was more responsive than the PRI had been.

Buenos Aires residents in areas that had strongly supported the UCI had lived in the colonia between ten and eighteen years. Here, many also had gained a fair amount of services. Where streets had been paved, they had been finished only two months earlier, while in other areas, paving was being done as I walked the area. Several blocks, which in 1994 relied on public hydrants for water, now enjoyed water in their houses. All residents shared the familiar complaint about garbage collection. The greatest difference was that when I asked how they received these services, almost all commented about the activity of the UCI, using both the organization's name and labels like "independent groups of neighbors." Several reminisced about how the residents themselves had initially installed infrastructure, which subsequently was slowly replaced by government-provided installations. Few in this area had positive things to say about the new government, answering that nothing had changed with the transition from the PRI to the PAN.

Nueva Santa María remains the largest colonia on Cerro del Cuatro, and like Buenos Aires, it was an area divided by conflict between UCI and PRI neighborhood groups. In walking the blocks that had not supported the UCI, householders complained bitterly that they still lacked sewers and water. In one neighborhood, streets had been paved in 2000, but in another, they were still hard-packed earth, punctuated by streams of sewage. Garbage collection was inadequate, although several residents noted that it had recently gotten better. Most attributed services to the earlier PRI government, although the paving and the limited sewer connections were attributed to the PAN. No residents mentioned UCI activity.

In the area of Nueva Santa María that had been affiliated with the UCI, memory of its activity was strong. Some of the earliest UCI mobilizations had occurred here, during the government attempt to dislodge residents. Both CEBS and the UCI had found willing participants in the wake of that threat. Here, too, most residents had lived in their homes between thirteen and eighteen years. About a third of residents still did not have running water in their homes, and about half remained unconnected to the sewer network. None of the streets in this area were paved, and again, garbage collection was "irregular," which meant every two weeks, at best, and sometimes only monthly. When asked how they had received their services, many residents commented on the activity of the UCI and "social organizations of colonos" and "united neighbors." Several people recognized me, reminded me of old struggles, and mourned the disappearance of the UCI from their neighborhood. They hoped it would come back to help them get the sewers connected.

In 2001, the only colonia with a UCI presence was Francisco I. Madero, where Hermano Javier Cruz continued to organize. This was also a neighborhood for which the UCI and the PRI had contested. The conditions in Francisco I. Madero were the least changed, with sewers unconnected, no evident street paving, and only intermittent garbage collection. Water, however, was available in every house where I inquired. In the priísta neighborhoods, the delivery of the services was attributed to the government. In the blocks where support for the UCI was strong, when asked how they had obtained their services, the residents responded that it was the UCI, or the "work of folks here," or "the UCI, but a lot of people don't recognize that."

THE UCI STRUGGLES, THEN DIES

The material quality of life had changed somewhat in the households of the people with whom I spoke. Some services had been installed, yet much was still lacking, especially sewer connections. For many, the PAN—in power in Jalisco since 1995—had made barely a dent in the provision of their material needs, and the services that do exist are attributed to either the PRI or the UCI. Many residents, when responding about the contributions of the UCI, articulated how much they missed the activity of the organization. The wish for the organization's ongoing presence was not nostalgia but residents' assessment that the democratic transition had left much unresolved at the neighborhood level.

The status of the UCI, however, was substantially changed by 2001. I spoke to several UCI leaders and members, and all agreed that the group in Colonia Francisco I. Madero led by Hermano Javier was the only one of the older groups that continued to function.

When I talked to Ana Mondragón, she showed me proudly around her home, and the improvements her family's hard work had accomplished. In 1994, her home had consisted of a kitchen, two rooms, and a large enclosed lot. In 2001, her family had built two new small homes on the lot. Ana had begun a small business selling snack foods and tacos. During my return trips, her clients constantly interrupted us. The subject of our discussion in 2001 was her departure from the UCI and various political changes on the hill.

Ana had ceased working with the UCI in 1998, when the work simply became too oppressive. "At the level of the personal [relationships] with the team, how do you say? We were so together, that the same togetherness made it difficult. . . . I think it was that we were really fed up with it—not tired, because I was way past tired. But that we were fed up. Fed up with the work and fed up with the group."

Ana mentioned that during her final years in the UCI, external support had diminished. The Jesuit students who were trying to help the UCI in 1994 halted their support work in 1995. Ana characteristically disparaged this final aid: "The students were never much help. They came when we were in crisis, but they were not much help. They never helped us much with advice—we had to advise them [she laughs]. They were good people, but they didn't have the knowledge that we already had gained."

According to Ana, the web of networks in which the UCI had been embedded, through its relationship with SEDOC, started unraveling in 1995. By 1997, the UCI was on its own, without external aid or counsel.

Ana also talked about her obligation to meet her family's and her own needs. In part, these were economically defined, but Ana also was working through a lot of personal issues: "I think, Jon, that the faith has stayed in my heart. And I think a lot of what I did was because of my faith. But now, I say to myself . . . I did this for so many years because I wanted to give to people. But I am thinking of myself more now. At least, a little bit."

Ana was enormously satisfied with her family's development, and she remained very interested in politics despite her removal from daily organizing. In her perspective, little had changed with the transition in power at the municipal, state, and federal levels. For her, the changes were manifested only in partisan affiliation. Indeed, other parties had recruited the very same PRI leaders the UCI had battled for a decade:

> Do you remember Doña Flora? She is now a militant of the PRD. The fights I had with that bitch! The PRD is now picking up all the [human] garbage that the PRI doesn't want, and it is the same with the PAN now. Because the PAN didn't create a [popular] base, they take them [leaders] from the PRD or PRI. So what ends up being the dynamic? The exact same as always. There is still the exchange of votes for stuff. They have these events that they bring people to, all the old practices of the PRI.

Ana mentioned that a UCI group still existed in Buenos Aires in 2001, and it was led by a member of the UCI, Maribel Castro. Buenos Aires continued to grow, up to the very crest of the hill, and newly arriving families continued to confront the same problems that had plagued earlier settlers. Although Maribel and her group used the UCI name and struggled with similar issues as did Hermano Javier, there was no contact between the groups.[3] When I asked Ana why, she responded: "I think one of the reasons is because of distance. But I also believe that [before] the Jesuits did much of the uniting. This was part of the work of the Jesuits."

During my visit in 2004, Ana gloried in being a grandmother, but she bemoaned the deterioration of the services the UCI had won. Her home continued to show evidence of the uneven changes brought about by democratization. Paving had never reached her area, and the streets bordering her property were still completely pitted and uneven. Ana fondly remembered the UCI and her work with it:

> It was an experience that was grand for me, a phase of my life that was very beautiful. It was a really good experience. For me, the UCI was not the best thing that has happened to me in my life, but something that I feel was very important. And I think that the efforts were a success in the end although there was a lot of pain. But I remember that we won the regularization, the water, the electricity, the buses. You can see that not all was finished. But it was an effort by a lot of people, and we had some gains, we made some changes.
> JS—What kinds of things weren't you able to change?
> AM—The things we weren't able to change were the thinking of more people. To understand why the people are like this. This is something that has stayed with me a lot.

For Ana, the UCI had played an important role on Cerro del Cuatro, and in her own life. Ana had changed markedly and did not understand why some of the changes she had experienced were not shared by many with whom she had worked for so long. She remained unimpressed with the impacts of electoral change on Cerro del Cuatro.

---

3. During my conversations with Hermano Javier, he did not even refer to the existence of the group in Buenos Aires.

In 2001, Hermano Javier continued to work with the UCI in Colonia Francisco I. Madero. His group had shrunk, although residents of Buenos Aires and Guayabitos had joined. During a conversation that lasted over several days in June of that year, Hermano Javier talked about why fewer residents were participating in the UCI, how the political process had changed, and how the lack of external supporters affected him and the group. Hermano's perspective on the level of services contrasted with the official statistics:

> The UCI continues to fight for services, for regularization—this whole area is still not regularized. For years the title deeds have been promised. They've [the municipio] done surveys; they come every six months, they look around, they say wait, and nothing [happens]. And so the UCI convoked meetings, and they paid attention to us—the municipio said they were going to arrange it—but it was just to calm us. Nothing has been done. The electricity is only 50 percent in place; the other 50 percent is stolen. I am one of them [he laughs]. All of us, the 50 percent who are robbing, we've contracted the work [with the municipio], but they haven't come to put it in. So, we steal it. The water—70 percent of the houses have water. We won this, that every house has its source of water. This again was a struggle of the UCI's. There are two blocks not on the water network . . . but those without water don't come to the meetings.

Those who did come to meetings were few in number. Javier commented both on poor turnout and why it had declined so precipitously since 1998. "There are fourteen people from here in the colonia. Fourteen who are very committed. In the group, we can count up to three hundred people [who can be mobilized]. But there are only fourteen who are always in the struggle. I think because of family problems, economic problems. Political problems, too. The political problems, I say, because many have gone over to the parties."

For Javier, the transition to PAN rule, which began in 1995, had not positively affected the local politics of demand making. "Look, it appears to me that it was better before. There was more recognition. It was easier to get an interview with the governor. Before the UCI was heard better—because of its size. Now, [it's] 'Hermano Javier and the UCI—send them away.' Before, when I tried to make a date for the next Thursday, I got to see them that same day."

Like Ana, Javier recognized that democratic transition had only minimally changed politics in the colonias. "The block representatives are now panistas, like they were priístas before. Now are they panistas. The government still tries to exchange votes for goods. The colonia representatives do what the government tells them to do. They are more representatives of the government than the colonia. So they get the people together to do what the government wants."

Javier observed that the UCI had lost power not only because of the decline in the popular base, but also because their former advisers had left:

> The UCI has less power. The people that are now in the UCI, we are not intellectuals. We are not the Jesuits; we are not the missionaries. It is people from here. Housewives, workers like me. We know little, and we struggle a lot. We don't have an adviser who says, "Look, let's go this direction, the other one, no." Without that kind of help, it's easier for them to hurt us. Before, in the meetings of the UCI, we had a wider vision. Fridays we knew what we were planning, and Wednesdays we went to the groups and worked. Now, no—all we have is the meetings on Wednesdays.

Like Ana, Javier was tired. His years of organizing added to his exhausting schedule as a baker:

> People need time to work, and to feed their kids. The days I work with the UCI, sometimes I don't sleep. I go from work, to a negotiation at 4, return at 6, then I have to work at 2 or 3 in the morning. I walk around like a zombie. Sometimes my wife gets angry [and] she says, "You don't sleep, and you can't work well [that way]."

> My dreams are that the UCI continues. That people continue struggling. But the reality is that I am tired. Every day, I feel more tired, I feel less supported. I'd like to continue until God says [otherwise]. Because I know the needs will continue, and I want to continue with the struggle because I benefit. But I see it as very difficult.

Despite his exhaustion and frustration, Hermano Javier was convinced of the utility of his time and efforts with the UCI over the years. "They were treating us like we were asleep. Here in the colonia, there are thirty awake, and three thousand asleep. But they are more afraid of the thirty than of the three thousand. I say this because we had a presence. When a candidate came, and I raised my hand, they listened to me, or listened to another brother from the UCI. When the people are asleep, they just [do what they want]. When there were one hundred asleep, and five awake, we said, 'Wake up, brothers!'"

When I returned to Cerro del Cuatro in the summer of 2004, I learned that the sole remaining neighborhood group of the UCI, the one led by Hermano Javier, had dissolved the previous December. I talked about this issue at length with him, both sitting down in his house and during an extended walk around the hill. Hermano and I agreed that one of the best ways to see the changes was to accompany him on his rounds. So, on an early Wednesday morning in July, Hermano Javier and I walked all over Cerro del Cuatro on his vending route. During that research visit, I had already taken several walks around the hill and talked with a variety of old friends and acquaintances. Hermano was the UCI stalwart, and I wanted to see the changes through his eyes. The following is a description of that walk, and what we saw.

CERRO DEL CUATRO, SUMMER 2004

Every morning, Monday through Friday, Hermano wakes early and bakes his wares. He fills a huge basket full of various kinds of bread and cookies, piles it in his red wheelbarrow, secures the plastic covering, and goes off on his route selling bread. Hermano was dressed in dirty blue jeans with the cuffs rolled up, a red Home Depot shirt, dusty hiking boots, and a yellow fishing hat. He usually wears a full beard, but that day his grizzled face was clean shaven. When he removed his hat, I saw that his head was shaved, too, with only an odd crown of hair around his ears and along the top of his neckline—sort of a monk's crown that had slipped down. He was still sweaty from his pre-dawn baking with his oven.

Throughout the morning, Hermano repeated his vendor's cry in a loud, deep voice: "Bolillos, birrotes, galletitas." People approached him, and Hermano greeted them all with great kindness, "Hello, sister, how are you? That's fine. Glory be to God! Stay well, brothers. What do you need, my queen?" Everyone knows Hermano Javier, even some people he does not know, and he shouted his greetings to all he passed.

As we walked, Hermano explained that sewers had been installed on several of the streets. However, the government had not connected house hookups. That had to be arranged with the permission of the government, although some residents had installed their own connections without governmental permission. In the early 2000s, the UCI sought and received permission as a group to connect the sewers on certain blocks, then they did the work collectively.

Hermano emphasized that the government had neither helped with the work itself nor provided the resources to complete it.

The sewers themselves were often left unconnected to the sewer main that finally was installed under the main street, Avenida 8 de Julio. Hermano showed me several storm drains that, according to him, always got stopped up with rocks and dirt. He further described how the sewer water would back up, pop the manhole covers, and run over the streets as if there were no sewers at all. This occurs constantly during the summer monsoon rains. To demonstrate his claim, Hermano showed me many places where water was pooling at the bottom of the hill where the streets intersected with 8 de Julio.

Some of the changes Hermano noted had to do with neighborhood safety. I was concerned when I saw him carrying a large walking stick, which I attributed to a health problem. He assured me he carried it for safety, because "there is a lot of vice around." His concern became more concrete when we reached a street where five young men sat around talking. They kept looking around, and four of them paid obvious deference to one man, who was seated in front of a house. They stared at me, briefly conversed among themselves, and immediately, one of the men walked over to buy a roll from Hermano. When the customer asked who I was, Hermano introduced me as one of the helpers or adviser of the uci. The man seemed satisfied and shook our hands. We started off, but as we reached the place where the five men were congregated, the seated one asked "Are they going to pave this street, Hermano?"

Hermano's response came almost as instinct after years of organizing: "If we organize ourselves, they will. If we don't, we'll be fucked."

"How many years have we been paying taxes, Hermano?" the man asked. Hermano agreed that paying taxes without receiving government services in return was unjust, and he reiterated that their only option was to organize. We moved on. When we were out of earshot, Hermano confirmed my suspicions that they were drug dealers. He explained that many work around the area: "They're all my customers. I know them all. Some sell marijuana, others crack, cocaine. Others listen to the radio to keep track of the police. They're very organized."

On the southernmost streets of Francisco I. Madero, Hermano showed me an area where no sewers had been installed and the lots were not regularized, and so the residents continued to fight for their titles. Hermano told me that, with the exception of this section, all of Cerro del Cuatro had been regularized. "It was through our effort, even though some on the hill didn't believe we could do it and still don't believe it was us," said Hermano.

As we walked and sold bread, a small man in a white cowboy hat approached to tell us how Mexico needed a left-leaning government. He talked at length, and with great passion, about the unmet needs of the proletariat. After we left him, Hermano commented that the man was currently working with the PRD but had been a priísta. Hermano, who voted for the PRD at every opportunity, said that the party doesn't do anything for the colonia, "It's just *arriba el* PRD—let's work for the party." Hermano Javier, a man I always thought of as one of the gentlest persons I have known, who over the years has always taken great pains to speak as uncritically as he could of others, dismissed the partisan effort with scorn.

Hermano commented that Cerro del Cuatro continued to attract new residents, many of whom faced the same infrastructure and land-title issues that he and others had faced when they moved to the hill twenty years ago. Hermano pointed out new areas, notable for the blue tarps that serve as roofs. Later, we walked by a small stand almost at the end of the paved section of 8 de Julio. There, Hermano Javier pointed out, worked some of the same land sellers who had collaborated with the PRI and fraudulently sold many of the lots decades before, and they continued now selling lots on the fringes of Cerro del Cuatro.

Walking on, two toddlers peeked outside the gate of their house, which was covered by red and blue plastic tarps. Dried mortar oozed from between the bricks, and the door was painted a bright green and held multiple locks. Their mother, dressed in a purple skirt, bought bread while commenting: "We need to work more, Hermano. But what can we do here, just three or four people?" Hermano agreed, "We need the majority with us, hermana." She remembered the struggle for regularization, which took fifteen years, during which time "we were in the offices of the government every two weeks." Despite the recent dissolution of the final UCI group, Hermano proselytized for the organization at every opportunity.

We passed by a typical row of houses, built side by side, reinforcement bar sticking out from the roofs and windows open to permit the entry of the breeze. Hermano noted a house with a red door and closed windows. It, too, was a drug house: "*puro marihuana*," said Hermano. As we passed, the door opened and a young man came out and stared after us. I wanted to take a picture of the rutted street with sewage pooling at the bottom, but I was reluctant to pull out the camera while he watched us. "They're watching us, Hermano," I said. He laughed, "That's normal." He commented that ten drug houses were located within a few blocks of his home.

"Hermano, don't you ever get a sore throat?" "Not in twenty-one years, Hermano Jon. For twenty-one years I have been walking the hill and selling bread." We stopped outside a mechanic's shop. "Hermano!" bellowed one of the mechanics, as he left the car he was working on. On Avenida 8 de Julio, Hermano stopped often to sell to people who approached him. "There have been no changes here," Hermano told me. "Everything we have we got before. Everything was already installed, but not connected to the houses—which was done by the UCI, only with the permission, not aid, of the government."

After walking on 8 de Julio for several blocks, we finally reached a sidewalk. Hermano walked in and out among pedestrians in a small, crowded tianguis. In the shoulder-to-shoulder crowd, people elbowed past stands and blankets where tianguistas sold their merchandise, from fake hair to clothes to ancient machine parts.

Hermano's route passes the Temple Nueva Santa María—the parish where Padre Andrés, the old scourge of the UCI, officiated and where the Foro Callejero was held in 1994. The temple was completed, with a wide patio, whitewashed and featuring a mural with Jesus Christ, John Paul II, and Mother Teresa juxtaposed over Cerro del Cuatro. After the 1994 Foro, Padre Andrés blamed Hermano publicly for the event, so he stopped going to that church. There is a new priest officiating there, who was warned about Hermano by Andrés. "We have no relationship" he said, criticizing the new priest as a charismatic and opposed to the theological and political contributions of liberation theology.

We were almost out of bread when we crossed the street to a hardware store where we sat and drank sodas and talked with the store manager. Although several people stopped to buy bread, it was clear that we were at the end of the route. "Some days are better than others; this has been a good day," Hermano explained. When sales are slow, he has to continue walking.

When we started back, we passed several men and a backhoe at a public works site. Because the pavement had been installed without sewer facilities, water streamed down the street. Hermano showed me another street that had been completed in 2002, and it was now entirely in ruins.

When we returned to Hermano's house, there was much to discuss. As in years past, we spoke about the past, present, and future of politics on Cerro del Cuatro and the nation. I asked him how local politics worked in Cerro del Cuatro now that the democratic transition was a reality. His answers demonstrated that old political processes are still largely in play: "The priísta groups work in sectors. The PRI manages eight sectors in Nueva Santa María. Every person in the group gets *dispensas* [bags of goods, especially food] every two weeks after they have attended ten meetings. There are meetings every week. You have to attend ten meetings in a row. If you don't go, they cut you off.

FIG. 15   A Cerro del Cuatro street after heavy rains, 2004

And the PAN manages four sectors, and certain groups in those sectors lend money to their supporters. For a small interest rate."

One important difference that Hermano noted was that block groups no longer mobilized to demand that local material needs be met. The parties did not bring groups to the government to make demands when running water was unavailable, which occurred three or four days a week, or when the sewage backed up. The focus of the neighborhood groups was on party building through individual exchange rather than the provision of community goods.

> Now, what the priístas are doing is first, uniting the people. And how? As we just said, through the dispensas. They are "organizing." They don't do anything for the colonia, because . . . how do I explain it? There are lots of things to do, but they aren't accustomed to working in this way.
> JS—So, are these new PRI leaders?
> HJC—They are the old ones. But now there are fewer lots to sell, and many [of the residents] have services. Now, all they can do is bring people together and give them dispensas.
> JS—And those from the PAN?
> HJC—The only thing they've managed is to lend money. You know, before this, they organized some meetings where they talked about

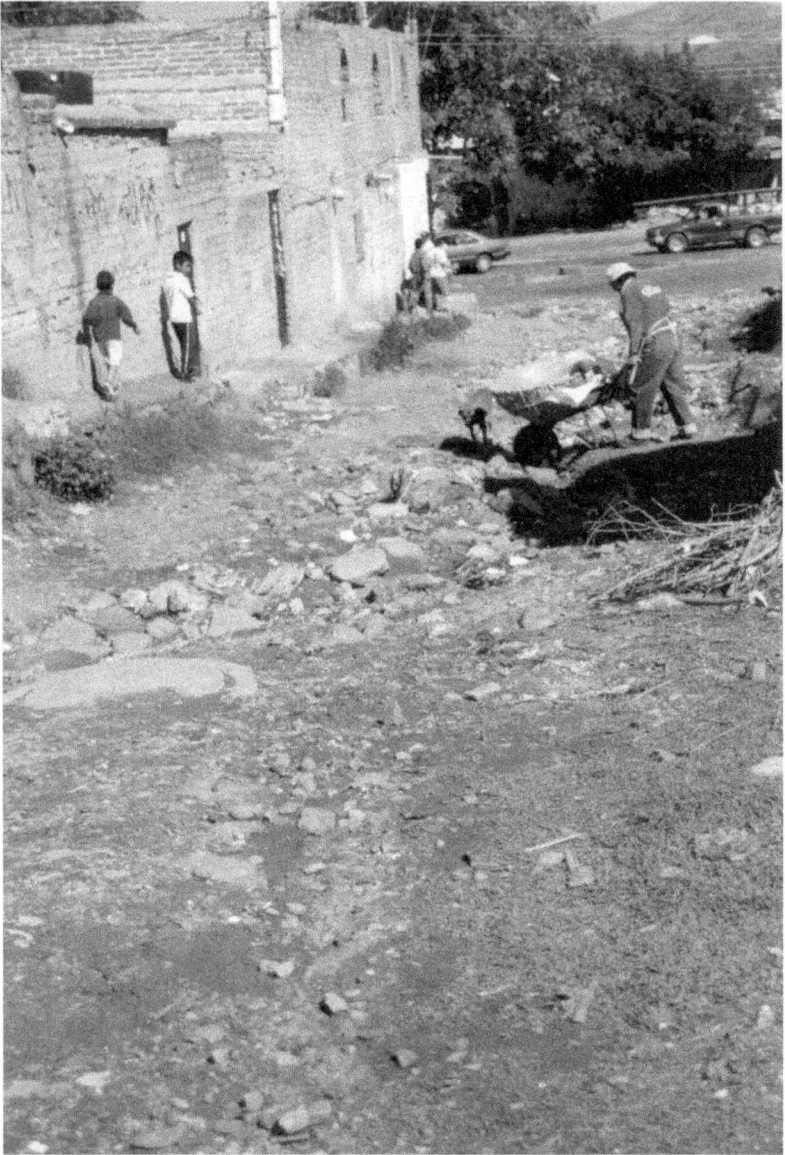

FIG. 16 Hermano Javier picks his way down a rutted Cerro del Cuatro street, 2004

FIG. 17   Sewage puddles near an unconnected sewer manhole, 2004

the panista doctrine, that [in a mocking lilt] "we want a new Mexico!" And the people leave—and possibly they leave with this message in their heads. Or they leave with the loaned money.

Javier found the previous PAN governments, and the even more recently elected PRI municipal administration, failing to resolve resident demands.

Look, here the PAN does not pay attention to us. The previous [PAN municipal] president was Antonio Alvarez. He didn't want to hear from us. We had to move him with the governor. We sent him a letter, and he did not answer. We sent a letter to the governor, saying what our problems and needs were, and he sent a letter to Antonio Alvarez, and then we got a call from the municipal president, who said, "Why did you do that? We already received your message." But without a response, what else could we do? It was twenty-two days after our letter that we got a response.

JS—And after receiving the letter from the governor, did he do anything?

HJC—Yeah, he did something. You saw when we were walking where the water pooled? There was another one over there, the same. We

FIG. 18   Hermano Javier selling his baked goods, 2004

sent two documents to Antonio Alvarez to fix the drainage problems, there were two, and it took two months to get fixed. But of two letters I sent to Marco Rosas [the current PRI municipal president]—neither got a response.

One reason that municipal administrations ignored the UCI was because of its declining strength, which led to the organization's eventual dissolution in 2004. Despite his ongoing efforts to talk up organizing as the way to resolve neighborhood problems, Hermano Javier harbored few illusions about the UCI's ability to revive. He attributed the UCI's end to its partial success.

First we struggled for the water, and we gained it. We struggled for the electricity, and now we have it. We struggled for the sewer, and there it is. Only part of it, but there it is. We struggled for streets, now there aren't streets in the way there should be, but . . . . And so, the people say we're "good." [He makes quotation marks in the air as he says "good."] There are many things for people to do, but with these they are consoled. JS—What else is there to do?

FIG. 19   Urban life meets rural life on Cerro del Cuatro, 2004

HJC—There is a lot yet to do. The bad paving, the bad sewers, which remain. Did you see the sewage flowing where we were walking? There is a lot to do.

His neighbors' and his own unsatisfied material needs provided Hermano Javier with serious grievances that a reinvigorated neighborhood organization could focus on. Yet it took little prompting to get Hermano to talk about the need for other, less tangible goods that local political work might also articulate. "There remains a lot for us to do, in addition to the services. Arriving at dignity [means] to begin to note that every Mexican citizen has the right to many benefits, which we have not been given. I've read the constitution, and I like it a lot. The rights in the constitution are very good, but they don't really exist. The government does not respect it. The Mexicans, we don't know our rights. And if we don't know them, we won't demand them."

For Javier, the struggle for wider political rights continued to be part of the local struggle. He held that same conviction over the years I have known him, but he recognized that the UCI was brought into the democratization struggle through the efforts of others. That support and aid had declined over the years.

FIG. 20   Paved and unpaved streets meet on the way to the top of Cerro del Cuatro, 2004

The UCI's partial success and subsequent loss of local support was compounded, in Hermano's view, by the fact that its external aid had disappeared:

> They [the Jesuit advisers] built the UCI to tell it to do what they wanted. But I continued working, and they did not give me the aid that they earlier promised they would. They stopped the aid. Some groups ceased existing because they lacked the will [to continue]. But those that did continue wanted to keep the aid, the support [of the advisers]. But no—they [the advisors] didn't want to continue with that. I imagine they said, "Well, they've finished; we're done, too." Under quotes, we won half of everything we fought for. Water there is, three or four times a week, but there is water. The electricity we've had. Now we have all the services, but various people left us—the Jesuits, and others.

For Javier, like other Cerro del Cuatro residents, even partial satisfaction of material necessities provided a significant contribution to quality of life. Yet throughout the existence of the UCI, the satisfaction of these material needs were discussed as the medium of political change, not as a final goal. Javier

FIG. 21   Avenida 8 de Julio, the main street bisecting Cerro del Cuatro, was paved by 2004

spoke of this process when he talked about how the UCI became a political force devoted to change beyond the colonia:

> JS—You told me that they [NGO organizers and others] wanted the UCI to do what they wanted. What did they want?
>
> HJC—Well, today, I see it this way. They bring people together, teach them that they have the right to services, and they teach them how to get them. We were taught, we acted, and we got the services. And I think this is what they wanted to do. "Let's go into a colonia that has no services, organize people so that they themselves take action. Get people to pay attention, to struggle for the services." Water, sewers, regularization, power. All that is here now, it is not done well, but it is here. I believe that they wanted to give to the people of the UCI this political injection. That is, they wanted to say—"Get involved!" and we got thrust into political life. That is, we were enlisted by those from the democracy movement.

New problems had emerged during the rule of the PAN, adding new grievances that might be addressed collectively. Hermano wondered if new forms of organizing, especially through youth sport activities, could offer new outlets

FIG. 22   Water being sold on Cerro del Cuatro, with Guadalajara in the distance, 2004

for mobilization. He was concerned about the youth, given his assessment of the biggest problem for the area:

> HJC—The drug addiction, hermano.
> JS—More than the badly made services?
> HJC—Yes. The drug addiction and robbery, the boys who take money. They stick a knife in your guts, and you give them what you're carrying. And sometimes they cut you. The insecurity is especially bad in the evenings. It's a really big problem to be out after nine or ten at the night.

Hermano saw the drug problems as just part of the vice that had increased in the zone. "Our panista brothers gave a lot of permits to put in liquor establishments. They start at 8 in the morning with 'table dances' (spoken in English), saloons where the women dance on the tables. In the stores, they sell a lot of beer and little milk. Me, I like my beer, but I would rather they sold more milk than beer. And there are a lot of houses where drugs are sold."

For Hermano Javier Cruz, the end of the UCI brought sadness and relief. He knew well the limits of what the UCI had accomplished, but he also recognized both the material and immaterial victories of the organized colonos. Hermano relished the fight and the fellowship, and he felt he had benefited immensely during the years of struggle. But he was tired. On our walk back up the hill, we stopped many times to rest from the exertion of pushing the cart up the hill.

Hermano felt angry at the departure of those whose counsel and advice he valued. He felt abandoned, and although he continued to think strategically about mobilization possibilities on Cerro del Cuatro, he recognized the drive to organize would have to come from others. In 2004, however, none emerged from either inside or outside of the colonia.

THE VIEW FROM INSIDE AND OUTSIDE

Talking with Tito was always an education. He was the first UCI organizer I met in 1994, and the person with whom I forged the closest friendship. We have been in continuous contact right up to the present day.

Listening to Tito's perspectives was always crucial for understanding the UCI. First, as a SEDOC-employed UCI organizer, he had worked with the UCI longer than any of his peers. Second, Tito was one of the links to many of the NGOs with whom the UCI had worked. He worked with the Alianza Cívica in 1994, observing the elections and helping integrate the UCI into this task, and he was embedded in a wide web of political groups. Additionally, Tito went on to become an election supervisor and a citizen commissioner for the reformed Mexican electoral system. Despite his later commitment to electoral politics, Tito had disagreed with the UCI's electoral turn, and he had argued against running candidates in 1991 and 1992.

Tito's perspective was also important because of his personal background. He cut his political teeth early, working in CEBs and neighborhood organizations in nearby Polanco. In Tito's youth, Polanco was the neighborhood farthest from the city center, and the organization with which he worked confronted many of the same issues of infrastructure as the UCI faced on Cerro del Cuatro. Although his family had attained lower-middle class status by his adulthood, his social background was much more similar to that of the UCI members than were the backgrounds of the other SEDOC organizers. Tito knew what it meant to struggle for survival; his eventual departure from the UCI in 1995 was caused by the financial needs of his family.

Spurred by my visits, Tito maintained contact with the UCI. He kept more substantial links with the NGO members he had known from his UCI days, as he continued to circulate in the political world increasingly defined by electoral competition. Tito's organizing career, and his forays into electoral politics, provided a wide set of experiences with which to analyze local and national Mexican politics. By 2004, he was simultaneously convinced that previous forms of popular organizing were dated and anxious about the electoral route. Tito saw very little popular organizing from the early 2000s on, and he attributed the decline in part to increasing economic need. "It has become very rare to see this in Guadalajara, the mobilization of people for their needs. Hermano told us that now people were not uniting because they had to work. Now when you return to your house, you do so tired. So, you don't have any energy to fight. So if you have been spending two, three years fighting for something that is not won, you get tired."

Tito had always endorsed the SEDOC belief that organizing to address the material needs of the poor provided a route to democratization. That strategy required consciousness-raising, to which the efforts of SEDOC and others had contributed:

> The moment the UCI was born was a whole experience, not just of struggle, but also of organizing. Of becoming a group, beginning with the base communities. So, the UCI harvested all that work as a social organization. All this process of consciousness raising has to be taken into account. I remember well, for example, about Carmen. Carmen was very much involved in the [base] groups. Also Ana, also Hermano. These people started being formed in groups of reflection, in base communities. So when the UCI was created, they found the way to express, in their personal terms, the social struggle. And part of this was through the services. What happened was the services were obtained, and these people continued mobilizing. But the people who came only for the water, when the water came, they returned to their homes, they stopped attending the meetings. The same with the electricity.

This kind of organizing, according to Tito, had ceased. "Mobilization for needs continues, but not as a project of citizen consciousness, which is what I think the UCI had. Not just to obtain the services for the sake of obtaining them, but whatever problem—as a colonia, as a block—we're going to resolve."

Tito's experience as a youth brought him into contact with political influences from outside his neighborhood, first in a popular group organized by

Jesuit clergy, and then, later, as an organizer with SEDOC. I asked him whether he thought poor people could organize independently without external support:

> Yes, but the mobilization will be rooted in a felt problem. Poor people can organize themselves around various felt needs. . . . When they feel the lack of water, they mobilize, but not from a consciousness of being a citizen, [not from the idea] that I am struggling for something more than just the services. That is one of the things that we did not win. Sure, this was won by certain folks, by Hermano, and other people, who have continued with this struggle after the necessities were won. But not by many.

Our discussion led us to talk about the declining participation of NGO organizers with organizations like the UCI. I mentioned the absence of organizers from the democratization movement on Cerro del Cuatro. In response, Tito talked about the changing form of struggle:

> The people who have been involved in the struggle continue to fight, but I think that the issue is that it has changed, and it had to change— the form of struggle. Certainly, there are people in the middle class, the intellectuals, the people working in the universities, who have done work with some of the poor. There are not many who are organizing now. I think that the people who were working in the NGOs, or with groups like the UCI, did it because they saw that there was a force capable of being mobilized, or they did it because it was seen that it could bear fruit. When it was apparent that the UCI was no longer a strong organization, little by little, these same people separated, looking for other forms of struggle.

Tito recognized that the organizing now centered on the new electoral landscape. Indeed, his own political activity currently focused on election supervision. He was, however, extremely conflicted. He believed in the fundamental importance of democratic formal elections, but he was cognizant these efforts had yielded only disappointments as of 2004. "In 2000, the expectations were very high. That there would be a change at the national level, and at the municipal level, too. When this change did not really occur, the people [thought], 'What difference does it make that I vote for a different party? Why should I vote? It's better if I abstain. The colors [party banners] are the only difference.' This, too, I think is part of the demobilization." The upcoming elections did not offer reason for optimism, according to Tito:

> People have grown very tired of politics. In this short period of time, the people have seen what the PAN really is. With the whole big mess of Toallagate, with the issue of Vamos Mexico Foundation, with all these things, the people are saying, "The PAN is the same." With all that is going on with the PRD at the national level and the local level, with the corruption. The same is happening with the PRD, the same with the Green Party, with the famous video.[4] So what is it that stays with the people? If we vote for the same, we will get the same treatment. So, there is no one to vote for.

In 2004, Tito faced a conundrum. He recognized the importance of both popular struggle and electoral democracy. He recognized that the urban poor had played a crucial role in democratization, yet he believed that the new political playing field required different strategies. And although Tito knew that formal democratic transition had brought little material change, he saw little opportunity for neighborhood organizations to be rejuvenated.

The story of the Unión de Colonos Independientes ended in 2004. The UCI had worked for fourteen years to improve both material conditions on Cerro del Cuatro and democratic governance in the nation. Its legacy, which was greatly influenced by wide-ranging political changes in Mexico, is paradoxical.

The UCI achieved some material benefits, especially legal land tenure and urban services. Yet the neoliberal policies of both PRI and PAN presidents had left Cerro del Cuatro residents in poor economic conditions. The UCI provided many residents with an alternative to the long-entrenched clientelism of the PRI, and the organization pushed forward the national democratization project by disrupting local power. Democratization did not dislodge clientelism as a political-control process, but significant changes in clientelism had certainly occurred on Cerro del Cuatro. The dominant PRI had new competitors from the PAN, although some of the local actors remained the same. The level of patronage used to entice party loyalty appeared to decrease markedly. Resources, such as those

---

4. Tito was referring to a series of political scandals, including the expensive towels used in the Mexican presidential residence, the allegations of misuse of funds by a foundation headed by President Fox's wife, Marta Sahagún, and a video released showing a Green Ecologist Party official accepting bribes.

provided by the Solidaridad program and other PRI-affiliated sources, declined, in part because of the infrastructure improvements that were won for Cerro del Cuatro after thirty years. But it was not only the patronage carrots that changed on Cerro del Cuatro; the sticks of threat appeared to have receded, too. Again, now that the long-awaited infrastructure was in place, the threat of providing or withholding urban services was no longer a viable medium of political exchange. But the removal of threat as one element of political life was a notable change.

Another marked shift was that democratization had not improved UCI leaders' and members' access to political functionaries. Some attributed the stagnant, and even declining, access to the UCI's waning power and finally, its disappearance, but it may additionally have been due to changes among officials and their different perspectives on the relevance of poor colonias to political power.

The UCI had won a measure of prestige and influence during the struggle for democratization. Yet the UCI received few, if any, benefits from the democratic transition. Although the PAN administrations are not considered to be as corrupt as were the PRI ones, the optimism and excitement of the transition was short-lived. By 2004, Cerro del Cuatro residents were less interested in democratic transition than they were in completing the installation of urban services that functioned reliably.

Over the organization's history, UCI leaders worked to obtain urban services to resolve their constituents' needs, but they used those efforts as the political medium to point out the corruption of the existing political process and the benefits that democracy would bring. SEDOC pushed democratization, as did many of the NGOs with which the UCI forged ties. With the formal democratic transition, achieved through PAN victories in Jalisco in 1995 and nationwide in 2000, a new political analysis came into play. Despite the contributions of popular organizations like the UCI to the process of democratic politics, many organizers pursued new strategies to attain political influence. In the wake of the electoral and strategic change, the UCI and the residents of Cerro del Cuatro were left more politically isolated than they had ever been. Democratization failed to ameliorate the material hardships of the urban poor on Cerro del Cuatro; it also left them with fewer allies and less access to formal political power.

What does the fourteen-year experience of the UCI tell us about the politics of the urban poor and the strategy of democratization? How can we understand the way neoliberal economics influences politics among neighborhood groups like the UCI and their supporters? Finally, what does this experience tell us about the much-discussed civil society? I turn to these questions in the next chapter.

8

DEMOCRATIZATION, CIVIL SOCIETY, AND CLASS CONFLICT

I returned to Guadalajara for a brief stay, en route to a new research project, in late June 2006. Visiting with Hermano Javier and Tito, it was apparent that their lives and Cerro del Cuatro had changed little. Both men thought the upcoming presidential election would bring the presidency of the leftist candidate and former Mexico City mayor, Andrés Manuel López Obrador. It had been a rough campaign, with López Obrador gaining support early as the result of politically generated legal wrangles with the federal government and popular disillusion with the administration of President Vicente Fox. In the spring, López Obrador had possessed a wide margin in the polls and appeared poised for an easy win. However, since then, his margin had slipped precipitously until he and PAN candidate Felipe Calderón were running almost even in the polls. Tito, again working as an election official, expected fierce partisan reaction regardless of the election outcome.

In my hotel room, packing to leave while listening to the television, I heard one of the reasons that López Obrador's election no longer seemed assured. Several commercials warned that a López Obrador victory would be disastrous. López Obrador would be a catastrophe for Mexico, according to the commercials' strident language. References to his purported mentor, Venezuelan President Hugo Chavez, were designed to make the point that if elected, López Obrador would be a populist dictator. Corporate-financed attacks had done their best to demonize the leftist candidate.[1]

On July 2, 2006, the Mexican presidential elections were held, and Felipe Calderón of the PAN was declared the apparent winner of the quick vote count.

---

1. López Obrador was the candidate of a coalition made up of the PRD, the Worker's Party (Partido del Trabajo), and the Convergencia de Organizaciones Civiles para la Democracia, or Convergencia, a coalition of NGOs focused on democracy that helped to create the Alianza Cívica.

But in the wake of election results showing them less than a quarter-of-a-million votes apart, both Calderón and López Obrador declared victory. The PRD organized weeks of protest and paralyzed Mexico City's downtown. Hundreds of thousands of protesters took to the streets from early July to mid-September. The PRD leveled charges of fraud, ranging from election officials burning ballots or throwing them in the garbage, to President Fox's active and illegal campaigning for the PAN, to the use of the federal welfare program Oportunidades to provide patronage in exchange for votes for the PAN candidate.[2] The protests reached from the streets into the Chamber of Deputies, when PRD Senators and Deputies disrupted President Fox's final state of the union speech and raucously called for a full recount of the vote. The Federal Election Tribunal examined the elections and accusations, and on September 5 issued its report. The Tribunal agreed there had been substantial voting irregularities, yet it declared Felipe Calderón to be the president-elect.

López Obrador's supporters remained in the streets until September 16, Mexican Independence Day, when they held a National Democratic Convention. Despite the mass turnout, the strategic decisions regarding further resistance were made by the ruling members of the coalition that had sponsored López Obrador's election. These groups declared López Obrador the "legitimate president of Mexico," and he assumed the leadership of a "shadow presidency." Once these decisions were made, the mass demonstrations were demobilized.

The economic policy of Felipe Calderón's presidency has followed the mold of its PAN and PRI predecessors. Former advisers from the Fox, Zedillo, and Salinas administrations were appointed to the cabinet, including the attorney general and the secretaries of the economy, communication and transportation, labor, and the interior.

Further indications that the Mexican government will continue to follow the neoliberal path came in January 2007, when unions, peasant organizations, and leftist parties converged on Mexico City to protest the 66 percent increase in corn prices that had occurred in just the first two months of Calderón's presidency. The surging tortilla prices, the staple of Mexican diet, especially drove the protests. Many linked the price hikes to increased demand in the United

---

2. Analysis by the Center for Economic and Policy Research substantiated charges of voting irregularities, including a widespread vote-count discrepancies and a tendency to underreport PRD votes. Without accusing anyone of outright fraud, the analysis suggests that the variety and extent of irregularities demonstrated a need for a full recount (Weisbrot, Sandoval, and Paredes-Drouet 2006). The Federal Election Tribunal refused a full recount in its September ruling in which Calderón was declared the winner.

States for corn-based ethanol, which had driven up the price of U.S.-grown corn, which now makes up about 25 percent of all corn sold in Mexico. This demonstrates that Mexico's position in the global economy continues to have grave consequences for economic well-being of Mexicans (Malkin 2007).

Whether López Obrador's shadow presidency will reinvigorate popular mobilization during Calderón's term in office is as yet unclear. Will we soon begin to hear that Mexican civil society has reemerged? We do not now have the answer to that question. We do know, however, that democratization in Mexico appears to have brought fierce partisan fights and all-too-familiar accusations of electoral fraud. Given the makeup of Calderón's cabinet, we also know the Mexican government remains firmly committed to the path of neoliberal economic globalization. The tortilla protests and other indications of ongoing inequality tell us that neoliberal policies and democratization have not addressed the needs of Mexico's poor and working class. The history of the UCI offers similar evidence.

The story of the UCI reveals that this popular organization worked on political issues that emerged from both its immediate locale and its national context. The UCI's history allows us to examine how the political economy of austerity influenced patron-client relations on Cerro del Cuatro. Austerity policies, one of the most consistent manifestations in the developing world of economic globalization, undercut the logic of clientelism for several reasons. One is that austerity policies play few favorites in determining which sectors of society will be harmed. Another reason is that the neoliberal imperative to shrink the state diminishes the resources that patrons rely on to elicit support.

The variety of actors that responded to the austerity measures and other abuses of the PRI state might be viewed as a clear-cut case of the often-discussed activity of civil society. This book has illustrated that a more careful empirical and conceptual examination of civil society—one that attempts to disaggregate its parts—is needed.

AUSTERITY AND CLIENTELISM

Clientelism relies on an exchange between more powerful state and party patrons and less powerful systemic supporters. Patrons offer a measure of security and material progress to clients, and in turn, clients legitimate the patron's rule by providing their support. Because clientelism is often place-based, patrons provide material goods that vary depending on the clients' needs and often their location.

The goods can include building lots, urban or social services, and jobs. The level of consolidation of the community determines what patronage is most useful for eliciting support.

Affective ties, through loyalty to individual brokers or parties, remain important elements of patron-client relations (Auyero 1999), but those ties are secondary to material benefits in generating support (Roniger and Günes-Ayata 1994). When a political economy of austerity limits patronage, affective ties are insufficient to maintain the patron-client relationship.

Thus, neoliberal globalization disrupts the logic of clientelism because a political economy of austerity pressures the state to limit social welfare spending, a key patronage resource. This is the context that has defined state-society relations in the developing world from the 1980s until today. On Cerro del Cuatro, the paucity of benefits helped an alternative political response emerge. When coupled with the ideological resource of liberation theology and the support of powerful actors, the limitation of resources undercut the logic of clientelism. Why be a client when patronage is not forthcoming, when the patron acts in a corrupt manner, and when powerful supporters demonstrate the possibilities of pursuing different kinds of political action?

Thus, the experience of the UCI and its nongovernmental allies demonstrates a change in the politics of the urban poor. The UCI, responding to hardships rooted in neoliberalism and exploding urbanization, pursued both new political activity and new strategies. In so doing, they resisted the fragmentation, isolation, and a focus on the local, which is so characteristic of clientelist neighborhood politics in Mexico and elsewhere. The UCI's focus on democratization brought them into common struggle with other political actors and integrated them into a successful movement that has substantially changed formal politics in Mexico.

SEDOC's presence on Cerro del Cuatro helped the UCI combat clientelism, yet the interactions between these organizations demonstrated differential power in the relationship. It is incorrect to characterize this relationship as clientelistic, because resources were shared in a different manner and used for a different purpose. The relationship did create a dependency, however, and a political process that, while not clientelistic, was not fully independent either. The UCI's reliance on powerful figures in SEDOC led the leaders of the neighborhood organization to make questionable policy choices that diminished popular support.

As others have demonstrated, Mexico's democratization could not have been achieved without the participation, voice, and mass pressure of the urban popular movement (Haber 2006). The democratization struggle coalesced similar and dissimilar groups into a cross-class movement that successfully demanded and won change in formal democratic representation. In the Guadalajara Metropolitan Zone, the UCI played an important role in that effort.

Yet after the UCI was integrated into the cross-class movement and some measure of victory was won, the democratization movement diverged from mass mobilization to incorporation within the new political landscape. With the transition, many of the UCI's networks dissolved. Neither the Jesuits, nor the secular NGOs with whom the UCI worked, remained at the UCI's side. The UCI had provided a mass base that helped its allies achieve democratization and, in turn, the NGOs aided the UCI in winning urban services and, generally, in gaining access to those in power. Access for the organized poor has not improved with democratization, nor has their material well-being. Instead, the quality of life for residents in Cerro del Cuatro has stagnated, and their access to elected officials has decreased.

Indeed, formal democratization has demonstrated the mutability of clientelism (Gay 2006; Fox 1994). On Cerro del Cuatro, new partisan efforts have followed the democratic transition. The new clientelism is less powerful and possesses fewer resources, as does the state in general. Yet for some of the organized poor, the new clientelist structures remain a viable solution to some of their problems.

The story of the UCI demonstrates the mutability of clientelism in other ways as well. The Solidaridad effort to incorporate and co-opt urban power contenders offers an example. The fight between local and federal Solidaridad reveals the attempt to rebuild centralized power even at the expense of local brokers. This suggests that diminishing patronage may split complementary patrons, forcing them to compete for resources. Patron-client politics builds on a hierarchy of expectations of patronage delivery and allegiance. Austerity policies may destabilize politics built on clientelism by destroying vertical links between the state and local brokers and patrons, especially during periods when there are viable independent political alternatives. Breaking links in that chain may provide opportunities for alternative politics to emerge. The UCI and SEDOC achieved that breach for a period on Cerro del Cuatro.

The political economy of austerity, then, had important influences on clientelism as a mode of control. For some sectors, the imposition of austerity simultaneously provided political mobilizing opportunities while it heightened material hardships. Such an outcome is by no means inevitable. The use of Solidaridad resources makes it clear that how clientelism will change is contingent on the distribution of resources, even when they have been reduced. Reducing resources does not necessarily create political opportunities. In contrast, when austerity leads to decreased availability of patronage, patrons may be able to consolidate their power if they are still the most likely source for the satisfaction of urban needs.

Several other resources must be present to challenge a state diminished in power by neoliberal policy. An alternative political claim requires an affective or ideological component, as social-movement-framing analysts have emphasized. New collective-action frames may be especially powerful when old ones prove empty. Thus, the emergence of liberation theology was especially useful when the PRI betrayed its revolutionary populist rhetoric by adopting neoliberal policies.

Powerful allies are another important resource facilitating an independent challenge. Even if they do not control the same level of material resources that previous patrons did, these allies may instead possess other ways to aid mobilization. SEDOC had a variety of resources, including money, education, and connections to the government, that were critical to the independent challenge on Cerro del Cuatro.

We can understand some of the changes in urban politics in Mexico by returning to Alejandro Portes's (1972) structural analysis of comparative struggles of the urban poor. During the long-ago debate about whether the poor were marginal to politics or were, instead, marginalized, Portes focused on how political systems structured the level and kind of participation of the urban poor. Far from being powerless, the urban poor always expressed agency with their political demands. Yet the process by which the poor pursued their needs was structurally limited by existing political and economic systems. With the limitations that neoliberalism has imposed on state domestic policy prerogatives, a different set of structural constraints now operate. In the case of Cerro del Cuatro, neoliberalism created opportunities for independent political organizing. Again, there is nothing inevitable about this direction of change. In other extended periods of neoliberal adjustment, opportunities for alternative political organizing may instead close, as households are forced to seek other strategies for survival rather than pursuing social change.

Austerity policies in Mexico have had wide effects, creating new coalition partners for neighborhood organizations seeking non-clientelist redress of material needs. What is new is not the "emergence" of civil society. Instead, civil-society actors have been evident throughout the struggles. However, in places like the streets of Cerro del Cuatro, under a globalized political economy, civil society now articulates in novel ways. New political contacts were driven, I have argued, by the cross-class immiseration resulting from two decades of neoliberal policies. Thus, organized actors worked together in ways that challenged the logical underpinnings of clientelist control, making a temporary alliance as the democratization movement.

DEMOCRATIZATION AS STRATEGY

It is important to note changes in urban politics, but I have emphasized that the changes in process have not been matched by changes in product, at least on Cerro del Cuatro. The UCI's participation in the democratization movement helped to heighten its profile and increase the networks on which it could rely. In turn, popular organizations like the UCI greatly benefited the democratization movement. Among other things, these organizations supplied the movement with the mass pressure, above and beyond the efforts of political parties, and offered an array of locales of contention. Yet the story of the UCI suggests that we ought to examine the utility of democratization as a strategy. One question is whether democratization can address the damages inflicted by neoliberalism. Another question is what the democratization strategy tells us about civil society.

Neoliberal policy makers suggest that democratization will increase material prosperity. In that view, democratic process allows greater freedom to act both politically and economically. Open markets will increase production and consumption, efficiency will increase, and employment growth will follow. Household incomes will rise with new employment, which of course will continue to drive consumption that will then repeat the whole happy cycle. Where economic expansion has accompanied neoliberal policy, however, the fruits have not been shared equally. The result has been burgeoning wealth for the few and immiseration for the many (Portes and Hoffman 2003).

The experiences of Cerro del Cuatro residents suggest that democratization's promise has remained unfulfilled because neoliberalism has diminished the Mexican state's ability to satisfy popular demands. In the economic arena, rather than creating mechanisms for nation-states to satisfy the material needs of their constituencies, neoliberal policy makers have provided a strict model that states must follow that decreases domestic policy-making prerogatives. In the political arena, democratization has failed to develop avenues to pressure for the alleviation of the economic harm that is being done. In terms of ideology, neoliberalism argues that private actors, not the state, should provide for those unable to avail themselves of the new global economy.

In Guadalajara, one clear result of democratization has been a change in the field of struggle. As multiple informants made clear, civil-society groups removed themselves from Cerro del Cuatro as formal democratic change progressed. The impact on the UCI was substantial. The organization's access to policy makers diminished, and its allies began to pursue new struggles in the newly democratized environment. The decline of the UCI and the removal of the links between actors also limited the use of protest as a pressure mechanism.

This decline in protest is a tactical mistake for the democratization movement. Similar errors followed the activity of poor people's movements in the United States, as Frances Fox Piven and Richard Cloward (1977) painstakingly documented. Piven and Cloward argued that the only means to secure real benefits is through disruptive protest, and that poor people's only weapon is the threat to withhold their participation in society. The shift to organized contestation often chills movement activity, as poor people's efforts to gain power must be rooted in the ability to disrupt the economy. Organizations play a mollifying role, becoming co-opted by new organizational rules of internal discipline, and they transform into tools of elite control, rather than expressions of mass dissent. Piven and Cloward also argued that channeling popular protest into electoral venues co-opts leaders, quieted calls for greater economic inclusion, and generated internal power struggles in the place of the pursuit of constituents' agendas. The history of the PRD, from 1989 until the 2006 mobilizations denouncing Andrés Manuel López Obrador's defeat, appears to confirm this line of argument.[3]

Despite important differences in context, Piven and Cloward's work is suggestive for the Mexican strategy of democratization. Times of governmental transition are exactly the moments when disruptive action is most threatening, and so such actions may exact even more concessions. At these moments, organizational focus on working within the electoral system may be counterproductive, as this will curb movement militancy just when elites are more likely to compromise. The abandonment of mass mobilization suggests that the democratization movement incorporated too readily within a system that may undermine demand making. Organizations may play an increasingly important role in political contention, but the value of disruption has not diminished.

3. The question of organization that Piven and Cloward raise must be reevaluated in the political and economic context of globalization. Globalization has made political organizing more complex for all movements, given the multiple roots of injustice against which people protest. Additionally, globalization has contributed a shifting set of actors that protestors must target, and it has altered the relationships between those actors and national states. Multinational corporations' threat of exit, for example, has increased with the opening of new labor markets and huge advances in communication and transportation technology. In the wake of these changes, movements face a need to act beyond their boundaries, which, for many struggles, may increase the importance of formal organization.

The experience of the UCI and its allies demonstrate that some of the tactics chosen by the democratization movement were problematic. Indeed, as a tactic to resist neoliberal policies, democratization itself may be given too much priority. In the context of Mexico's political legacy of clientelism and corporatism, the high priority placed on strategies that focus on political inclusion is logical. Political inclusion, however, does not necessarily address the damage inflicted by neoliberal policies. As Elizabeth Jelin states, "The transition to democracy brings with it confusion and bewilderment. A new space opens up for democratic discourse, for elections and participation. . . . Indeed, there is a double discourse: a discourse of (political) participation and a non-discourse of economic exclusion" (1997, 83). Jelin further articulates the questionable relationship between democracy and basic needs: "The issue is a classic: Can there be political democracy without guaranteeing a basic minimum level of economic well-being? . . . Can people enjoy their civil and political rights if they do not have access to the basic conditions (eliminating hunger and pain, but also access to the relevant information) that ensure the possibility of exercising such rights?" (1997, 80).

In fetishizing democracy, we commit analytical errors similar to those that Karl Polanyi (2001) pointed out. Those who espouse the free market emphasize the economic over all other spheres of human life; those who advocate for democratization overemphasize the political. Both foci ignore the contradictions between the rhetoric of inclusive democratization and the exclusionary reality of the global economy. Norbert Lechner points out Polanyi's warning about the dangers of privileging of the market over other social institutions, and he sees tragedy and irony in the neoliberal project which "in pursuit of imposing in unrestrained fashion the rationality of the market, the neoliberal strategy seeks to withdraw the economy from all processes of democratic decision making" (1998, 29).

The political aim of neoliberalism is exclusion of the state from the economy. The objective of democratization is to enhance citizens' influence over the state. But if the state continues to be pressured to abandon the economy to "market forces," democratizing is unlikely to alleviate the neoliberal injuries, since gaining access to decision makers means little when they barely control the economy. The current neoliberal trajectory thus calls into question the strategy of gaining influence over the state in order to address economic hardships. Terry Karl (2000) notes the clear sharpening of inequality in Latin America that has occurred concurrently with increased democratization. Even more ironically, a democratization process lacking any but formal channels to articulate popular demands may lessen political access for those who once relied on clientelist networks to voice their needs. Ongoing poverty and diminished political access for the poor force us to look critically at democratization as a strategy of inclusion.

Governments pressured by neoliberal globalization may find that political inclusion is the easiest movement strategy to confront. Creating an image of increased political access may undercut the impetus for more significant economic changes needed to address poverty. Focusing on budgetary transparency, for example, directs opposition attention to bureaucratic processes of budget design. Yet an overemphasis on transparency may displace a struggle over governmental spending priorities and how they have been defined by neoliberal imperatives. Inclusion into a limited discussion of bureaucratic process can channel opposition groups away from posing more significant challenges to government policy. Absent such a challenge, little resistance can be made to a global system that has impoverished so many, and with which national governments have been complicit. Cleaning up politics and creating structures of potential political representation are important, but these strategies may not expand resource availability. Democracy is a necessary condition to address Mexico's ills, but it is clearly insufficient to provide a cure.[4] Economic policy that provides more citizens with a better quality of life by addressing urban service needs, education, health care, and higher wages must accompany formal democratization. So far, neoliberal democratization has provided exactly the opposite in Mexico and elsewhere.

More generally, democratization as the remedy for neoliberalism is a problematic strategy given current definitions of democratic politics. Democratization cannot challenge neoliberalism while conceptions of economic and political participation remain segregated. With only political democratization on the table and under the hegemonic influence of neoliberal thought, there is little impetus for economic redistribution. Limiting choice in this way allows preexisting power holders to dominate decision making.

Indeed, formal democratization is consistent with neoliberalism. Democratization of formal institutions does not challenge class rule nor does it eradicate class-based inequalities. When we widen participation and make elections fairer, many hope that economic opportunities will grow. But there is nothing intrinsic to democracy that controls the abuses of privilege; privilege may instead be readily perpetuated. The real challenge to neoliberalism will come from pressing not just political inclusion but also for economic inclusion.

---

4. I am grateful to Philip Oxhorn for his comments on these issues.

THE STRATA OF CIVIL SOCIETY

I have argued throughout this book that the story of the UCI and SEDOC reveals some of the basic characteristics of civil society. My analysis suggests that—rather than weakness or strength, emergence or unification—the defining characteristic of civil society is its division. When we examine social movements, unions, NGOs, or other groups acting in concert, I suggest that we need to look more carefully in order to understand how individual organizations have joined forces. In this case study, the two allied organizations were very different in terms of class, status, and legitimacy. That resulting hierarchy led to differential power within the coalition and manifested in decision making that addressed one group's interests more than those of the other. SEDOC's and the UCI's original focus on obtaining basic infrastructure for the Cerro del Cuatro residents was derailed by the adoption of an electoral strategy. The unity of civil society in this case, and I suggest in others, proved to be illusory and temporary.

Two basic questions help us recognize the stratification in civil society: What is politics for? And how is politics different for different groups? The experience of UCI and SEDOC tell us that the divisions within civil society make the political demands of various groups diverge dramatically. Groups increasingly unite because of shared injuries stemming from globalization, but that does not erase or even diminish their class and status differences. Instead, the injuries differ depending on the location of a group's stratum, whether that be defined by class or another collective identity. Groups may unite around shared injuries, but the specifics of those injuries for each group—as well as the differences in resources and power available to them—result in distinct experiences of globalization. Such differences affect groups' abilities to unify in the struggle against globalization or other shared hardships.

When coalesced groups (another way to say civil society) comprise organizations with different levels of social power, how does that influence the setting of goals? How are the goals of coalesced groups influenced when they are made up of organizations with different levels of social power? Shared injuries do not neatly translate into the equivalence of demands nor into the equal articulation of those demands. Civil society is stratified in terms of the power of its constituent actors; the coalescence of these actors does not lessen their differences. The examination of the UCI and its allies demonstrates that despite the seemingly inclusionary label of "civil society," the ways in which organized groups are stratified, by class, education, and other status markers, defines the ways in which they work together in coalesced efforts. In this case, the stratified power of the coalesced actors explains why certain strategies were followed to the detriment of one organization.

Observing the strata of civil society forces us to recognize the overreach of civil-society analysis. Coalitions of organized groups, with varied levels of power and varied demands, must be examined for the fault lines these relationships reveal. In fact, the way such coalitions are lauded for their confrontations with unjust power, and the kind of romantic analysis we have engaged in for decades, papers over potential fault lines in a way that allows us to ignore their stratified layers.

The influential literature detailing both clientelist and independent neighborhood activity demonstrates the overreach of civil-society analysis. Whether demands are made deferentially, and ultimately bolster the state, or made uncompromisingly, in language of citizenship that challenges the state, depends on many factors: material needs; the history of community politics; and the presence of parties, patrons, and alternatives, to name just a few. Such differences influence the political processes of separate communities that possess similar class and status backgrounds. Thus, potential political activity of groups defined by similar class and status will differ widely given the presence or absence of these factors.

If the political activity of neighborhood groups of largely similar background can differ to such a great extent, the political activity of dissimilar actors is likely to diverge even more. The differences between neighborhood groups and other actors included under the label of civil society are substantial. When we label the united action of groups as "civil society," despite their divergence in class and status, we ignore the likelihood that these long-lasting differences may be as important as more fleeting similarities in political agenda. Our search for similarity, both empirical and theoretical, imposes a false unity, which blinds us to organizational and constituent dynamics that hold important implications for how organized groups work together.

SEDOC's and UCI's interests diverged on the electoral question. More broadly, different groups are posed to exploit formal democratization to different degrees. Civil society actors make varied demands on political institutions, not all of which can be addressed by greater formal processes of democratic governance. Many activists in the front lines of the democratic struggle demand not just human rights but also economic rights, not just freedom from repression and political violence but also access to commodities that have traditionally been exchanged for support of clientelist and corporatist systems. Many movement supporters, if UCI's experience is any indication, wanted democratic governments to supply more democratically distributed goods. Differences among the actors manifest in the expression of different needs and design of strategy. Examining these differences provides answers to my question about the purpose of politics for these diverse groups. But these differences are obscured if such groups remain undifferentiated in our analysis.

Our focus on civil society may also lead us to a false belief that states and civil society must be in opposition. This has multiple roots (see Chapter 2): post–Cold War triumphalism; the neoliberal position that states cannot resolve what are cast as "market problems"; and the complicity of states in the creation of neoliberal global economy and the injury it inflicts. This perspective creates a false dualism, ignoring the fact that a mobilized citizenry is one of the few reasons that states pursue progressive policies. Citizen groups must push states, but the states can then take progressive stances in a way that reciprocally strengthens both actors. We err in assuming that the state is, or must be, the enemy of a mobilized citizenry. It can be—it need not be. The demands of a mobilized citizenry can strengthen states so that they can gain more leverage in a global system. This dynamic, I would argue, helps explain the "pink tide" in Latin America. Collective action condemning austerity policies in separate nations led to electoral changes in Venezuela, Brazil, Argentina, and Ecuador. Transition in these governments may now provide regional leverage as these nations renegotiate the demands of the global economy.

The concept of civil society is particularly problematic when addressing hardships imposed by class. As Steffan Lindberg and Árni Sverrisson comment, "class divisions, the controversies and conflicts they create, and their negotiation and settlement are integral elements of 'civil society,' although the self-image and demands of the movements and organizations involved are not necessarily cast in interest group or class terms" (1997, 6). The de-emphasizing of class in civil-society analysis obscures our understanding of the impact of neoliberalism on various sectors. Neoliberalism is, in its essence, a class project (Harvey 2005). As Alejandro Portes and Kelly Hoffman (2003) document, neoliberalism has exacerbated class divisions in Latin America. Leslie Sklair (2001), Miguel Centeno (1994), and Sarah Babb (2001) demonstrate how neoliberalism provides ideological and policy cover for class fragments and institutions that have legitimated the thinning of the state, which has done away with those programs that previously provided poor and working people with a modicum of support that facilitates survival and allowed the middle class to progress. Civil-society analysis obscures the class nature of neoliberal policy.

Civil-society analysis also obscures the nature of the resistance to neoliberalism. Coalitions always pose questions: To what extent are certain goals shared? And which goals are to be given priority? Those issues create further difficulties in forming strategies to achieve the intended social change. When made by a coalition of groups rent by class and status hierarchies, decisions are likely to be based on the differential social power embedded in those hierarchies. Those possessing greater resources, knowledge, expertise, and legitimacy will influence those with less power. A civil-society coalition may hold together, and exert pressure on the state. Yet to fully understand outcomes of state-society conflicts, we must still examine how those organizations work in relation to each other, and whose goals and strategies are given priority.

Such differences are especially salient for the analysis of democratization struggles. Given discourses of shared and increased participation, the expectation may be that such movements should carefully examine differential levels of group power and accommodate those differences in decision-making processes. The democratization movement in Guadalajara, however, demonstrated instead the re-creation of social hierarchy, especially as defined by class.

Portes and Hoffman (2003) allude to a masking of the class project when they pose the puzzle of an absence of class-based response in Latin America. In the wake of such an assaultive class project as neoliberalism, they ask, why are class-based political parties relatively weak? The answer comes, at least in Mexico, in the form of struggle that has emerged. The very fact that multiple groups have been injured creates the possibility of cross-class coalition building. However, in their internal organizational relations, such coalitions run the risk of re-creating, rather than overturning, class-based hierarchy.

In *The Eighteenth Brumaire of Louis Bonaparte,* Karl Marx noted how coalitions of actors with conflicting interests might satisfy the needs of some at the expense of others. Yet recognizing the strata of civil society does not preclude the formation of coalitions as one strategy to pressure states. The very fact that multiple groups suffer harm from neoliberal policies creates the possibility of coalition formation, and coalitions may force substantial change given a constellation of factors. These include the power of coalition partners and the power of state actors. Important also is the form of appeal, and whether an appeal may generalize across disparate social groups. The history of state control over potentially independent actors will affect how coalitions form and their effectiveness in pressing change. The level of hardship and the breadth of its spread also affect the likelihood of coalition formation. All of these factors influence what kinds of coalitions may form, and how effective they may prove to be. Yet the example of SEDOC and the UCI caution us to recognize that coalitions are likely to be temporary and fragment along preexisting strata of class and status.

What constitutes the illusion of civil society to which I refer? First, that somehow civil society can be understood as less stratified than society in general. Examining coalesced groups reveals class and status strata that manifest in strategic decision making. The decisions may demonstrate the choice of strategies that yield differential results for the partners of coalesced groups. If we can overcome our affection for the presumed theoretical unity of civil society, we can better understand differentiation of interests, opportunities, and capacities that exist in groups within a mobilized citizenry.

Second, it is an illusion to believe that a single civil society strategy—for example, democratization or coalition building—will comprehensively address the needs of all sectors at all times. Recognizing the strata of civil society forces us to understand that the successful accomplishment of a single strategy will still yield differential results for different actors. It may be that certain strategies allow certain, more powerful, sectors to retain their privilege while less powerful groups' interests remain unmet. In contrast, other strategies may be able to force the state to make concessions. There is a wide continuum of possible outcomes, and where a specific coalition ends up on that continuum will depend on its makeup and dynamics, as well as on a set of variables stemming from the inter-section of states and the global economy.

Third, it is an illusion to assume that unity and coherence exist in coalitions. That assumption tends to hide genuine and important divisions among coalesced actors. The way civil society works together on shared strategies may build bridges or create fissures, depending on relations among members, compatibility of goals, ability to recognize differential outcomes, and willingness to augment or abandon strategies in the face of different outcomes.

The final illusion is that when united action occurs among groups in civil society, it will be ongoing. The threats to which organized groups respond may indeed be sustained, but the coalitions and alliances are likely to be temporary because the flexibility of state actors allows for a selective response that more readily resolves the concerns of certain strata than others. State flexibility to address the needs of more powerful opposition members fractures the unity of civil society in such a way that systemic legitimacy may be maintained rather than achieving social justice.

The concept of civil society obscures societal difference by assuming that there is a unity among actors, which research denies is the case. Understanding the illusion of civil society highlights the multitude of varying social categories, all of which are identified with structured hierarchies and inequality. My emphasis on the inadequacy of civil-society analysis of neoliberal economics and politics does not mean I want to return to defining class as the master status, above and beyond various other categories. Instead, I emphasize that if we are looking at organized efforts to resist, change, or even overturn hierarchies, we must examine the social bases of those hierarchies. The social basis of the neoliberal project is class. Because neoliberalism is a class project, organized response to that project must be assessed in class terms: how people act from their class positions to resist, implement, or accommodate the class project. Which particular hierarchy penetrates a specific society at a specific time is a case of historical contingency, to be examined within various cases. Certainly, people often act from an intersection of their lived experiences. If we are to understand the roots and emergence of different contentious communities, we have to recognize the many oppressions—race, gender, ethnicity, and others—that characterize current and historical social structures. Understanding the multitude of oppressions and contentions, however, is obscured when we impose the false theoretical unity of civil society.

The concept of civil society has run its course. Civil-society analysis interferes with our understanding of what kinds of conflicts exist, who the constituents of varied groups embroiled in these conflicts are, and the differential results of varied strategies and struggles.

What do we do if we leave the concept of civil society behind? Must we create a concept that acts as a placeholder that will help us recognize the political activity of organized groups that do not fit neatly into the formal democratic arena?[5] I think substituting a new category will, before long, confront us with the same analytic mess that the concept of civil society has. Instead, after years of addiction to the concept of civil society, the analytic change I advocate is a return to specificity. If labor proves to be the locus of resistance and alternative policy, we examine labor. If ethnic resistance proves to be the locus of resistance in another society, we examine ethnic movements as they pose a challenge to domination. Clearly, we must look at the complex intersections of these structured inequalities—how people experience their lives as members of multiple groups, often disadvantaged in layered and compounded ways. The hardships imposed by structurally disadvantaged positions, and the subsequent ways that resistance is generated and alternatives are articulated, depend on aggrieved social groups' resources, culture, power, allies, and so forth. The more we understand these differences, the better placed we will be to understand such struggles.

I do not argue that no shared bases of solidarity exist, or that groups must always clash during common work. Instead, I believe the places and issues on

5. I am grateful to Saskia Sassen and Fred Block for posing these questions.

which we can forge common agendas must be understood through careful examination of real moments of domination. These will be more effective in laying foundations for alliances than an illusory imposition of unity. Mobilized citizens, organized in a variety of forms, bring about social change. But to trace, understand, and aid these groups, we have to understand their actions and potential in terms specific to them and the systems against which they struggle.

References

Adams, Jacqueline. 1998. "The Wrongs of Reciprocity: Fieldwork Among Chilean Working-Class Women." *Journal of Contemporary Ethnography* 27, no. 2: 219–41.

Aguilar Camín, Héctor, and Lorenzo Meyer. 1993. *In the Shadow of the Mexican Revolution.* Austin: University of Texas Press.

Alarcón, Diana. 2003. "Income Distribution and Poverty Alleviation in Mexico: A Comparative Analysis." In Middlebrook and Zepeda 2003.

Alianza Cívica de Jalisco. 1992. *Informe de la observación electoral en Jalisco.* Guadalajara: Alianza Cívica.

Almond, Gabriel, and Sidney Verba. 1963. *The Civic Culture.* Princeton: Princeton University Press.

Alvarez, Sonia, Evelina Dagnino, and Arturo Escobar. 1998. *Cultures of Politics, Politics of Cultures: Re-visioning Latin American Social Movements.* Boulder, Colo.: Westview Press.

Amsden, Alice. 1985. "The State and Taiwan's Economic Development." In *Bringing the State Back In,* ed. Peter B. Evans, Dietrich Rueschemeyer, and Theda Skocpol. New York: Cambridge University Press.

Austin Memorandum. 1994. "The Austin Memorandum on the Reform of Article 27 and Its Impact upon the Urbanization of the Ejido in Mexico." *Bulletin of Latin American Research* 13, no. 3: 327–35.

Auyero, Javier. 1999. "From the Client's Point(s) of View: How Poor People Perceive and Evaluate Political Clientelism." *Theory and Society* 28, no. 2: 297–334.

Avritzer, Leonardo. 2006. "Civil Society in Latin America in the Twenty-first Century: Between Democratic Deepening, Social Fragmentation, and State Crisis." In Feinberg, Waisman, and Zamosc 2006.

Ayuntamiento de Guadalajara. 2003. *Anuario socioeconómico y demográfico de Guadalajara, 2002.* Guadalajara: Ayuntamiento de Guadalajara.

Aziz Nassif, Alberto. 2001. "Alternation and Change: The Case of Chihuahua." In Middlebrook 2001.

Babb, Sarah. 2001. *Managing Mexico: Economists from Nationalism to Neoliberalism.* Princeton: Princeton University Press.

Baer, Delal. 1990. "Electoral Trends." In *Prospects for Democracy in Mexico,* ed. George W. Grayson. New Brunswick, N.J.: Transaction Publishers.

Bailey, John, and Jennifer Boone. 1994. "National Solidarity: A Summary of Program Elements." In Cornelius, Craig, and Fox 1994.

Ballinas, Victor. 1994. "Se realizaron más de 500 mil obras mediante PRONASOL: Rojas." *La Jornada,* September 20.

Barry, Tom. 1992. *Mexico*. Albuquerque, N.M.: Inter-Hemispheric Education Resource Center.

Bellah, Robert. 2000. "The Good Society: We Live Through Our Institutions." In *The Essential Civil Society Reader*, ed. Don Eberly. Boulder, Colo.: Rowman and Littlefield.

Berrueto Pruneda, Federico. 1994. "1994: Nueva geografía electoral." *Voz y Voto* 20 (October): 44–52.

Berryman, Philip. 1987. *Liberation Theology*. New York: Pantheon.

Blair, Harry. 1997. "Donors, Democratisation, and Civil Society: Relating Theory to Practice." In *NGOs, States, and Donors: Too Close for Comfort?* ed. David Hulme and Michael Edwards. London: Macmillan.

Boltvinik, Julio. 2003. "Welfare, Inequality, and Poverty in Mexico, 1979–2000." In Middlebrook and Zepeda 2003.

Broad, Robin. 2002. *Global Backlash: Citizen Initiatives for a Just World Economy*. Boulder, Colo.: Rowman and Littlefield.

Bruhn, Kathleen. 1997. *Taking on Goliath: The Emergence of a New Left Party and the Struggle for Democracy in Mexico*. University Park: Pennsylvania State University Press.

Camp, Roderic. 1993. *Politics in Mexico*. New York: Oxford University Press.

———. 2007. *Politics in Mexico: The Democratic Consolidation*. 5th ed. New York: Oxford University Press.

Campbell, John L., and Ove K. Pederson, eds. 2001. *The Rise of Neoliberalism and Institutional Analysis*. Princeton: Princeton University Press.

Carr, Barry. 1986. "The Mexican Left, the Popular Movements, and the Politics of Austerity, 1982–1985." In *The Mexican Left, the Popular Movements, and the Politics of Austerity*, ed. Barry Carr and Ricardo Anzaldúa Montoya. La Jolla: Center for U.S.-Mexican Studies, University of California, San Diego.

Castañeda, Jorge. 1993. *Utopia Unarmed: The Latin American Left After the Cold War*. New York: Vintage Books.

Castells, Manuel. 1983. *The City and the Grassroots*. Berkeley and Los Angeles: University of California Press.

Centeno, Miguel Angel. 1997. *Democracy Within Reason: Technocratic Revolution in Mexico*. 2nd ed. University Park: Pennsylvania State University Press.

Clark, Janine A., and Remonda B. Kleinberg. 2000. "Introduction: The Impact of Economic Reform on Civil Society, Popular Participation, and Democratization in the Developing World." In Kleinberg and Clark 2000.

Cohen, Jean, and Andrew Arato. 1992. *Civil Society and Political Theory*. Cambridge, Mass.: MIT Press.

Colclough, Christopher. 1991. "Structuralism Versus Neoliberalism: An Introduction." In *States or Markets? Neoliberalism and the Development Policy Debate*, ed. Christopher Colclough and James Manor. Oxford: Clarendon Press.

Consejo Electoral de Estado de Jalisco. 2003. *Votación emitida en distritos*. Guadalajara: CEEJ.

Cornelius, Wayne. 1975. *Politics and the Migrant Poor in Mexico City*. Stanford, Calif.: Stanford University Press.

———. 1999. "Subnational Politics and Democratization: Tensions Between Center and Periphery in the Mexican Political System." In *Subnational Politics and Democratization in Mexico*, ed. Wayne Cornelius, Todd A. Eisenstadt, and Jane Hindley. La Jolla: Center for U.S.-Mexican Studies, University of California, San Diego.

Cornelius, Wayne A., and Ann L. Craig. 1991. *The Mexican Political System in Transition.* La Jolla: Center for U.S.-Mexican Relations, University of California, San Diego.

Cornelius, Wayne A., Ann L. Craig, and Jonathan Fox, eds. 1994. *Transforming State-Society Relations in Mexico: The National Solidarity Strategy.* La Jolla: Center for U.S.-Mexican Studies, University of California, San Diego.

Cornelius, Wayne A., J. Gentleman, and P. H. Smith, eds. 1989. *Mexico's Alternative Political Futures.* La Jolla, Calif.: Center for U.S.-Mexican Studies, University of California, San Diego.

Correa, Guillermo. 1991. "Alcaldes no priístas dicen que se les hace a un lado del PRONASOL." *Proceso* 776, September 16.

Corro, Salvador. 1991. "PRONASOL, el instrumento de rescate de posiciones e imagen presidencial." *Proceso* 782, October 28.

Covarrubias, Ana Cristina. 1994. "Hubo Fraude?" *Voz y Voto* 20 (October): 22–27.

Dagnino, Evelina. 1998. "Culture, Citizenship, and Democracy: Changing Discourses and Practices of the Latin American Left." In Alvarez, Dagnino, and Escobar 1998.

Dauvergne, Peter. 1998. "Corporate Power in the Forests of the Solomon Islands." *Pacific Affairs* 71, no. 4: 524–38.

de la Peña, Sofia. 1991. "Los significados de la participación en la Unión de Colonos Independientes del Cerro del Cuatro (UCI-C4)." Guadalajara: EDOC; ITESO. Photocopy.

del Castillo, Agustín. 1994. "Expropriación, 'lo mejor' para el Cerro del Cuatro." *Siglo 21,* February 24.

de León Arias, Adrián. 1988. "La gran industria y el desarollo industrial." In *Crecimiento industrial y manufacturero, 1940–1980,* ed. Rogelio Luna, Cristina Padilla, Adrián de León, and Jesús Arroyo. Vol. 13 of *Jalisco desde la Revolución.* Guadalajara: Gobierno de Jalisco/Universidad de Guadalajara.

Delgado, Gary. 1986. *Organizing the Movement: The Roots and Growth of ACORN.* Philadelphia: Temple University Press.

Diamond, Larry, Jonathan Hartlyn, and Juan Linz. 1999. "Introduction: Politics, Society, and Democracy in Latin America." In *Democracy in Developing Countries: Latin America,* 2nd ed., ed. Larry Diamond, Jonathan Hartlyn, Juan Linz, and Seymour Martin Lipset. Boulder, Colo.: Lynne Rienner.

Díaz Betancourt, José. 1993. "La Liconsa 118 es oficina del PRI." *Siglo 21,* January 18.

Díaz-Cayeros, Alberto. 2004. "Decentralization, Democratization, and Federalism in Mexico." In *Dilemmas of Political Change in Mexico,* ed. Kevin Middlebrook. La Jolla: Center for U.S.-Mexican Studies, University of California, San Diego.

Dresser, Denise. 1991. *Neopopulist Solutions to Neoliberal Problems: Mexico's National Solidarity Program.* La Jolla: Center for U.S.-Mexican Studies, University of California, San Diego.

———. 1994. "Bringing the Poor Back In: National Solidarity as a Strategy of Regime Legitimation." In Cornelius, Craig, and Fox 1994.

Dussel Peters, Enrique. 2000. *Polarizing Mexico: The Impact of Liberalization Strategy.* Boulder, Colo.: Lynne Rienner.

Eberly, Don. 2000. *The Essential Civil Society Reader.* Boulder, Colo.: Rowman and Littlefield.

Eckstein, Susan. 1988. *The Poverty of Revolution: The State and the Urban Poor in Mexico.* Princeton: Princeton University Press.

Economist Intelligence Unit. 2002. *Country Profile: Mexico.* London: EIU.

Eisentadt, Todd. 2004. *Courting Democracy in Mexico: Party Strategies and Electoral Institutions.* New York: Cambridge University Press.

Elshtain, Jean Bethke. 2000. "Democracy on Trial: The Role of Civil Society in Sustaining Democratic Values." In Eberly 2000.

Evrensel, Ayse Y. 2002. "Effectiveness of IMF-Supported Stabilization Programs in Developing Countries." *Journal of International Money and Finance* 21, no. 5: 565–87.

Fagen, Richard, and William S. Tuohy. 1972. *Politics and Privilege in a Mexican City*. Stanford, Calif.: Stanford University Press.

Feinberg, Richard, Carlos H. Waisman, and Leon Zamosc, eds. 2006. *Civil Society and Democracy in Latin America*. New York: Palgrave.

Fernández-Kelly, Patricia, and Jon Shefner, eds. 2006. *Out of the Shadows: Political Action and the Informal Economy in Latin America*. University Park: Pennsylvania State University Press.

Fox, Jonathan. 1994a. "Targeting the Poorest: The Role of the National Indigenous Institute in Mexico's Solidarity Program." In Cornelius, Craig, and Fox 1994.

———. 1994b. "The Difficult Transition from Clientelism to Citizenship: Lessons from Mexico." *World Politics* 46, no. 2: 151–84.

Freire, Paolo. 1970. *Pedagogy of the Oppressed*. New York: Herder and Herder.

Friedmann, Santiago, Nora Lustig, and Arianna Legovini. 1995. "Mexico: Social Spending and Food Subsidies During Adjustment in the 1980s." In *Coping with Austerity: Poverty and Inequality in Latin America*, ed. Nora Lustig. Washington, D.C.: Brookings Institution.

Galli, Christof, ed. 2007. "NGO Research Guide: Key Resources." Available: http://docs.lib.duke.edu/igo/guides/ngo/. Last accessed on March 13, 2008.

Gamboa Rodríguez, Irma Adriana, and Mónica del Carmen Mancilla Soto. 1991. *Proyecto de la reconstrucción histórica de la Unión de Colonos Independientes del Cerro del Cuatro: Taller de integraccion*. Photocopy. Guadalajara: ITESO.

Gay, Robert. 1994. *Popular Organization and Democracy in Rio de Janeiro*. Philadelphia: Temple University Press.

———. 1998. "Rethinking Clientelism: Demands, Discourses, and Practices in Contemporary Brazil." *Revista europea de estudios latinamericanos y del Caribe* 65:7–24.

———. 2006. "The Even More Difficult Transition from Clientelism to Citizenship: Lessons from Brazil." In Fernández-Kelly and Shefner 2006.

Gilbert, Alan, ed. 1989. *Housing and Land in Urban Mexico*. La Jolla: Center for U.S.-Mexican Studies, University of California, San Diego.

Gilbert, Alan, and Ann Varley. 1989. "From Renting to Self-Help Ownership? Residential Tenure in Urban Mexico Since 1940." In Gilbert 1989.

———. 1991. *Landlord and Tenant: Housing and the Poor in Urban Mexico*. London: Routledge.

Glendon, Mary Anne. 2000. "Rights Talk: The Impoverishment of Political Discourse." In Eberly 2000.

Gomá, R. G., R. González, S. Martí, L. Peláez, M. Truñó, P. Ibarra, M. J. Monteserín, and A. Blas. 2003. "Participation, Public Policies, and Democracy." In *Social Movements and Democracy*, ed. Pedro Ibarra. New York: Palgrave.

González de la Rocha, Mercedes. 1994. *The Resources of Poverty*. Oxford: Blackwell.

———. 2000. *Private Adjustments: Household Responses to the Erosion of Work*. UNDP Conference Paper Series, Social Development and Poverty Elimination Division. New York: United Nations Development Program.

———. 2001. "From the Resources of Poverty to the Poverty of Resources? The Erosion of a Survival Model." *Latin American Perspectives* 28, no. 4: 72–100.

Gramsci, Antonio. 1971. *Selections from the Prison Notebooks.* Edited and translated by Quintin Hoare and Geoffrey Nowell Smith. New York: International Publishers.

Grupo Santa María. 1989a. Monthly Newsletter. Photocopy.

———. 1989b. *II Jornada de Lucha: Evaluacion.* Photocopy.

Guillén López, Tonatiuh. 2001. "Democratic Transition in Baja California: Stages and Actors." In Middlebrook 2001.

Gustafson, Lowell S. 1994. *Economic Development Under Democratic Regimes: Neoliberalism in Latin America.* Westport, Conn.: Praeger.

Gutiérrez, Gustavo. 1973. *A Theology of Liberation.* Maryknoll, N.Y.: Orbis.

Guzmán Anell, José Teódulo. 1992. A todos los miembros de la asamblea directiva de SEDOC. Internal letter to the members of Assembly of Directors of SEDOC. October 28.

———. 1993. Internal letter to the members of Assembly of Directors of SEDOC. February 26.

Haber, Paul Lawrence. 1997. "Social Movements and Social Change in Latin America." *Current Sociology* 45, no. 1: 21–40.

———. 2006. *Power from Experience: Urban Popular Movements in Late Twentieth-Century Mexico.* University Park: Pennsylvania State University Press.

Hammersley, Martyn, and Paul Atkinson. 1983. *Ethnography: Principles in Practice.* London: Tavistock Publications.

Harris, Richard L., and Melinda J. Seid. 2000. "Critical Perspectives on Globalization and Neoliberalism in the Developing Countries." *Journal of Developing Societies* 16, no. 1: 1–26.

Harvey, David. 2005. *A Brief History of Neoliberalism.* New York: Oxford University Press.

Hedman, L. E. 1997. "Constructing Civil Society: Election Watch Movements in the Philippines." In Lindberg and Sverrisson 1997.

Hellman, Judith Adler. 1997. "Social Movements: Revolution, Reform, and Reaction." *NACLA Report on the Americas* 30, no. 6: 13–18.

Hernández, Luis, and Jonathan Fox. 1995. "Mexico's Difficult Democracy: Grassroots Movements, NGOs, and Local Government." In *New Paths to Democratic Government in Latin America,* ed. Charles A. Reilly. Boulder, Colo.: Lynne Rienner.

Hollifield, James F., and Calvin Jillison, eds. 2000. *Pathways to Democracy: The Political Economy of Democratic Transitions.* New York: Routledge.

Howell, Jude, and Jenny Pearce. 2001. *Civil Society and Development: A Critical Exploration.* Boulder, Colo.: Lynne Rienner.

IFE (Instituto Federal Electoral). 2006. *Elecciones Federales 2006: Encuestas y resultados electorales.* Mexico City: Instituto Federal Electoral.

INEGI (Instituto Nacional de Estadística Geografía e Informática). 1990. *XI Censo general de población y vivienda, 1990.* Mexico City: INEGI.

———. 2000. *XII Censo general de población y vivienda, 2000.* Mexico City: INEGI.

———. 2003. *Anuario estadístico del Estado de Jalisco, edición 2003.* Guadalajara: INEGI.

Jelin, Elizabeth. 1997. "Emergent Citizenship or Exclusion? Social Movements and Non-Governmental Organizations in the 1990s." In Smith and Korzeniewicz 1997.

Karl, Terry Lynn. 1990. "Dilemmas of Democratization in Latin America." *Comparative Politics* 23, no. 1: 1–21.

———. 2000. "Economic Inequality and Democratic Instability." *Journal of Democracy* 11, no. 1: 149–56.

Kleinberg, Remonda B., and Janine A. Clark, eds. 2000. *Economic Liberalization, Democratization, and Civil Society in the Developing World*. London: Macmillan.

Klesner, Joseph. 1987. "Changing Patterns of Electoral Participation and Official Party Support in Mexico." In *Mexican Politics in Transition*, ed. Judith Gentleman. Boulder, Colo.: Westview Press.

La Botz, Dan. 1995. *Democracy in Mexico: Peasant Rebellion and Political Reform*. Boston: South End Press.

Laurell, Ana Cristina. 2003. "The Transformation of Social Policy in Mexico." In Middlebrook and Zepeda 2003.

Lechner, Norbert. 1998. "The Transformation of Politics." In *Fault Lines of Democracy in Post-Transition Latin America*, ed. Felipe Agüero and Jeffery Stark. Coral Gables, Fla.: North-South Center Press.

Leeds, Anthony, and Elizabeth Leeds. 1976. "Accounting for Behavioral Differences: Three Political Systems and the Responses of Squatters in Brazil, Peru, and Chile." In *The City in Comparative Perspective: Cross-National Research and New Directions in Theory*, ed. J. Walton and M. H. Masotti, 193–248. New York: Sage/Halsted.

Levine, Daniel H. 1992. *Popular Voices in Latin American Catholicism*. Princeton: Princeton University Press.

Levy, Daniel, and Kathleen Bruhn. 1999. "Mexico: Sustained Civilian Rule and the Question of Democracy." In *Democracy in Developing Countries: Latin America*, 2nd ed., ed. Larry Diamond, Jonathan Hartlyn, Juan Linz, and Seymour Martin Lipset, 519–73. Boulder, Colo.: Lynne Rienner.

———. 2001. *Mexico: The Struggle for Democratic Development*. Berkeley and Los Angeles: University of California Press.

Lindberg, Steffan, and Árni Sverrisson. 1997. *Social Movements in Development*. London: Macmillan.

Linz, Juan, and Alfred Stepan. 1996. *Problems of Democratic Consolidation: Southern Europe, South America, and Post-Communist Europe*. Baltimore: Johns Hopkins University Press.

Lipset, Seymour Martin. 1959. "Some Social Requisites of Democracy: Economic Development and Political Legitimacy." *American Political Science Review* 53, no. 1: 69–105.

Lomnitz, Larissa. 1977. *Networks and Marginality: Life in a Mexican Shantytown*. San Francisco: Academic Press.

López Rangel, Rafael. 1987. *Urbanización y vivienda en Guadalajara*. Guadalajara: Centro de Ecodesarollo.

Lustig, Nora. 1992. *Mexico: The Remaking of an Economy*. Washington, D.C.: Brookings Institution.

———. 1998. *Mexico: The Remaking of an Economy*. 2nd ed. Washington, D.C.: Brookings Institution.

Malkin, Elizabeth. 2007. "Thousands in Mexico City Protest Rising Food Prices." *New York Times*, February 1. Available: http://www.nytimes.com/2007/02/01/world/americas/01mexico.html. Last accessed on January 29, 2008.

McMichael, Philip. 1996. *Development and Social Change: A Global Perspective*. Thousand Oaks, Calif.: Pine Forge Press.

Mexican Labor News and Analysis. 2004. *Mexican Labor News and Analysis* 7 (2). E-mail listserv accessed at http://socrates.berkeley.edu/~border/list_articles/031402_mlna_mexico.html.

Middlebrook, Kevin, ed. 2001. *Party Politics and the Struggle for Democracy in Mexico: National and State-Level Analyses of the Partido Acción Nacional.* La Jolla: Center for U.S.-Mexican Studies, University of California, San Diego.

Middlebrook, Kevin, and Eduardo Zepeda, eds. 2003. *Confronting Development: Assessing Mexico's Economic and Social Policy Challenges.* Stanford, Calif.: Stanford University Press.

Migdal, Joel. 1988. *Strong Societies and Weak States: State-Society Relations and State Capabilities in the Third World.* Princeton: Princeton University Press.

Molinar Horcasitas, Juan, and Jeffrey Weldon. 1994. "Electoral Determinants and Consequences of National Solidarity." In Cornelius, Craig, and Fox 1994.

Navarro Fierro, Carlos. 1994. "Elementos para una lectura e interpretación de los resultados electorales de 1994." *El Cotidiano* 65.

Nef, Jorge, and Wilder Robles. 2000. "Globalization, Neoliberalism, and the State of Underdevelopment in the New Periphery." *Journal of Developing Societies* 16, no. 1: 27–48.

Nelson, Joan. 1979. *Access to Power: Politics and the Urban Poor in Developing Nations.* Princeton: Princeton University Press.

Nuñez, Carlos. 1993. "Las voces de la sociedad civil." In *¿Quién nos hubiera dicho?* ed. Cristina Padilla and Rossana Reguillo. Guadalajara: ITESO.

O'Donnell, Guillermo, Philippe Schmitter, and Laurence Whitehead, eds. 1986. *Transitions from Authoritarian Rule: Prospects for Democracy.* Baltimore: Johns Hopkins University Press.

OECD (Organisation for Economic Co-operation and Development). 2002. OECD *Economic Surveys: Mexico.* No. 7. Paris: OECD.

Olvera Rivera, Alberto. 2001. "Movimientos sociales prodemocráticos, democratización y esfera pública en México: El caso de Alianza Cívica." *Cuadernos de la Sociedad Civil,* no. 6. Xalapa, Veracruz: Instituto de Investigaciones Históricos-Sociales, Universidad Veracruzana.

Ortiz, Juan Diego. 1992. "Informe y balance de la campaña electoral en Tlaquepaque, Jalisco." Guadalajara: SEDOC. Photocopy.

Otero, Gerardo, ed. 1996. *Neoliberalism Revisited: Economic Restructuring and Mexico's Political Future.* Boulder, Colo.: Westview Press.

Oxhorn, Philip. *Organizing Civil Society: The Popular Sectors and the Struggle for Democracy in Chile.* University Park: Pennsylvania State University Press.

———. 2006. "Conceptualizing Civil Society from the Bottom Up: A Political Economy Perspective." In Feinberg, Waisman, and Zamosc 2006.

Perlman, Janice E. 1976. *The Myth of Marginality: Urban Poverty and Politics in Rio de Janeiro.* Berkeley and Los Angeles: University of California Press.

Piven, Frances Fox, and Richard A. Cloward. 1977. *Poor People's Movements: Why They Succeed, How They Fail.* New York: Vintage Books.

Polanyi, Karl. 2001. *The Great Transformation: The Political and Economic Origins of Our Time.* Boston: Beacon Press.

Polaski, Sandra. 2004. Brief Submitted to the Canadian Standing Senate Committee on Foreign Affairs. February 25. Available: http://www.carnegieendowment.org/publications/index.cfm?fa=view&id=1473&proj=zted. Last accessed on March 12, 2008.

Portes, Alejandro. 1972. "Rationality in the Slum: An Essay on Interpretive Sociology." *Comparative Studies in Society and History* 14, no. 3: 268–86.

Portes, Alejandro, and Kelly Hoffman. 2003. "Latin American Class Structures: Their Composition and Change During the Neoliberal Era." *Latin American Research Review* 38, no. 1: 41–82.

Presidencia de la República. 1992. *El esfuerzo nacional de Solidaridad*. Mexico City: Dirección General de Comunicación Social.

PRONASOL (Pronasol Unidad de Desarollo Regional). 1994. *Programa operativo anual—inversión aprobada*. Guadalajara: PRONASOL.

Pye, Lucian. 2000. "Democracy and Its Enemies." In Hollifield and Jillson 2000.

Ramírez Sáiz, Juan Manuel. 2006. "Informal Politics in the Mexican Democratic Transition: The Case of the People's Urban Movement." In Fernández-Kelly and Shefner 2006.

Ramírez Sáiz, Juan Manuel, and Héctor Nuncio Hermosillo. 1994. *Entre la iglesia y la izquierda: El Comité Popular del Sur*. Guadalajara: Universidad de Guadalajara.

Regalado Santillán, Jorge. 1986. "El movimiento popular independiente en Guadalajara." In *Perspectivas de los movimientos sociales en la región Centro-Occidente*, ed. Jesús Tamayo. Mexico City: Editorial Línea.

Riding, Alan. 1989. *Distant Neighbors*. New York: Vintage Books.

Roberts, Kenneth. 1997. "Beyond Romanticism: Social Movements and the Study of Political Change in Latin America." *Latin American Research Review* 32, no. 2: 137–51.

Robinson, William I. 1996. *Promoting Polyarchy: Globalization, U.S. Intervention, and Hegemony*. New York: Cambridge University Press.

Rodríguez, Victoria. 2003. *Women in Contemporary Mexican Politics*. Austin: University of Texas Press.

Rodríguez, Victoria, and Peter Ward, eds. 1995. *Opposition Government in Mexico*. Albuquerque: University of New Mexico Press.

Román, Luis Ignacio, Rodrigo Flores, and Roberto Govela. 2004. *Planes, políticas, y actores económicos en Jalisco en el marco de la liberalización económica*. Guadalajara: ITESO.

Ronfeldt, David. 1973. *Atencingo: The Politics of Agrarian Struggle in a Mexican Ejido*. Stanford, Calif.: Stanford University Press.

Roniger, Luis. 1990. *Hierarchy and Trust in Modern Mexico and Brazil*. New York: Praeger.

Roniger, Luis, and Ayse Günes-Ayata, eds. 1994. *Democracy, Clientelism, and Civil Society*. Boulder, Colo.: Lynne Rienner.

Roxborough, Ian. 1997. "Citizenship and Social Movements Under Neoliberalism." In Smith and Korzeniewicz 1997.

Rucht, Dieter. 1999. "The Transnationalization of Social Movements: Trends, Causes, Problems." In *Social Movements in a Globalizing World*, ed. Donatella della Porta, Hanspieter Kriesi, and Dieter Rucht. New York: St. Martin's Press.

Sawyer, Suzana. 2004. *Crude Chronicles: Indigenous Politics, Multinational Oil, and Neoliberalism in Ecuador*. Durham, N.C.: Duke University Press.

Schock, Kurt. 2005. *Unarmed Insurrections: People Power Movements in Nondemocracies*. Minneapolis: University of Minnesota Press.

SEDESOL. 1993a. *Los Comités de Solidaridad: Organización social*. Mexico City: SEDESOL.

———. 1993b. "Talleres para la planeación participativa." Cuaderno de trabajo [working paper]. Mexico City: SEDESOL.

SEDOC. 1986. Estatuos de Servicios Educativos de Occidente, A.C. Guadalajara: SEDOC. Photocopy.

————. 1989. Planeación de Servicios Educativos de Occidente, 1989–1993. Guadalajara: SEDOC. Photocopy.

————. 1991. Postura del Equipo Sur. Guadalajara: SEDOC. Photocopy.

————. 1992a. Asamblea directiva ampliada. March 23. Guadalajara: SEDOC. Photocopy.

————. 1992b. A todos los miembros de la asamblea directiva de SEDOC. October 28. Guadalajara: SEDOC. Photocopy.

————. 1992c. Acta de la asamblea directiva de SEDOC. November 4. Guadalajara: SEDOC. Photocopy.

————. 1992d. Propuestas alternativas para la desincorporacion de los proyectos y organizaciones sociales vinculadas a SEDOC. December 7. Guadalajara: SEDOC. Photocopy.

Shadlen, Kenneth C. 2004. *Democratization Without Representation: The Politics of Small Industry in Mexico.* University Park: Pennsylvania State University Press.

Shefner, Jon. 1999a. "Sponsors and the Urban Poor: Resources or Restrictions?" *Social Problems* 46, no. 3: 376–97.

————. 1999b. "Legitimacy Crisis, Contentious Supporters, and Post-Disaster Instability: A Case Study of Political Ferment." *International Journal of Mass Emergencies and Disasters* 17, no. 2: 137–60.

————. 2001. "Coalitions and Clientelism in Mexico." *Theory and Society* 30, no. 5: 593–628.

Shefner, Jon, and Robert Gay. 2002. "The Politics of Field Research: Lessons from Brazil and Mexico." *Canadian Journal of Latin American and Caribbean Studies* 27, no. 54: 199–214.

Shefner, Jon, and John Walton. 1993. "The *Damnificados* of Guadalajara: The Politics of Domination and Social Movement Protest." *International Journal of Urban and Regional Research* 17, no. 4: 611–22.

Shirk, David. 2005. *Mexico's New Politics: The PAN and Democratic Change.* Boulder, Colo.: Lynne Rienner.

Silliman, G. S., and L. G. Noble, eds. 1998. *Organizing for Democracy: NGOs, Civil Society, and the Philippine State.* Honolulu: University of Hawaii Press.

Sklair, Leslie. 1993. *Assembling for Development: The Maquila Industry in Mexico and the United States.* La Jolla: Center for U.S.-Mexican Studies, University of California, San Diego.

————. 2001. *The Transnational Capitalist Class.* Oxford: Blackwell.

————. 2002. *Globalization: Capitalism and Its Alternatives.* Oxford: Oxford University Press.

Smith, William C., and Roberto P. Korzeniewicz, eds. 1997. *Politics, Social Change, and Economic Restructuring in Latin America.* Coral Gables, Fla.: North-South Center Press.

Stiglitz, Joseph. 2006. *Making Globalization Work.* New York: W. W. Norton.

Stokes, Susan. 1995. *Cultures in Conflict: Social Movements and the State in Peru.* Berkeley and Los Angeles: University of California Press.

Tangeman, Michael. 1995. *Mexico at the Crossroads: Politics, the Church, and the Poor.* Maryknoll, N.Y.: Orbis.

Taylor, Lance. 1999. *After Neoliberalism: What Next for Latin America?* Ann Arbor: University of Michigan Press.

Teichman, Judith A. 1995. *Privatization and Political Change in Mexico.* Pittsburgh: University of Pittsburgh Press.

UCI–Cerro del Cuatro. 1990. Por qué luchamos en la UCI-C4? Document of the Asamblea Constitutiva. August 12. Photocopy.

———. 1990–94. *Abriendo Camino.* Monthly newsletter of the UCI—Cerro del Cuatro. Photocopy.

———. 1991. Balance del trabajo en el primer aniversario y sugerencias de trabajo 1991–1992. Photocopy.

Vásquez, Daniel. 1989. "Rural-Urban Land Conversion on the Periphery of Guadalajara." In Gilbert 1989.

Vega, Gustavo, and Luz María de la Mora. 2003. "Mexico's Trade Policy: Financial Crisis and Economic Recovery." In Middlebrook and Zepeda 2003.

Vélez-Ibáñez, Carlos. 1983. *Rituals of Marginality: Politics, Process, and Culture Change in Central Urban Mexico, 1969–1974.* Berkeley and Los Angeles: University of California Press.

Veltmeyer, Henry, and Anthony O'Malley, eds. 2001. *Transcending Neoliberalism: Community-Based Development in Latin America.* Bloomfield, Conn.: Kumarian Press.

Waisman, Carlos H. 2006. "Autonomy, Self-Regulation, and Democracy: Tocquevillean-Gellnerian Perspectives on Civil Society and the Bifurcated State in Latin America." In Feinberg, Waisman, and Zamosc 2006.

Walton, John. 1977. *Elites and Economic Development: Comparative Studies on the Political Economy of Latin American Cities.* Austin: University of Texas.

———. 1978. "Guadalajara: Creating the Divided City." In *Metropolitan Latin America: The Challenge and the Response,* ed. W. A. Cornelius and R. V. Kemper. Latin American Urban Research 6. Beverly Hills, Calif.: Sage.

Walton, John, and David Seddon. 1994. *Free Markets and Food Riots.* Oxford: Blackwell.

Ward, Peter. 1986. *Welfare Politics in Mexico: Papering over the Cracks.* London: Allen and Unwin.

———. 1994. "Social Welfare Policy and Political Opening in Mexico." In Cornelius, Craig, and Fox 1994.

Ward, Peter, and Victoria Rodríguez. 1999. *New Federalism and State Government in Mexico: Bringing the States Back In.* Austin: LBJ School of Public Policy, University of Texas.

Weaver, Frederick Stirton. 2000. *Latin America in the World Economy.* Boulder, Colo.: Westview Press.

Weisbrot, Mark, Luis Sandoval, and Carla Paredes-Drouet. 2006. "An Analysis of Discrepancies in the Mexican Presidential Election Results." *Center for Economic and Policy Research Issue Brief 2006–18.* Washington, D.C.: CEPR.

White, Gordon. 1996. "Civil Society, Democratization, and Development." In *Democratization in the South: The Jagged Wave,* ed. Robin Luckham and Gordon White. Manchester, U.K.: Manchester University Press.

Wood, Robert. 1986. *From Marshall Plan to Debt Crisis.* Berkeley and Los Angeles: University of California Press.

World Bank. 1995a. *World Debt Tables, 1994–1995.* Washington, D.C.: World Bank.

———. 1995b. *World Development Report, 1995: Workers in an Integrating World.* Washington, D.C.: World Bank.

———. 2001. *World Development Indicators.* Washington, D.C.: World Bank.

Yúdice, George. 1998. "The Globalization of Culture and the New Civil Society." In Alvarez, Dagnino, and Escobar 1998.

Index

www.ingramcontent.com/pod-product-compliance
Lightning Source LLC
Chambersburg PA
CBHW021901020426
42334CB00013B/422